VERBAL
FRACTIONS
without pencil or paper

Michael Levin
Charan Langton

MOUNTCASTLE COMPANY
Fourth book in the Verbal Math Lesson Series

VERBAL
FRACTIONS
without pencil or paper

Michael Levin
Charan Langton

Edited by Ashley Kuhre

Copyright 2010 Mountcastle Company
First Print Edition Sep 2010

ISBN 978-0-913063-12-5
Manufactured by BookMasters, Inc. Ashland, OH USA
Job# M7125 March 2010
Cover Photo from BigStockPhotos

MOUNTCASTLE COMPANY
mntcastle@earthlink.net
www.mathlesson.com
www.readinglesson.com

Contents

Introduction

One day while browsing in an antiquarian book store in San Francisco, we noticed a tattered old book called Mental Math. The idea of the book was to teach math verbally, without writing the problems down. Intrigued, we bought the book and tried it with our son who disliked worksheets. He loved it. Suddenly math became more like a game for him than work.

We learned that mental math used to be a very popular method of teaching children math. It was free of the tediousness of writing while teaching children efficient methods of solving math problems. Wanting to reintroduce this method in a step-by-step fashion, we have created a series of books using this approach. We call it verbal math. This simple idea will free your child from the drudgery of handwriting and will turn math into a mental game.

In this book, we bring this time-honored approach to help your child become proficient with fractions. After the four basic arithmetic operations, fractions are the most fundamental of math concepts. All progress in math will depend on how well the child understands and is able to work with fractions. If your child is not proficient with fractions, it is likely that he or she will begin to dislike math in higher grade levels. The fractions are the first significant roadblock in math education and if not mastered, will have negative future impact.

With Verbal Fractions, your child will learn, in a gradual manner, what fractions mean. Follow the lessons and see your child do even complex-looking problems quickly and accurately. All without pencil or paper. When time comes to learn algebra, your child will be miles ahead of his or her peers.

Here is an example of the type of problem your child will be able to do quickly by the end of this course, without any figuring on paper.

The distance from Mount Joy to Harrisburg is 25 miles, and $\frac{4}{5}$ of this distance is $\frac{5}{8}$ of $\frac{4}{9}$ of the distance from Harrisburg to Minton. What is the distance to Minton?

This course introduces a special way of analyzing math problems. The method is based on understanding of unit values. The first couple of problems in each lesson show the process.

Please instruct your child to follow this method even though he or she may know of other strategies. Using this method will make more complicated problems easier to solve. The purpose of this course is to help child develop a conceptual understanding of fractions.

SOME GUIDELINES

1. You must start this course at lesson one, even if the problems seem very simple to your child.

2. This course requires a teacher or parent to work with the student. Problems *must* be read to the student. You may need to guide the student, helping as needed with difficult problems, and using the solutions and methods given in the book. The answers are there just for *you*. (If you feel it necessary to give your student a copy of the problems, this book - without the answers - is available for purchase in eBook form at our website.)

3. All of these problems can be done mentally. When you read the problem to the child, he or she may write down the numbers but all calculations should be done mentally.

4. Follow the method that is given at the beginning of each lesson. The solutions given should be explained to the child if she has difficulty.

5. Most children can easily do half a lesson a day. Some longer lessons can be spread over a week. The problems do get more difficult towards the end of the book. The child will not be able to do the problems in the later chapters until he or she has done the preceding ones.

6. Subordinate speed to accuracy, but do not neglect speed. The ability to answer these problems quickly results in mastery of the concepts.

7. The course is suitable for children in 4th-6th grades and above depending on the child's ability with arithmetic.

8. Older children who are not confident with fractions will benefit from this course as well. College entrance exams often have problems of this type on the tests.

9. After you have done approximately two-thirds of this book, please consider starting the companion book on Percents.

Please let us know how this book works for you.

With best wishes,

Michael Levin
Charan Langton
mntcastle@earthlink.net
www.mathlesson.com

Lesson one – *Halves, Thirds, and Fourths*

IF I divide an apple into two equal parts, what is one of these parts called? What are two of these parts called? **Ans:** One-half; a whole or one.

1. How many halves are in one apple? **Ans:** 2.

2. What is one-half of 4? of 8? of 10? of 12? **Ans:** 2; 4; 5; 6.

3. What is one-half of 14? of 16? of 18? of 20? **Ans:** 7; 8; 9; 10.

4. What is one-half of 22? of 26? of 28? of 32? **Ans:** 11; 13; 14; 16.

5. If one pound of sugar costs 100 cents, what will one-half pound of sugar cost? **Ans:** 50 cents.

6. If a pound of coffee costs $10, then how many half pounds can you buy for $10? **Ans:** Two half-pounds.

7. If a pound of sugar costs $15, then how many half-pound boxes can you buy for $15? **Ans:** Two half-pound boxes.

8. Paul picked 20 apples and gave one-half to his brother. How many apples did he give to his brother? **Ans:** 10 apples.

9. Thompson bought 24 books, and sold one-half of them when the school term was over. How many of his books did he sell? **Ans:** He sold one-half of 24, which is 12 books.

10. Phoebe had 40 peaches and gave one-half of them away. How many does she have left? **Ans:** 20.

11. If I divide an apple into 3 equal parts, what is one of these parts called? **Ans:** Each part is called one-third.

12. How many thirds are in one apple? **Ans:** 3.

13. What are 2 parts and 3 parts of an apple cut into three pieces called? **Ans:** Two parts are called 2 thirds and 3 parts make a whole.

14. How many one-thirds do you need to make a whole? **Ans:** Three-thirds make a whole.

15. What is one-third of 6? of 9? of 12? of 15? **Ans:** 2; 3; 4; 5.

16. What is one-third of 21? of 24? of 30? of 36? **Ans:** 7; 8; 10; 12.

17. James had $30 and spent one-third of it. How much did he spend? **Ans:** One-third of $30 is $10. He spent $10.

18. Sanjay had 9 pears and Thomas had one-third as many as Sanjay. How many pears did Thomas have? **Ans:** Thomas had one-third of 9, which is 3 pears.

19. Lucy had 21 pins and gave Mary one-third of them. How many pins did she give to Mary? **Ans:** One-third of 21 is 7. Mary received one-third, or 7 pins.

20. Anil bought 42 stamps, and sold one-third of them to Bob. How many does he have now?
Ans: One-third of 42 is 16. So 2 thirds is twice that many, or 32. After selling one-third, he has 2 thirds left, which is 32 stamps.

21. What is 2 thirds of 9? **Ans:** One-third of 9 is 3. If one-third of 9 is 3, then 2 thirds of 9 is 2 times 3, which is 6.
Note—*In doing these problems, we will first find the unit fraction value and then multiply it with the numerator to get the answer. The unit fraction in problem 22 is 3.*

22. What is 2 thirds of 6? of 12? of 15? of 18? **Ans:** 4; 8; 10; 12.
Note—*Ask child to first find the unit value then multiply it by 2.*
Ans: One-third of 6 is 2. Two-thirds is twice that many, or 4.

23. What is 2 thirds of 24? of 30? of 27? of 33? **Ans:** 16; 20; 18; 22.
Ans: One-third of 24 is 8. Two-thirds is twice that many, or 16. One-third of 30 is 10. Two-thirds is twice that many, or 20. One-third of 27 is 9. Two-thirds is twice that many, or 18. One-third of 30 is 11. Two-thirds is twice that many, or 22.

24. What is one-third of 123? What is two-thirds of 123? **Ans:** 41: 82.

25. What is one-third of 222? What is two-thirds of 222? **Ans:** 74: 148.

26. John had $21, and gave 2 thirds of his money to Sarah. How many dollars did he give to Sarah? **Ans:** One-third of 21 is 7. Two-thirds is twice that many or 14. So Sarah received $14.

27. There were 27 cherries in the bowl. You ate 2 thirds of them. How many did you eat? **Ans:** One-third of 27 is 9. Two-thirds is twice that many, or 18. I ate 18 cherries.

28. If you give away one-third of something, how many thirds do you have left? **Ans:** 2 thirds.

29. Sanjay had a CD collection of 33 CDs. He gave his sister 2 thirds of it. How many did he keep? **Ans:** He has one-third left which is 11. Sanjay kept 11 CDs.

30. Daniel had $36 and lost 2 thirds of it somewhere. How much money does he have left? **Ans:** After losing 2 thirds, Daniel has one-third left. One-third of 36 is 12.

31. If I divide an apple into 4 equal parts, what are 1, 2, and 3, of these parts called? **Ans:** One = one-fourth, 2 = two-fourths or one-half, 3 = three-fourths.

32. How many fourths of an apple are in a whole apple? **Ans:** 4 fourths are in one whole apple.

33. What is one-fourth of 4? of 8? of 20? of 32? **Ans:** 1; 2; 5; 8.

34. What is one-fourth of 12? of 24? of 16? of 48? **Ans:** 3; 6; 4; 12.

35. What is 2 fourths of 24? of 16?; of 28? of 36? **Ans:** 12; 8; 14; 18.

36. If one-fourth of 20 is 5, then what is 2 fourths? **Ans:** It is 2 times 5 or, 10.

37. What is 3 fourths of 20? of 24? of 12? of 16?
Ans: One-fourth of 20 is 5. Three-fourth is 3 times one-fourth, which is 15. One-fourth of 24 is 6. Three-fourths is 3 times one-fourth, which is 18. One-fourth of 12 is 3. Three-fourths is 3 times one-fourth, which is 9. One-fourth of 16 is 4. Three-fourths is 3 times one-fourth, which is 12.
Note—*The fraction one-fourth in this problem is called the unit fraction. To compute three-fourths, we first computed one-fourth and then multiplied it by the 3.*

38. What is 3 fourths of 120? **Ans:** One-fourth of 120 is 30. Three-fourths is 3 times that or 90.

39. The ski shop had 44 snow boards. The shop rented 2 fourths of them on Friday. How many snow boards are left in the shop?
Ans: One-fourth of 44 is 11. Two-fourths is twice that much, or 22. The shop has 22 snow boards left.

40. If a meter of cloth costs $8, then what will 3 fourths of a meter cost?
Ans: One-fourth of 8 is 2. Three-fourths is 3 times as much or 6. The cloth will cost $6.

41. If I give away one-third of some thing, how many thirds do I have left? **Ans:** two-thirds.

42. What is one-half and one-third of 24? **Ans:** 12 and 8.

43. Jessica had 24 gumballs. She gave half of them to Margie and a third of them to Cathy. How many gumballs does she have left?
Ans: One-half of 24 is 12. One-third of 24 is 8. She gave 12 gumballs to Margie and 8 balls to Cathy, or a total of 20 gumballs. She had 24, so she has $24 - 20 = 4$ gumballs left.

44. Harley is 24 years old and Townsend is 8 fourths as old. How old is Townsend?
Ans: One-fourth of 24 is 6. Eight-fourths is 8 times as much, or $6 \times 8 = 48$. Townsend is 48 years old.

45. What is the sum of one half and one-third of 36? **Ans:** 18 plus 12, 30.

46. A farmer harvested 36 melons. A shop bought half of them, and one-third were too green to be sold. How many ripe melons does the farmer have left?
Ans: The number of melons sold plus those he can not sell is $18 + 12 = 30$. So he has 6 ripe melons left.

47. A store owner has 40 boxes of sneakers. He sold 3 fourths of them. How many does he have left? He then bought one-third as much as he sold. How many boxes of sneakers does the store have now?
Ans: One-fourth of 40 is 10. The owner sold 3 fourths of 40, which is 3 times 10, or 30. Then he buys one-third of 30, which is 10. He had 40, sold 30 and bought 10 boxes. So the total number of boxes he has now is $40 - 30 + 10 = 20$ boxes.

48. A store owner has 20 jackets. She sold 2 fourths of them. How many does she have left? She then bought one-half as much as she sold. How many are there now? **Ans:** 15.

49. What is an another way of saying one-fourth? **Ans:** One quarter, or just a quarter.

50. Why is the coin called a quarter?
Ans: The coin called quarter is worth 25 cents. There are 100 cents in a dollar and 25 cents is one-fourth of that. That is why the coin is called a quarter, or a quarter dollar. ⌣

Lesson 2 – *Fifth, Sixth, and Seventh*

IF you divide an orange into 5 equal parts, what are 1, 2, 3, and 4 of these parts called?

Ans: One-fifth, 2 fifths, 3 fifths. 4 fifths.

1. How many fifths are in one orange? **Ans:** 5.

2. What is one-fifth of 10? of 25? of 15? of 30?
   Ans: 2; 5; 3; 6.

3. What is 2 fifths of 15? of 30? of 45? of 20?
   Note—*First compute one-fifth and then multiply it by 2.*
   Ans: 6; 12; 18; 8.

4. What is 3 fifths of 10? of 30? of 25? of 55?
   Note—*First compute one-fifth and then multiply it by 3.*
   Ans: 6; 18; 15; 33.

5. What is 4 fifths of 55? of 35? of 40? of 50?
   Note—*First compute one-fifth and then multiply it by 4.*
   Ans: 44; 28; 32; 40.

6. Mary has 15 blue beads, and Rachel has 2 fifths as many. How many blue beads does Rachel have?
   Ans: One-fifth of 15 is 3, so Rachel has 6 blue beads.

7. Susan is 25 years old, and her sister is 4 fifths as old. How old is her sister? **Ans:** 20 years.

8. Rowland is 35 years old, and his sister is 4 fifths as old. How old is his sister? **Ans:** 28 years.

9. A horse cost $1000, and a saddle cost 3 fifths as much as the horse. What is the cost of the saddle?
   Ans: One-fifth of $1000 is $200. Three-fifths is three times as much or $600. The cost of saddle is $600.

10. Mary had 40 lambs and she lost 20 of them. After a lot of searching, she found 3 fifths of her lambs. How many lambs does she have now?
    Ans: If Mary lost 20 lambs, she had left 40 − 20, or 20 lambs. One-fifth of 20 is 4, so 3 fifths of 20 is 12. So she has 20, and the 12 she found or, 12 + 20 = 32, the number of lambs Mary has left.

11. A dairyman owned 50 cows. He sold 4 fifths of them, and then bought 32 new cows. How many does he have now? **Ans:** 42 cows.

12. If you divide a melon into 6 equal parts, what are 1, 2, 3, 4, and 5 of these parts called? **Ans:** One-sixth, 2 sixths, 3 sixths, 4 sixths, 5 sixths.

13. How many sixths are there in a single thing? **Ans:** 6.

14. What is 2 sixths of 24? of 18? of 36? of 60?
Ans: 8; 6; 12; 20.

15. What is 3 sixths of 12? of 42? of 30? of 66?
Ans: 6; 21; 15; 33.

16. What is 4 sixths of 6? of 36? of 48? of 54?
Ans: 4; 24; 32; 36.

17. What is 5 sixths of 18? of 54? of 24? of 72?
Ans: 15; 45; 20; 60.

18. Rob went to a festival and brought back 48 flags. He gave 3 sixths of the flags to Megan and 2 sixths to Morgan. How many flags did he give to both? **Ans:** 24 flags to Megan, 16 to Morgan.

19. What will 5 sixths of 36 meters of cloth cost at the rate of $2 a meter? **Ans:** One-sixth of 36 is 6. Five-sixths is 5 times that or, 30 meters. 30 meters of cloth at $2 per meter will cost $60.

20. Warren had 12 shirts, and Oliver had 5 sixths as many less 4. How many shirts did Oliver have?
Ans: Five-sixths of 12 shirts is 10 shirts. $10 - 4 = 6$, the number of shirts that Oliver has.

21. Dana had 60 special cards. She gave 2 sixths of them to her friend Barton, and 3 sixths to Benton. How many did she keep for herself? **Ans:** 10 cards.

22. If one meter of speaker wire costs 5 sixths of 36 cents, how many meters can you buy for 60 cents? **Ans:** 2 meters.

23. Two-thirds of $30 is $10 less than what Anil had. How much does Anil have? **Ans:** $30.

24. Frazier had 40 color pens. He gave 10 to Brown, and 2 sixths of the remaining to Seal. How many pens does he have left? **Ans:** 20 pens.

25. If a melon is divided into 7 equal parts, what are 1, 2, 3, 4, 5, and 6 of these parts called?
Ans: One-seventh, 2 sevenths, 3 sevenths, 4 sevenths, 5 sevenths, 6 sevenths.

26. How many sevenths are there in a whole? **Ans:** 7.

27. If you give away one-seventh of something, how much do you have left? **Ans:** 6 sevenths.

28. If you give away 5 sevenths of something, how much do you have left? **Ans:** 2 sevenths.

29. What is one-seventh of 21? of 28? of 42? of 56?
Ans: 3; 4; 6; 8.

30. What is 2 sevenths of 28? of 49? of 63? of 70?
Ans: 8; 14; 18; 20.

31. What is 3 sevenths of 14? of 35? of 49? of 28?
Ans: 6; 15; 21; 12.

32. What is 4 sevenths of 70? of 77? of 63? of 84?
Ans: 40; 44; 36; 48.

33. What is 5 sevenths of 77? of 91? of 42? of 28?
Ans: 55; 65; 30; 20.

34. What is 6 sevenths of 35? of 42? of 49? of 140?
Ans: 30; 36; 42; 120.

35. Jim bought a bicycle and sold it for 6 sevenths of its cost. What portion of the cost did he lose? **Ans:** One-seventh.

36. Jim paid $70 for his bike, and sold it for 6 sevenths of its cost. How much money did he lose? **Ans:** $10.

37. Andy saw a bike for $210 and was told that the discount would be 2 sevenths of the cost. How much is the discount and what did Andy have to pay for the bike?
Ans: One-seventh of $210 is $30. So the discount is $60 and Andy paid $150 for the bike.

38. Andy saw an another bike for $200 and was told that the discount on this bike would be one-fifth of the cost. How much is the discount and what did Andy have to pay for the bike?
Ans: One-fifth of $200 is $40. So Andy would have to pay $150 for the bike.

39. What is the sum of one-sixth and one-seventh of 42? **Ans:** 13.

40. What is the sum of one-fifth and two-fifths of 20? **Ans:** 12.

41. What is the sum of one-third and one-sixth of 96? **Ans:** 48.

42. A student paid $70 for her math book, and 3 sevenths as much for her science book. After the term was over, she sold them both for $90. What was her loss?

Ans: Three-sevenths of $70 is $30. $70 + $30 is $100, the whole cost. $100 − $90 is $10, the loss.

43. Three-sevenths of $56 is $6 more than what one book cost. What will 2 books cost at the same rate? **Ans:** $36.

44. Ben had $240, one-third of which he spent on a suit, one-fourth for a watch, and one-sixth for shoes. How much does he have left?

Ans: One-third of 240 is 80, one-fourth is 60, and one-sixth is $40. So he spent 80 + 60 + 40 = 180 and has left 240 -180 = $60.

45. A repair station has 40 barrels of oil. It used 3 fourths of it and then bought one-third as much as it sold. How many barrels of oil does the station have now?

Ans: One-fourth of 40 is 10. The station used 3 fourths of 40, which is 3 times 10, or 30. Then it buys one-third of 30, which is 10. It had 40, used 30 and bought 10 more barrels. The total number of barrels it has now is 40 − 30 + 10 = 20 barrels.

46. Ashok had $140. He gave 3 sevenths of it to his cousin, and spent 3 fourths of the rest on books. How much does he have left?

Ans: He gave 3 sevenths of 140, or 60 to his cousin. He had left 140 − 60 = 80. He then spent 3 fourths of 80, or 60, and had left 80 − 60 = $20.⌣

Lesson 3 − *Eighths and Ninths*

IF anything is divided into 8 equal parts, what is one of these parts called? **Ans:** One-eighth.

1. What are 2, 3, 4, 5, 6 and 7 of these parts called, and how many eighths are in a whole or one? **Ans:** 2 eighths, 3 eighths, 4 eighths, 5 eighths, 6 eighths, 7 eighths.

2. What is one-eighth of 24? 48? 72? 88? **Ans:** 3; 6; 9; 11.

3. What is 2 eighths of 32? 40? 56? 72? **Ans:** 8. 10; 14; 18. One-eighth of 32 is 4. So 2 eighths is 2 times 4 or 8.

4. What is 3 eighths of 16? 64? 80? 32? **Ans:** 6; 24; 30; 12.

5. What is 5 eighths of 8? 24? 48? 64? **Ans:** 5; 15; 30; 40.

6. One-eighth of 24 is how many times 3?
   Ans: One-eighth of 24 is 3 which is one times 3.

7. Three-eighths of 40 is how many times 5?
   Ans: One-eighth of 40 is 5 which is 3 times 5.

8. Four eighths of 80 is how many times 8?
   Ans: One-eighth of 80 is 10. Four-eighths is 4 times that, or 40, which is 5 times 8.

9. Five-eighths of 56 is how many times 7?
   Ans: One eighth of 56 is 7. 5 eighths is 5 times that, or 35, which is 5 times 7.

10. Six-eighths of 64 is how many times 12?
    Ans: One-eighth of 64 is 8. Six-eighths is 8 times that, or 48, which is 4 times 12.

11. Seven-eighths of 72 is how many times 3? **Ans:** 21.

12. Three-eighths of 32 is how many times one-third of 12?
    Ans: One-eighth of 32 is 4, and 3 eighths is 3 times 4, or 12. One-third of 12 is 4. The first part is 12, the second part of the problem is 4. 12 is 3 times 4.

13. Six-eighths of 40 is how many times one-fourth of 24?
    Ans: One-eighth of 40 is 5, and 6 eighths is 6 times 5, or 30; one-fourth of 24 is 6; 30 is 5 times 6.

14. Four-eighths of 48 is how many times 2? **Ans:** 7.

15. One-eighth of 96 is how many times 6? **Ans:** 2.

16. Five-eighths of 56 is how many times 35? **Ans:** 1.

17. Two-thirds of 27 is how many times 2? **Ans:** 1.

18. Three-eighths of 48 is how many times 9? **Ans:** 2.

19. Seven-eighths of 72 is how many times 3? **Ans:** 13.

20. Five-eighths of 32 is how many times 5? **Ans:** 4.

21. Three-eighths of 48 is how many times 9? **Ans:** 2.

22. Two-eighths of 160 is how many times 8? **Ans:** 5.

23. Three-eighths of 320 is how many times 4? **Ans:** 30.

24. Two-thirds of 81 is how many times 9? **Ans:** 3.

25. Three-eighths of 16 is how many times 1? **Ans:** 6.

26. Five-eighths of 72 is how many times 5? **Ans:** 9.

27. Three-eighths of 64 is how many times 3? **Ans:** 8.

28. Two-thirds of 27 is how many times 3 fourths of 12? **Ans:** 2.

29. What is 2 ninths of 18? 27? 45? 36? **Ans:** 4; 6; 10; 8.

30. What is 3 ninths of 63? 72? 81? 27? **Ans:** 21; 24; 27; 9.

31. What is 4 ninths of 9? 36? 54? 81? **Ans:** 4; 16; 24; 36.

32. What is 5 ninths of 54? 72? 63? 27? **Ans:** 30; 40; 35; 15.

33. What is 6 ninths of 81? 18? 36? 90? **Ans:** 54; 12; 24; 60.

34. What is 7 ninths of 18? 99? 27? 108? **Ans:** 14; 77; 21; 84.

35. How much is three times 6 plus 2 thirds of 6?
Ans: 3 times 6 is 18. One-third of 6 is 2, and 2 thirds of 6 is 2 times 2, or 4. 18 and 4 is 22.

36. How much is four times 12 plus 3 fourths of 12?
Ans: 4 times 12 is 48; 3 fourths of 12 is 9; $48 + 9 = 57$.

37. How much is 5 times 10 plus 3 fifths of 10? **Ans:** 56.

38. How much is 6 times 12 plus 3 sixths of 12? **Ans:** 78.

39. How much is 5 times 7 plus 4 sevenths of 7? **Ans:** 39.

40. How much is 9 times 8 plus 5 eighths of 8? **Ans:** 77.

41. Two times 18 plus 7 ninths of 18 is how many? **Ans:** 50.

42. Two-ninths of 18 is how many times 2 thirds of 3?
Ans: 2 ninths of 18 is 4; 2 thirds of 3 is 2; 4 is as many times 2 as 2 is *contained in* 4, or 2.
Contained in is a concept that means division. It is great for developing a comprehensive understanding of the process of division. We start with asking "what is contained in" and then move to direct division later.

43. Five-ninths of 27 is how many times 5 sixths of 6?
Ans: 5 ninths of 27 is 15; 5 sixths of 6 is 5; 15 is as many times 5 as 5 is contained in 15, or 3.

44. Six-ninths of 54 is how many times 4 fifths of 15? **Ans:** 3.

45. Three-ninths of 72 is how many times 2 eighths of 16? **Ans:** 6.

46. Seven-eighths of 24 is how many times 7 eighths of 8? **Ans:** 3.

47. Lucy bought 60 DVDs, and sold one-third of them to Bob, and 3 fifths of the remaining to Carl. How many DVDs does she have now?
Ans: Lucy sold Bob one-third of 60 DVDs, or 20 DVDs, and had 60 − 20, or 40 left. Three-fifths of 40 is 24. So she then has 40 − 24, or 16 DVDs left.

Which is bigger?

48. One-third of 24 or 2 thirds of 12? **Ans:** Same.

49. One-third of 48 or 2 thirds of 24? **Ans:** Same.

50. Two-thirds of 36 or one-third of 72? **Ans:** Same.

51. One-third of 81 or 2 thirds of 57? **Ans:** Second

52. One-third of 90 or 2 thirds of 60? **Ans:** Second.

53. Two-thirds of 72 or one-third of 96? **Ans:** First.

54. Two-fifths of 50 or 3 fifths of 40? **Ans:** Second.

55. Two-fifths of 35 or 2 thirds of 18? **Ans:** First.

56. Three-fifths of 60 or 2 thirds of 45? **Ans:** First.

57. Four-fifths of 100 or one-third of 240? **Ans:** Same.

58. Three-fifths of 80 or 2 thirds of 48? **Ans:** First.

59. One-third of 72 or 2 fifths of 60? **Ans:** First.

60. Three-sevenths of 21 of 2 fifths of 40? **Ans:** Second.

61. Three-sevenths of 42 or 2 less than 2 fifths of 50? **Ans:** Second.

62. Four-sevenths of 63 or 20 more than 3 fifths of 200? **Ans:** First.

63. Three-eighths of 54 or 8 less than 2 thirds of 72? **Ans:** First.

64. Three-sevenths of 70 or 10 less than 4 fifths of 50? **Ans:** Same.

65. Four-fifths of 600 or 200 less than 3 fifths of 800? **Ans:** First.

66. Three-eighths of 40 or 3 less than one-third of 57? **Ans:** First.

Note—*Repeat problems that the student did incorrectly or very slowly.*

Lesson 4 – *Addition, Subtraction*

HARRY gave one-third of an apple to his brother, and 2 thirds of the apple to his sister. How much did he give away?
Ans: 3 thirds or all of it.

1. Matthew gave 2 fifths of a peach to Eliot, and 3 fifths to Morris. How much did he give to both? **Ans:** 5 fifths or all of it.

2. James gave 3 sevenths of a melon to Harry, and 4 sevenths to Henry. How much did he give away? **Ans:** 7 sevenths or all of it.

3. Danny ate 3 eighths of a bag of cashews yesterday, and 4 eighths of the bag today. How much of the bag did he eat in two days? **Ans:** 7 eighths.

4. Ella gave one-fourth of a melon to Peggy, 2 fourths to Carrie, and 3 fourths to Kate. How much did she give away? **Ans:** 6 fourths or $1\frac{1}{2}$ melons.

5. Philip gave 2 sixths of a candy bar to Jay, 3 sixths to Sarah, and 5 sixths to Eliza. How many sixths did he give away? **Ans:** 10.

6. Victor lost 7 fifths of a dollar, but has 8 fifths of a dollar left. How much did he have at first?
Ans: If Victor lost 7 fifths of a dollar and had 8 fifths left, then before his loss he had 7 + 8, or 15 fifths of a dollar, which is 3 dollars.

7. Matthew lost 6 eighths of his coins, and then 12 eighths later, and then had 6 eighths left. How many did he have at first?
Ans: If he lost 6 eighths + 12 eighths, which is 18 eighths of the coins, and has 6 eighths left. He had 18 + 6, or 24 eighths of coins.

8. Dora gave 3 ninths of a pound of raisins to Ellen, and 7 ninths to Daisy, and then had 3 ninths left. How many did she have at first? **Ans:** 13 ninths.

9. Jane had 7 eighths of a pound of candies, and gave Maria 5 eighths of a pound. How many eighths are left? **Ans:** 2 eighths.

10. Frank took one-seventh of a melon, and gave Drew 4 sevenths of the melon. How much is left? **Ans:** 2 sevenths of the melon.

11. How many beads are there in one-fourth of 80 beads? **Ans:** 20.

12. What is the difference between the 6 sevenths and 5 sevenths? **Ans:** One-seventh.

13. Sallie had 24 pears. She gave Ben 2 eighths of the pears and Amanda 3 eighths of them. How many does she have left? **Ans:** 9 pears.

14. Jake had one-third cup of peanuts. He bought 4 thirds of a cup more, and then threw away one cup. If the cup holds 3 thirds, what part of a cup is left?
Ans: One-third + 4 thirds is 5 thirds. The cup contains 3 thirds; 5 thirds − 3 thirds is 2 thirds of a cup left

15. Peter had 5 sixths of a basket of apples, then he gave away 3 sixths, and then bought 2 sixths of a basket, how many sixths does he have now?
Ans: 5 sixths − 3 sixths is 2 sixths; 2 sixths + 2 sixths is 4 sixths.

16. What is the difference between the sum of 3 eighths and 7 eighths, and the sum of 4 eighths and 5 eighths? **Ans:** One-eighth.

17. A shop bought 20 tires, and sold 2 tenths of them to customer A, 3 tenths to customer B and 4 tenths to customer C. How many tires are left?
Ans: 2 tenths + 3 tenths + 4 tenths are 9 tenths; they had left 10 tenths − 9 tenths, or one-tenth of 20 tires, or 2 tires.

18. A woman had 36 meters of carpet. She gave 5 ninths of it to one person, and 3 ninths of it to another. How much does she have left?
Ans: 5 ninths + 3 ninths is 8 ninths. So she has left 9 ninths − 8 ninths, or one-ninth of 36 meters, or 4 meters.

19. Mariana had 3 fourths of a pint of nuts, Elaine had twice as much, and Kevin had 3 times as much. How much did they all have? **Ans:** 18 fourths.

20. Alex bought 4 ninths of a bag of rice, and Bill bought 3 times as much. How much did Bill buy? **Ans:** 12 ninths.

21. At 7 fifths of a dollar each, how much will 5 candies cost? **Ans:** 35 fifths, or $7.

22. How many fifths are there in one of something? **Ans:** 5.

23. Mary had one and one-fifth of a melon. How many fifths of melon is that? She gave 2 fifths of it to Sarah, and 4 fifths to Sophia. How much is left?
Ans: She had 5 plus 1 or 6 fifths of a melon. She gave Sarah 2 fifths and Sophia 4 fifths; both receive 2 fifths + 4 fifths, or 6 fifths of a melon; she gave all of it and none is left.

24. If I give away 2 sixths of something, how many sixths do I have left? **Ans:** 4.

25. If I give away 2 times one third of something, how many thirds do I have left? **Ans:** 1.

26. If I give away 5 times one seventh of something, how many sevenths do I have left? **Ans:** 2.

27. What is the sum of one third of something and three thirds? **Ans:** 4 thirds.

28. What is the sum of two thirds of something and three thirds? **Ans:** All.

29. What is the sum of 2 fifths of something and 3 thirds? **Ans:** 5 fifths.

30. What is the sum of 3 sevenths of something and 2 sevenths? **Ans:** 5 sevenths.

31. What is the sum of one-half and one-half? **Ans:** 1.

32. What is the sum of one-third and one-third? **Ans:** 2 thirds.

33. What is the sum of one-fourth and one-fourth? **Ans:** 2 fourths or One-half.

34. If Jake has two-thirds of $36 and Anna has three-sixths of $60, how much do they have together? **Ans:** $54.

35. If Henry has one-third of $30 and David has one-sixth of $30, how much do they have together? **Ans:** $15.

36. Jill and Jack start from the same place and in opposite directions. If Jill walks $2\frac{1}{5}$ miles, and Jack walks $1\frac{4}{5}$ miles, how far are they from each other? **Ans:** 4 miles.

37. One game costs $20\frac{1}{7}$ dollars, and the other costs $22\frac{3}{7}$ dollars. What do both cost together? **Ans:** $44\frac{4}{7}$ dollars.

38. A wall is $8\frac{3}{8}$ inches thick. The carpenter added drywall which added $\frac{5}{8}$ inch to the thickness of the wall. How thick is the wall now? **Ans:** 9 inches.

39. How do you write 3 thirds, 4 fifths, 3 eighths and 2 ninths. **Ans:** $1; \frac{4}{5}; \frac{3}{8}; \frac{2}{9}$.

40. If one-half of a number is 1, then what is that number? **Ans:** 2.

41. If one-half of a number is 6, then what is that number? **Ans:** 12.

42. If one-third of a number is 6, then what is that number? **Ans:** 18.

43. If one-third of a number is 7, then what is that number? **Ans:** 21.

44. If one-third of a number is 9, then what is that number? **Ans:** 27.

45. If one-third of a number is 12, then what is that number? **Ans:** 36.

46. If one-fifth of a number is 10, then what is that number? **Ans:** 50.

47. If one-fifth of a number is 7, then what is that number? **Ans:** 35.

48. If one-fifth of a number is 9, then what is that number? **Ans:** 45.

49. If one-fifth of a number is 12, then what is that number? **Ans:** 60.

50. If one-fifth of a number is 10, then what is that number? **Ans:** 50.

51. If one-sixth of a number is 10, then what is that number? **Ans:** 60.

52. If one-sixth of a number is 7, then what is that number? **Ans:** 42.

53. Andy took 5 sevenths of a bag of peanuts, Nina took 2 sevenths of the bag. How much is left? **Ans:** None.

54. How many days are there in one-fourth of a month? **Ans:** $\frac{15}{2}$ days.

55. What is the difference between the 6 sevenths and 1 sevenths? **Ans:** Five-sevenths.

56. A bird picked up 24 seeds, lost some on the way to her nest and then and fed her babies the remaining 2 eighths. How many seeds did she lose?
Ans: She fed them 2 eighths, so she lost 4 eighths. One-eighth of 24 is 3 seeds, and 4 eighths is 12 seeds.

57. Michael had one-third of a cup of cereal. He liked it and asked for 4 thirds of a cup more, and then left third of a cup uneaten. What part did he eat?
Ans: One-third + 4 thirds is 5 thirds. The cup contains one-thirds; 5 thirds − 1 thirds is 4 thirds of a cup is what he ate.

58. A squirrel found 3 fourths of a pinecone, she ate one fourth and hid the rest of the pinecone. How much did she hide? **Ans:** 2 fourths or one-half.

59. A mouse saved 4 ninths of a bag of crackers, and then ate half of it. How much is left? **Ans:** 2 ninths.

Note—*Repeat problems that the student did incorrectly or very slowly.* ☺

Lesson 5 – *Rates*

HOW much will 4 pencils cost if 3 pencils cost 90 cents?

Ans: *We must figure out how much one pencil costs first.* If 3 pencils cost 90 cents, one pencil will cost one-third of 90 cents, which is 30 cents. If one pencil costs 30 cents, 4 pencils will cost 4 times 30, which is 120 cents.

1. What will 5 erasers cost at the rate of 3 for 120 cents?
    Ans: One eraser costs 120 cents divided by 3, which is 40 cents. So 5 erasers will cost 200 cents.

2. If 3 pairs of shoes cost $60, how much will 5 pairs cost? **Ans:** One pair of shoes costs $\frac{60}{3} = \$20$. Five pairs will cost $100.

3. If 4 peaches cost 80 cents, what do 8 peaches cost? **Ans:** 160 cents.

4. What are 10 oranges worth if 8 oranges cost 160 cents? **Ans:** 200 cents.

5. If 7 pounds of plaster costs 420 cents, what will 9 pounds cost?
    Ans: 540 cents.

6. What is the cost of 10 bags of fertilizer at the rate of 5 bags for $33?
    Ans: $66.

7. How far can a camel travel in 12 days at the rate of 36 miles in 4 days? **Ans:** 108 miles.

8. How many tons of hay will a rancher need for 11 weeks, if his animals eat at the rate of 10 tons of hay in 5 weeks? **Ans:** 22 tons.

9. What is the cost of 5 games at the rate of $12 for 3 games?
    Ans: $20.

10. Kim paid $3 for apples at the rate of $1 for 3. How many apples did she buy? **Ans:** 9.

11. Rena paid $8 for some tickets at the rate of $5 for 15 tickets. How many tickets did she buy? *Hint: How many tickets can she buy for $1?* **Ans:** 24 tickets.

12. Cesar walked 7 hours at the rate of 12 miles in 4 hours. How far did he walk? *Hint: How far did he walk in one hour?* **Ans:** 21 miles.

13. Robert traded 12 mangoes for apples at the rate of 3 mangoes for 9 apples. How many apples did he get in exchange? **Ans:** 36 apples.

14. At the rate of 3 ladybugs for 12 worms, how many worms can be exchanged for 10 ladybugs?
Ans: Four worms are worth as much as one ladybug. So 10 ladybugs are worth 40 worms.

15. If 6 tractors can mow 12 acres of grass in a day, how much can 8 tractors mow in the same time?
Ans: One tractor can mow 2 acres in a day. Eight tractors would mow 2 times 8 or, 16 acres in the same time.

16. If 4 workers can paint a house in 4 days, how long would one worker take? *Hint: Would it take one day? No. One worker would take longer than the time it took 4 workers.*
Ans: If it takes 4 workers 4 days, then one worker will need 4 times that much, or 16 days.

17. If 4 workers can paint a house in 4 days, how long would 2 workers take? **Ans:** 8 days.

18. If 3 workers can paint a house in 5 days, how much of the house do they paint in one day? **Ans:** $\frac{1}{5}$ of the house.

19. If 3 workers can paint a house in 5 days, how much of the house does one worker paint in one day? **Ans:** $\frac{1}{15}$ of the house.

20. If 1 worker can paint $\frac{1}{15}$ of the house in 1 days, how long will it take him to paint the whole house? **Ans:** 15 days.

21. If 5 workers can paint a house in 8 days, how much of the house do they paint in one day? **Ans:** $\frac{1}{8}$ of the house.

22. If 5 workers can paint a house in 8 days, how much of the house does one worker paint in one day? **Ans:** $\frac{1}{40}$ of the house.

23. If 1 worker can paint $\frac{1}{40}$ of the house in 1 days, how long will it take him to paint the whole house? **Ans:** 40 days.

24. If 1 worker can paint a house in 10 days, how long will it take 2 workers? **Ans:** 5 days.

25. If 5 workers can paint a house in 5 days, how long would one worker take? **Ans:** 25 days.

26. If 4 workers can paint a house in 5 days, how long would two workers take? **Ans:** 10 days.

27. If 2 workers can paint a house in 5 days, how long would 5 workers take? **Ans:** 2 days.

28. If 10 excavators can lay 30 meters of pipeline in one day, how much can 12 excavators lay in the same time? **Ans:** 36 meters.

29. How long will it take 4 students to use a box of tea if 6 students can use it in 12 days?
Ans: If 6 students can use a box of tea in 12 days, it will take one student 6 times longer, or 72 days. Four students will drink it in one-fourth of 72 days, or 18 days.

30. If 5 boys can do a piece of work in 16 days, how long will it take 20 boys to do it?
Ans: If 5 boys do the work in 16 days, 20 boys, or 4 times 5 boys, will take one-fourth of 16 days, or 4 days.

31. In what time will 8 girls pick a basket of berries if 4 girls can do it in 8 hours?
Ans: If 4 girls pick a basket of berries in 8 hours, 8 girls, or 2 times 4 girls, will take one-half of 8 hours, or 4 hours.

32. How many machinists will it take to build a robot in 6 days, if 3 machinists can do it in 12 days? **Ans:** 6 machinists.

33. How many machinists will it take to build a robot in 3 days, if 3 machinists can do it in 12 days? **Ans:** 12 machinists.

34. If 10 workers need 8 days to build a wall, how many workers are needed to build it in 1 day? **Ans:** 80 workers.

35. If 5 workers build a boat in 20 days, how many workers will be needed to do it in one-fourth the time?
Ans: If 5 workers build a boat in 20 days, to do it in one-fourth of the time will require 4 times 5 workers, or 20 workers.

36. If 7 meters of wire cost $21, what will 2 thirds of 15 meters cost?
Ans: Two thirds of 15 meters is 10 meters. If 7 meters cost $21, one meter will cost $3, and 10 meters will cost 10 times 3, or $30.

37. Jack exchanged 7 roses for 21 daisies. At this rate how many daisies could he get for 8 roses? **Ans:** 24 daisies.

38. If 8 lemons are worth 16 cucumbers, how many cucumbers can you get for 10 lemons? **Ans:** 20 cucumbers.

39. At the rate of 6 grapefruits for 18 oranges, how many oranges can be purchased for 11 grapefruits? **Ans:** 33 oranges.

40. If 9 kiwis are worth 27 chestnuts, how many chestnuts can you get for 12 kiwis? **Ans:** 36 chestnuts.

41. The price of 4 boxes of popcorn is same as 6 cups of apple juice. What do two cups of apple juice cost, if 4 boxes of popcorn cost $4.80?
Ans: Four boxes of popcorn cost $4.80, so 6 cups of apple juice cost $4.80. One cup of apple juice is one-sixth of that or 80 cents, and 2 cups will cost $1.60.

42. Albert can get 5 boxes of popcorn for the same price as 2 candy bars. What is a box of popcorn worth if 3 candy bars cost $3?
Ans: If 3 candy bars are worth 3 dollars, then one is worth $1. So 5 boxes of popcorn are worth $2, and one box is worth one-fifth of that or 40 cents.

43. Simmi bought a shirt for $21, and instead of payment agreed to work at the store for $7 per hour. How many hours did she work? **Ans:** 3 hours.

44. How many coconuts will be needed if we give each of the 12 boys one-third of an coconut? **Ans:** 4 coconuts.

45. How many points did Jack get if out of 100, Ann got one-half the points, Jill got one-quarter of the remaining points. **Ans:** 25 points.

46. If 5 mangoes cost 7 dollars, then how much does 1 mango cost? **Ans:** $\frac{7}{5}$ of a dollar.

47. If Jake has completed 2 fifths of his classes, how many fifths does he have left? **Ans:** 3 fifths.

48. Mom gave Allisa one-third and Adrian one-fifth of the money she had. If she had 150 dollars, how much did she give to each child? **Ans:** $50 to Allisa and $30 to Adrian.

49. Victor exchanged 6 red tickets for 18 blue tickets. At this rate how many blue tickets could he get for 8 red tickets? **Ans:** 24.

50. If 8 oranges are worth 16 lemons, how many oranges can you get for 6 lemons? **Ans:** 3 oranges.

51. At the rate of 6 pencils for 18 erasers, how many erasers can be purchased for 11 pencils? **Ans:** 33 erasers.

52. If 9 macadamia nuts are worth 27 almonds, how many almonds can you get for 12 macadamia nuts? **Ans:** 36 almonds.

Lesson 6 – *Rates to Fractions*

HOW much will one meter of wire cost if 2 thirds of a meter costs $4?

In this lesson, we begin to teach the concept of unit rates. Computing unit rates is fundamental to doing fraction problems. A unit rate in this problem is the cost of one meter of wire.

Ans: If 2 thirds of a meter of wire cost $4, one-third of a meter will cost one-half of $4, or $2, and 3 thirds, or one meter, will cost 3 times $2, which is $6.

1. What will one box of soap cost if 3 fourths of a box costs 3 fourths of a dollar? **Ans:** One dollar.

2. What will one box of erasers cost if 2 thirds of a box costs $2? **Ans:** $3.

3. What will one box of paper cost if 3 fourths of a box costs $6? **Ans:** If 3 fourths of a box of paper cost $6, one-fourth of a box will cost one-third of $6, or $2, and 4 fourths, or one box, will cost 4 times $2, or $8.

4. If 3 fifths of a ticket cost $9, what will one ticket cost? **Ans:** If 3 fifths of a ticket cost $9, one-fifth of a ticket will cost one-third of $9, or $3, and 5 fifths, or one ticket, will cost 5 times $3, or $15.

5. If 3 fourths of a cake cost $12, what will the whole cake cost? **Ans:** If 3 fourths of a cake cost $12, then one-fourth of the cake will cost one-fourth of $12, or $4, and 4 fourths, which is the whole cake, will cost 4 times $4, or $16.

6. If 4 fifths of a box of tea cost $8, what will one box cost? **Ans:** If 4 fifths of a box cost $8, one-fifth of a box will cost one-fourth of $8, or $2, and 5 fifths, or one box, will cost 5 times $2, or $10.

7. If 3 fifths of a meter of speaker wire cost $6, what will one meter cost? **Ans:** If 3 fifths of a meter cost $6, one-fifth of a meter will cost one-third of $6, or $2, and 5 fifths, or one meter, will cost 5 times $2, or $10.

8. What will two pounds of coffee cost if 5 sixths of a pound cost 10 dollars? **Ans:** If 5 sixths of a pound cost 10 dollars, one-sixth of a pound will cost one-fifth of 10 dollars, or 2 dollars, and 6 sixths, or one pound,

will cost 6 times 2 dollars, or 12 dollars. And 2 pounds will cost 2 times 12, or 24 dollars.

9. What is the cost of 2 bags of soil at the rate of $4 for 4 sixths of a bag?
   Ans: If 4 sixths of a bag cost $4, one-sixth of a bag will cost one-fourth of $4, or one dollar, 6 sixths, or one bag, will cost $6, and 2 bags will cost 2 times $6, or $12.

10. What is the cost of one of an item, if 2 of them cost one-sixth of a coin? **Ans:** One twelfths.

11. What is the cost of one of an item, if 3 of them cost 4 fifths of a coin? **Ans:** 12 fifths.

12. What is the cost of one of an item, if 2 of them cost 5 thirds of a coin? **Ans:** 5 sixths of a coin.

13. What is the cost of 3 meters of cloth if 3 sevenths of a meter costs $6? **Ans:** $42.

14. How far can Alan walk in 4 days if in 5 sixths of a day he can walk 20 miles? **Ans:** He can walk 4 miles in one-sixth of a day and 24 miles in a day and in 4 days, 96 miles.

15. What is the cost of 5 pounds of steak if 3 fifths of a pound cost $6? **Ans:** $50.

16. What is 5 times the distance to Lancaster if 3 fourths of the distance is 3 miles? **Ans:** 20 miles.

17. How much will 4 bags of secret potion cost if 5 tenths of a bag cost 50 cents? **Ans:** 400 cents.

18. Mary bought 9 bags of beads at the rate of 12 cents for 6 sevenths of a bag. What is the cost of the beads?
    Ans: If 6 sevenths of a bag cost 12 cents, then one-seventh of a bag will cost one-sixth of 12 cents, or 2 cents, 7 sevenths, or one bag, will cost 14 cents, and 9 bags will cost 9 times 14 cents, or 126 cents.

19. How much will 5 bunches of roses cost if $10 will buy 5 sixths of a bunch?
    Ans: If 5 sixths of a bunch cost $10, one-sixth of a bunch will cost one-fifth of $10, or $2, 6 sixths, or one bunch, will cost $12, and 5 bunches will cost 5 times $12, or $60.

20. Huan bought 4 dozen eggs at the rate of 80 cents for 2 thirds of a dozen. How much did they cost?
Ans: If 2 thirds of a dozen cost 80 cents, one-third of a dozen will cost one-half of 80 cents, or 40 cents, 3 thirds, or a dozen, will cost 120 cents, and 4 dozen will cost 480 cents.

21. What is the cost of 3 bags of cherries, at the rate of $2 for 2 thirds of a bag? **Ans:** $9.

22. If 3 fourths of a bottle of perfume costs $6, what will 5 eighths of a bottle cost? **Ans:** $5.

23. A new watch cost $300. 4 fifths of its cost is twice the cost of the old watch. What was the cost of the old watch?
Ans: 4 fifths of $300 is $240. If $240 is twice the cost of the old watch, then its cost was one-half of $240, or $120.

24. Billy's ski boots cost $200. Three-fifths of the cost of the boots is 4 times the cost of the lift tickets. What is the cost of the lift tickets?
Ans: Three-fifths of $200 is $120, which is 4 times the cost of the lift tickets. So the cost of the lift tickets will be one-fourth of $120, or $30.

25. Mina is 25 years old, and 4 fifths of her age is 4 years less than twice Tina's age. What is Tina's age?
Ans: Four-fifths of 25 years are 20 years, which is 4 years less than twice Tina's age. So twice Tina's age is 20 + 4, or 24 years, and her age is one-half of 24, or 12 years.

26. A store had 20 barrels of monkeys, sold 3 fourths of it to a customer A, and 3 fifths of the rest to customer B. How much is left?
Ans: The store sold 3 fourths of 20 barrels, or 15 barrels, to customer A and had left 20 − 15, or 5 barrels. They sold to the second customer 3 fifths of 5 barrels which is, 3 barrels. So they then had left 5 − 3, or 2 barrels of monkeys.

27. Think of a number, multiply it by 8, divide by 4, multiply by 3, divide by 6, add 20, subtract the number thought of, divide by 4, and name the result. **Ans:** 5.

28. Think of a number, multiply by 12, divide by 3, divide again by 4 and name the result. **Ans:** Same as the number.

29. What is 24 multiplied by 6, divided by 8, multiplied by 4, divided by 3, multiplied by 8, divided by 4? *Ask student to do it one step at a time.*

30. If 8 pounds of cleverness cost $12, how much will 2 pounds cost? **Ans:** It will cost one-fourth of $12 or $3.

31. If 11 pounds of niceness cost $44, how much will 2 pounds cost? **Ans:** $8.

32. If 8 ounces of kindness cost $21, how much will 16 ounces cost? **Ans:** $42.

33. If 3 pounds of happiness cost $4, how much will 2 thirds of a pounds cost?
    Ans: One pound of happiness will cost 4 thirds of a dollar and one-third of a pound will cost one third of that or 4 ninths of a dollar. The 2 thirds will cost 2 times that or 8 ninths of a dollar.

34. What is the cost of 4 bags of fun at the rate of $2 for 2 thirds of a bag?
    Ans: If 2 thirds of a bag cost $2, then one-third will cost 1 dollar. Three thirds or one bag will cost 3 times that of $3. Four bags will cost $12.

35. If 3 fourths of a pound of tea cost $12, what will one-eighth of a pound cost?
    Ans: If 3 fourths of a pound of tea cost $12, then one-fourth will cost $4 and one-eighth will cost half of that or $2.

36. If 3 fourths of a pound of tea costs $12, what will 5 eighths of a pound cost? **Ans:** $10.

37. A new computer game cost $30. The old game cost 4 fifths of the cost of the new one. What was the cost of the old game? **Ans:** $25.

38. If one-sixth of a pound of a spice cost $2, then how much can you buy for $12? **Ans:** One pound.

39. If you divide one-half of an apple into 3 equal pieces, what part of the whole will be each piece? **Ans:** One-sixth.

40. One cake is cut in five equal pieces and the other is cut in seven pieces. Which cake has bigger pieces? **Ans:** The first cake.

41. Which is bigger; one-third of something or two fourths? **Ans:** 2 fourths, because it is a half and half is bigger than one-third. ⌣

Lesson 7 – *Reducing Fractions*

HOW many thirds are contained in 4?

   Ans: In one there are 3 thirds, and in 4 there are 4 times as many 3 thirds, which is 12 thirds.

1. How many thirds are in 2? 3? 5? 7? 8
   Ans: 6; 9; 15; 21; 24.

2. How many fourths are in 3? 5? 6? 4? 7?
   Ans: 12; 20; 24; 16; 28.

3. How many fifths are in 5? 4? 8? 2? 8?
   Ans: 25; 20; 15; 10; 40.

4. How many sixths are in 3? 2? 5? 6? 4?
   Ans: 18; 12; 30; 36; 24.

5. How many sevenths in 2? 5? 4? 7? 9?
   Ans: 14; 35; 28; 49; 63.

6. How many eighths are in 3? 6? 4? 5? 7?
   Ans: 24; 48; 32; 40; 56.

7. How many ninths are in 8? 4? 6? 3? 10?
   Ans: 72; 36; 54; 27; 90.

8. How many thirds are in 3 and 2 thirds? in 4 and one-third?
   Ans: In one there are 3 thirds, and in 3 there are 9 thirds; 9 thirds and 2 thirds are 11 thirds. In 4 there are 12 thirds, and 12 thirds plus one-third is 13 thirds.

9. How many fifths are in 4 and 3 fifths? in 6 and 3 fifths?
   Ans: In one there are 5 fifths, and in 4 there are 4 times 5, or 20 fifths; 20 fifths + 3 fifths are 23 fifths. In 6 there are 30 fifths, and 30 fifths + 3 fifths are 33 fifths.

10. How many fourths are in 2 and one-fourth? in 7 and 3 fourths?
    Ans: In one there are 4 fourths and in 2 there are 2 times 4 fourths, or 8 fourths; 8 fourths + one-fourth are 9 fourths. In 7 there are 7 times 4 fourths, or 28 fourths; 28 fourths + 3 fourths is 31 fourths.

11. How many sevenths are in 5 and 6 sevenths? in 3 and 4 sevenths?
    Ans: 41; 25.

12. How many sixths are in 7 and 5 sixths? in 3 and 2 sixths? **Ans:** 47; 20.

13. How many eighths are in 5 and 3 eighths? in 5 and 7 eighths? **Ans:** 43; 47.

14. If 5 meters of cloth cost 2 and one-half dollars, what will six meters cost?
Ans: Two and one-half dollars is 5 halves of a dollar. If 5 meters cost 5 halves of a dollar, one meter will cost one-half of a dollar, and 6 meters will cost 6 halves, or $3.

15. If 2 items cost one-third, how much will one item cost? **Ans :** 1 sixths.

16. If 2 items cost two-thirds, how much will one item cost? **Ans:** One third.

17. If 2 items cost 3 eighths, how much will one item cost? **Ans:** 3 sixteenth.

18. If 2 items cost 5 sevenths, how much will one item cost? **Ans:** 5 fourteenth.

19. If 2 items cost 3 fourths, how much will one item cost? **Ans:** 3 eighth.

20. If 3 items cost one-thirds, how much will one item cost? **Ans:** 1 ninth.

21. If 3 items cost two-thirds, how much will one item cost? **Ans:** One ninth.

22. If 3 items cost 3 eighths, how much will one item cost? **Ans:** one eighth.

23. If 3 items cost 3 sevenths, how much will one item cost? **Ans:** 1 seventh.

24. If 3 items cost 3 fourths, how much will two items cost? **Ans:** 1 fourth.

25. If 3 items cost two-thirds, how much will one items cost? **Ans:** 2 ninths.

26. If 3 items cost 3 eighths, how much will two items cost? **Ans:** 2 eighth.

27. If 3 items cost 3 sevenths, how much will two items cost? **Ans:** 2 seventh.

28. If 3 items cost 3 fourths, how much will two items cost? **Ans:** 2 fourth.

29. If 4 cups cost 2 and 2 third dollars, what do 7 cups cost?
Ans: Two and 2 thirds dollars are 8 thirds dollars. If 4 cups cost 8 thirds, one cup will cost 2 thirds of a dollar, and 7 cups will cost 7 times 2 thirds, or 14 thirds dollars.

30. What is the cost of 10 biscuits at the rate of 30 cents for 3 biscuits?
Ans: If 3 biscuits cost 30 cents, one biscuit will cost 10 cent, and 10 biscuits will cost 10 times 10 halves, or 100 cents.

31. If 11 cookies cost 4 and 2 fifths dollars, what will 12 cookies cost?
Ans: There are 20 fifths in 4. 11 cookies cost 22 fifths. One cookie costs 2 fifths, so 12 cookies will cost 24 fifths.

32. If one-half of eight meters of cloth cost 3 and one-fifth dollars, what will 9 meters cost?
Ans: 3 and one-fifth is same as 16 fifths. If 4 meters cost 16 fifths, then one meter will cost one-fourth of that or 4 fifths and 9 meters will cost 9 times that of 45 fifths dollars.

33. If 2 thirds of 9 baskets of flowers cost 4 and 4 fifths dollars, what will 3 fourths of 12 baskets cost? **Ans:** 45 fifths dollars.

34. If 4 fifths of ten pounds of snowflakes cost 5 and one-third dollars, what will 10 pounds cost? **Ans:** 20 thirds dollars.

35. How many ones are in 6 thirds?
Ans: In one there are three thirds. So, in six thirds there are 2 ones.

36. How many ones are in 6 halves? 9 thirds? 12 thirds?
Ans: 3; 3; 4.

37. How many ones are in 12 fourths? 20 fourths? 8 fourths?
Ans: 3; 5; 2.

38. How many ones are in 10 fifths? 12 sixths? 14 sevenths?
Ans: 2; 2; 2.

39. How many ones are in 16 eighths? 21 sevenths? 24 eighths?
Ans: 2; 3; 3.

40. How many ones are in 18 ninths? 15 thirds? 25 fifths?
Ans: 2; 5; 5.

41. How many ones are in 28 sevenths? 36 ninths? 24 fourths?
Ans: 4; 4; 6.

42. How many ones are in 15 thirds? 20 tenths? 33 elevenths?
Ans: 5; 2; 3.

43. If 2 batteries cost 6 fifths of a dollar, what will 5 batteries cost?
Ans: If 2 batteries cost 6 fifths of a dollar, one battery will cost one-half of 6 fifths, or 3 fifths of a dollar, and 5 batteries will cost 15 fifths dollars, or $3.

44. What is the cost of 5 pairs of pens if 4 pairs of pens cost 12 fifths dollars?
Ans: If 4 pairs of pens cost 12 fifths dollars, one pair will cost one-fourth of 12 fifths, or 3 fifths of a dollar, 5 pairs will cost 15 fifths, or three dollars.

45. How much are 8 pies worth if 3 pies are 15 fourths dollar? **Ans :** $40.

46. What is the cost of 12 eggs if 3 eggs cost 3 fourths of a dollar? **Ans** : $3.

47. How much do 9 tickets cost if 5 tickets cost 10 thirds of a dollar? **Ans:** $6.

48. What is the cost of 8 buttons if 6 buttons cost 12 fourths of a dollar? **Ans:** $4.

49. How much are 4 disks worth if 7 disks are worth 14 half dollar? **Ans:** $4.

50. What is the cost of 3 halves of a meter of rope if 5 meters cost 10 ninths of a dollar?
Ans: If 5 meters cost 10 ninths of a dollar, then one meter costs one-fifth of 10 ninths or 2 ninths. Three times that costs 6 ninths and half of that cost 3 ninths, or one-third.

51. What is the cost of 7 halves of a meter of rope if 5 meters cost 5 sevenths of a dollar? **Ans:** One-half dollar.

52. What is the cost of one-half of 8 meters of pipe if one-half of 6 meters cost one-third of $27?
Ans: If one-half of 6 meters, or 3 meters, cost one-third of $27, or $9, then one meter will cost one-third of 9, or $3. One-half of 8 meters, or 4 meters, will cost 4 times $3, or $12.

53. What is the cost of one-half of 12 boxes of mangoes if one-third of 12 boxes cost one-fourth of $12?
Ans: Since one-third of 12 boxes, or 4 boxes, cost one-fourth of $12, or $3, one box will cost 3 fourths of a dollar, and one-half of 12, or 6 boxes, will cost 6 times 3 fourths, or 18 fourths dollar.

54. A girl had 10 books of tickets to sell. She sold one-fifth to her friends, and two fifths to her parents. How many books of tickets does she still have? **Ans:** 4 books.

55. Eight is 2 fifths of what number?
Ans: If 8 is 2 fifths of a number, then one-fifth of the number is one-half of 8 or 4. So the whole number is 5 fifths of 5 times 4 or 20.

56. By what number do you divide 30 to get one-fifth of 30? **Ans:** 5.

57. If you have $25 and you spend 4 fifths of it, how much money do you have left? **Ans:** $5.

58. How many fifths are in $\frac{2}{5} + \frac{1}{5}$? **Ans:** 3 fifths.

59. How many fifths are in $\frac{2}{5} + \frac{5}{5}$? **Ans:** 7 fifths.

60. How many fifths are in $\frac{3}{5} - \frac{1}{5}$? **Ans:** 2 fifths.

61. How many fifths are in $2 + \frac{1}{5}$? **Ans:** 11 fifths.

62. If Nadia bought 2 dozen eggs but broke $\frac{1}{8}$ of them on the way home; how many eggs did she bring home? **Ans:** 21 eggs.

63. If Charles can finish $\frac{3}{8}$ of a project in one day and Joe can finish $\frac{1}{8}$, then how much can they get done in 2 days?
Ans: In one day, they can do $\frac{3}{8} + \frac{1}{8} = \frac{4}{8}$ or one-half, so in two days they can finish the project.

64. By what do you divide 32 to get one eighth of 32? **Ans:** 8.

65. How much is $\frac{1}{2}$ of $\frac{1}{4}$? **Ans:** $\frac{1}{8}$.

66. Since one is equal to $\frac{8}{8}$, how much is $1 - \frac{8}{8}$? **Ans:** 0.

67. Since one is equal to $\frac{8}{8}$, how much is $1 - \frac{3}{8}$? **Ans:** $\frac{8}{8} - \frac{3}{8} = \frac{5}{8}$.

68. One half of an hour is equal to how many tenths of an hour?
Ans: 5.

69. If it costs $150 to paint $\frac{3}{10}$ of a building, what will it cost to paint $\frac{1}{10}$? **Ans:** $50.

70. How many fourths of a inch are there in 2 eighths of an inch?
Ans: 1.

71. How many sixths are there in 2 twelfths? **Ans:** 1.

72. How many sevenths are there in $\frac{4}{14}$? $\frac{6}{14}$? $\frac{8}{14}$? $\frac{12}{14}$?
Ans: 2; 3; 4; 6.

73. How many eighths are there in $\frac{4}{16}$? $\frac{8}{16}$? $\frac{14}{16}$? $\frac{10}{16}$?
Ans: 2; 4; 7; 5.

74. How many tenths are there in $\frac{9}{30}$? $\frac{15}{30}$? $\frac{24}{30}$? $\frac{45}{30}$?
Ans: 3; 5; 8; 15.

75. What is $\frac{1}{2}$ of $\frac{1}{2}$ of 20? **Ans:** 5.
Note—*Do the last fraction first.*

76. What is $\frac{1}{2}$ of $\frac{1}{4}$ of 16?
Ans: 2. One-quarter of 16 is 4, one-half of that is 2.

77. What is $\frac{1}{2}$ of $\frac{1}{2}$ of 10?
Ans: $\frac{5}{2}$. One-half of 10 is 5, one-half of that is $\frac{5}{2}$.

78. What is $\frac{1}{2}$ of $\frac{1}{4}$ of 8? **Ans:** 1.

79. What is $\frac{4}{5}$ of $\frac{10}{5}$ of 2? **Ans:** $\frac{16}{5}$.

80. What is $\frac{1}{2}$ of $\frac{1}{3}$ of 30? **Ans:** 5.

81. What is $\frac{1}{2}$ of $\frac{2}{3}$ of 3? **Ans:** 1.

82. What is $\frac{1}{3}$ of $\frac{1}{2}$ of 10? **Ans:** $\frac{10}{6}$.

83. What is $\frac{1}{3}$ of $\frac{1}{3}$ of 90? **Ans:** 10.

84. What is $\frac{1}{3}$ of $\frac{2}{3}$ of 9? **Ans:** 2.⌣

Lesson 8 – *Number Analysis*

THREE is one-half of what number?
    Ans: If one-half of some number is 3, then two halves of that number is 2 times 3, or 6.

1. Four is one-third of what number?
   Ans: If one-third of some number is 4, then 3 thirds of that number is 3 times 4, or 12.

2. Six is one-fourth of what number?
   Ans: If one-fourth of some number is 6, 4 fourths, or that number, is 4 times 6, or 24.

3. Five is one-sixth of what number? **Ans:** 30.

4. Six is one-half of what number? **Ans:** 12.

5. Eight is one-seventh of what number? **Ans:** 56.

6. Nine is one-fifth of what number? **Ans:** 45.

7. Eight is one-ninth of what number? **Ans:** 72.

8. Five is one-seventh of what number? **Ans:** 35.

9. Ten is one-sixth of what number? **Ans:** 60.

10. Nine is one-third of what number? **Ans:** 27.

11. Eleven is one-fourth of what number? **Ans:** 44.

12. Nina is 10 years old, which is one-fifth of Michael's age. What is Michael's age?
    Ans: If one-fifth of Michael's age is 10 years, 5 fifths, is 5 times 10, or 50 years.

13. An apple costs 30 cents, which is one-fourth of the cost of a melon. What is the cost of the melon?
    Ans: If one-fourth of the cost of a melon is 30 cents, 4 fourths, or the whole cost, is 4 times 30 cents, or 120 cents.

14. A jacket cost $60, which is one-fifth of the cost of a coat. What was the cost of the coat? **Ans:** $300.

15. John has 20 gold stars, which is one-third of the number Daniel has. How many gold stars does Daniel have? **Ans:** 60 gold stars.

16. Nancy's scarf cost $7, which is one-fourth of the cost of her dress. What is the cost of her dress? **Ans:** $28.

17. Kevin found 5 shells, which is one-third of what he already had. How many shells did he have at first? **Ans:** 20 shells.

18. Six is one-half of 3 times what number?
    Ans: If one-half of 3 times some number is 6, then 2 halves of 3 times the number is 12. Since 12 is 3 times some number, then that number is one-third of 12, or 4.

19. Five is one-fourth of 2 times what number?
    Ans: If one-fourth of 2 times some number is 5, then 4 fourths of 2 times that number is 20. Four-fourths is same as the number. Since 20 is 2 times that number, then the number will be one-half of 20, or 10.
    Note—*In these problems, ask child to work on the first relationship first. So we would tackle the issue of "5 is one-fourth of." Multiply 5 by 4, we get 20. Once we have figured that out, we go on to the second part. Now we can change the problem to read, 20 is equal to 2 times some number and the number is 10.*

20. Eight is one-third of 4 times what number?
    Ans: If one-third of 4 times some number is equal to 8, then 3 thirds of 4 times that number is equal to 8 times 3 or, 24. Now 24 is 4 times some number, so that number will be one-fourth of 24 or, 6.

21. Nine is one-half of 6 times what number? H*int: Nine times 2 is equal to what?* **Ans:** 3.

22. Nine is one-half of 3 times what number? **Ans:** 6.

23. Seven is one-sixth of 3 times what number? H*int: Seven times 6 is equal to what?* **Ans:** 14.

24. Seven is one-sixth of 7 times what number? **Ans:** 14.

25. Seven is one-fifth of 5 times what number? **Ans:** 7.

26. Twelve is one-third of 9 times what number? **Ans:** 4.

27. Eleven is one-sixth of 3 times what number? **Ans:** 22.

28. Pam's purse cost $10, which is one-third of 6 times the cost of her shoes. What is the cost of her shoes?
    Ans: If one-third of 6 times the cost of the purse is $10, then 3 thirds

of 6 times the cost is 3 times $10, or $30. If 6 times the cost of the shoes is $30, the cost of the cap would be one-sixth of $30, or $5.

29. A teacher bought a book for $20, which is one-third of 4 times what the rest of his books cost. What is the cost of the rest of the books he bought? **Ans:** $15.

30. The head of a fish is 6 inches long, which is one-fourth of 3 times the length of its body. What is the length of the fish's body? **Ans:** 8 inches.

31. A boy lost $15, which is one-fourth of 5 times the money he had left. How much money did he have at first? **Ans:** $27.

32. Eight is one-third of one-half of what number?
Ans: If one-third of one-half of some number is 8, then 3 thirds of one-half of that number is 3 times 8, or 24. If one-half of some number is 24, 2 halves of that number equals 2 times 24, or 48.

33. Four is one-third of one-fifth of what number?
Ans: If one-third of one-fifth of some number is 4, then 3 thirds of one-fifth of that number is 3 times 4, or 12. If one-fifth of some number is 12, then 5 fifths of that number equals 5 times 12, or 60.

34. Three is one-fifth of one-fourth of what number? **Ans:** 60.

35. Two is one-eighth of one-fourth of what number? **Ans:** 64.

36. Two is one-seventh of one-sixth of what number? **Ans:** 84. Four is one-tenth of one-fifth of what number? **Ans:** 200.

37. Twelve is one-third of half of what number? **Ans:** 72.

38. Six is 2 thirds of one-third of what number? **Ans:** 27.

39. Four is two fifths of one-third of what number? **Ans:** 30.

40. Five is one-half of one-seventh of what number? **Ans:** 70.

41. 1 is $\frac{1}{2}$ of what number? **Ans:** 2.

42. 1 is $\frac{1}{3}$ of what number? **Ans:** 3.

43. 1 is $\frac{1}{4}$ of what number? **Ans:** 4.

44. 1 is $\frac{1}{6}$ of what number? **Ans:** 6.

45. 1 is $\frac{1}{7}$ of what number? **Ans:** 7.

46. 1 is $\frac{1}{9}$ of what number? **Ans:** 9.

47. 3 is $\frac{1}{2}$ of what number? **Ans:** 6.

48. 4 is $\frac{1}{3}$ of what number? **Ans:** 12.

49. 5 is $\frac{1}{4}$ of what number? **Ans:** 20.

50. 6 is $\frac{1}{6}$ of what number? **Ans:** 36.

51. 7 is $\frac{1}{7}$ of what number? **Ans:** 49.

52. 10 is $\frac{1}{9}$ of what number? **Ans:** 90.

53. 1 is $\frac{1}{10}$ of what number? **Ans:** 10.

54. 1 is $\frac{2}{10}$ of what number? **Ans:** 5.

55. 6 is $\frac{1}{3}$ of what number? **Ans:** 18.

56. 6 is $\frac{2}{3}$ of what number? **Ans:** 9.

57. 10 is $\frac{1}{5}$ of what number? **Ans:** 50.

58. 10 is $\frac{2}{5}$ of what number? **Ans:** 25.

59. 12 is $\frac{1}{3}$ of what number? **Ans:** 36.

60. 12 is $\frac{2}{3}$ of what number? **Ans:** 18.

61. 9 is $\frac{1}{4}$ of what number? **Ans:** 39. 36

62. 9 is $\frac{3}{4}$ of what number? **Ans:** 12.

Lesson 9 — *Arithmetic Analysis*

1. SIX is 2 thirds of what number?
   Ans: If 2 thirds of some number is 6, then one-third of that number is one-half of 6, which is 3, and so 3 thirds of that number, is 3 times 3, or 9.
   Note—*Although your child may know of other ways of solving these problems, we ask that your child think these problems out-loud using the unit method given here.*

2. Nine is 3 fourths of what number?
   Ans: If 3 fourths of some number is 9, then one-fourth of that number is one-third of 9, or 3 (One-third because 3 fourths only has 3 fourths.) and 4 fourths of that number, is 4 times 3, or 12.

3. Six is two-thirds of what number?
   Ans: If one-third of some number is 6, 2 thirds of that number is 2 times 6, or 12.

4. Ten is 2 fifths of what number? **Ans:** 25.

5. Twelve is 4 sixths of what number? **Ans:** 18.

6. Ten is 5 sevenths of what number? **Ans:** 14.

7. Eight is 4 ninths of what number? **Ans:** 18.

8. Nine is 3 fifths of what number? **Ans:** 15.

9. Fifteen is 5 sixths of what number? **Ans:** 18.

10. Ten is 5 eighths of what number? **Ans:** 16.

11. Sixteen is 8 ninths of what number? **Ans:** 18.

12. Fourteen is 7 thirds of what number? **Ans:** 6.

13. Frank is 12 years old, and his age is 3 fifths of Danny's age. How old is Danny?
    Ans: If 3 fifths of Frank's age is 12 years, one-fifth of his age is one-third of 12 years, or 4 years, and 5 fifths is 5 times 4 years, or 20 years.

14. Andy gave his brother 10 coins, which is 2 thirds of all the coins he had. How many coins did he have?
    Ans: If 2 thirds of his coins number 10, then one-third is one-half of 10 coins, or 5 coins, and 3 thirds is 3 times 5 coins, or 15 coins.

15. A girl received $12 from her mom, which is 4 sixths of the money she had before. How much did she have at first? **Ans:** $18.

16. Leslie got too big for her bike and sold it for $24, which was 6 fifths of the cost of the bike. What was its cost? **Ans:** $20.

17. A student sold his car for $3000. His profit is one-fifth of what he paid for the car. What did he pay for the car? **Ans:** $2500.

18. Frank broke 12 of his models, which is 2 fifths of the number he had. How many models does he have left?
    Ans: If 2 fifths of his models are 12, one-fifth of his number will be one-half of 12 models, or 6 models, and 5 fifths, or the whole number, is 5 times 6, or 30 models. 30 − 12 equals 18, the number of models left.

19. Martin is 20 years old, and 4 fifths of his age is twice his brother's age. What is the age of his brother?
    Ans: Four-fifths of 20 years is 16 years. If 16 years is twice his brother's age, the brother's age will be one-half of 16 years, or 8 years.

20. Ten is one-half of 4 fifths of what number?
    Ans: If one-half of 4 fifths of some number is 10, then 2 halves of 4 fifths of that number, is twice 10, or 20. If 20 is 4 fifths of some number, then one-fifth of that number is one-fourth of 20, or 5, and 5 fifths, is 5 times 5, or 25.

21. Twelve is one-third of 6 sevenths of what number?
    Ans: If one-third of 6 sevenths of some number is 12, then 3 sevenths of that number will be 3 times 12, or 36. If 36 is 6 sevenths of some number, one-seventh is one-sixth of 36, or 6, and 7 sevenths, or the number, is 7 times 6, or 42.
    Note—*The following problems should be solved using the methodology shown in problem 21. Do not introduce concepts of algebra.*

22. Sixteen is 2 fifths of 10 fourths of what number? **Ans:** 16.

23. Fifteen is 5 sixths of 6 sevenths of what number? **Ans:** 21.

24. Fourteen is 7 fourths of 4 thirds of what number? **Ans:** 6.

25. Eighteen is 9 eighths of 4 sevenths of what number? **Ans:** 28.

26. Twenty is 5 fourths of 8 thirds of what number? **Ans:** 6.

27. One is one-fourth of one-third of what number? **Ans:** 1 twelfths.

hirds of what number? **Ans:** 2 twelfths.

ds of what number? **Ans:** 1 half.

; of what number? **Ans:** 2.

hs of what number? **Ans:** 16 thirds.

for $400 which is 4 fifths of 5 sixths of the
hat did the computer cost?
xths of the cost is $400, one-fifth of 5 sixths
rth of $400, or $100. If one-fifth of 5 sixths, or
ost is $100, 6 sixths, or the cost, is 6 times $100, or

33. Mr. Johnson sold his tractor for $1400, which is 7 eighths of 4 thirds
of its original cost. What was the cost of the tractor?
Ans: If 7 eighths of 4 thirds of the cost of the tractor is $1400, one-
eighth of 4 thirds of its cost will be one-seventh of $1400, or $200,
and 4 thirds of its cost will be 8 times 200, or $1600. If 4 thirds of
the cost is $1600, one-third will be one-fourth of $1600, or $400, and
3 thirds, will be 3 times $400, or $1200.

34. Alan's hat cost $6, which is 3 fourths of 4 fifths of the cost of his sun
glasses. What is the cost of his sun glasses?
Ans: One-fourth of 4 fifths is one-fifth, and 3 fourths of 4 fifths are
3 fifths. If $6 is 3 fifths of the cost of his sun glasses, one-fifth of the
cost is one-third of $6, or $2, and 5 fifths are 5 times 2, or $10.

35. Twenty meters of a pole is in the water, which is 2 fifths of 5 sevenths
of the length in the air. What is the length of the pole?
Ans: Two-fifths of 5 sevenths is 2 sevenths. If 2 sevenths of the
length in the air is 20 meters, one-seventh of the length is one-half of
20, or 10 meters, and 7 sevenths is 7 times 10 meters, or 70 meters,
the length in the air. When added to 20 meters, the length in the
water, gives 90 meters, the length of the pole.

36. A pole is 30 meters in the air, which is 3 fifths of its height. What is
the length of the pole? **Ans:** 50 meters.

37. A book cost $24, which is 3 fourths its cost. What was the cost of
the book? **Ans:** $32.

38. Anna's new bike cost $200. The special biking outfit she bought cost
4 fifths of the cost of the bike. What did her biking outfit cost? **Ans:**
$160.

39. A park has 24 geese, and 3 fourths of the number of geese equals 2 times the number of ducks. How many ducks are in the park? **Ans:** 9 ducks.

40. A man bought a jacket for $60, which is 5 fourths of 2 times what the shirt cost. What was the cost of shirt?
Ans: Five-fourths of 4 times the cost of the jacket is 5 times the cost of the shirt. If 5 times the cost of the shirt is $60, the cost of the shirt is one-fifth of $60, or $12.

41. Ten is 2 thirds of what number? **Ans:** 15.

42. Twelve is 3 fourths of what number? **Ans:** 16.

43. Fifteen is one-third of what number? **Ans:** 45.

44. Twenty is 5 sixths of what number? **Ans:** 24.

45. Eighteen is 3 eighths of what number? **Ans:** 48.

46. 2 is $\frac{2}{3}$ of what number? **Ans:** 3.

47. 6 is $\frac{2}{3}$ of what number? **Ans:** 9.

48. 8 is $\frac{2}{3}$ of what number? **Ans:** 12.

49. 10 is $\frac{2}{3}$ of what number? **Ans:** 15.

50. 12 is $\frac{2}{3}$ of what number? **Ans:** 18.

51. 20 is $\frac{2}{3}$ of what number? **Ans:** 30.

52. 60 is $\frac{2}{3}$ of what number? **Ans:** 90.

53. 1200 is $\frac{2}{3}$ of what number? **Ans:** 1800.

54. Which is bigger; $\frac{2}{3}$ of a number or one-half? **Ans:** One-half.

55. What's the difference between one-half of 30 and two-thirds of 30? **Ans:** 5.

56. I gave my mom 20 coins, which is 2 thirds of all the coins I had. How many coins did I have?
Ans: If 2 thirds of the coins number 20, then one-third is10 coins, and 3 thirds is 3 times 10 coins, or 30 coins.

57. A girl received $15 from her mom, which is 3 fifths of the money she had before. How much did she have at first? **Ans:** $25.

58. Jose bought a bike. $24 is 2 thirds of the cost of the bike. What was its cost? **Ans:** $36.

59. A woman sold her car for $2400. Her loss is one-fourth of what she paid for the car. What did she pay for the car? **Ans:** $3000.

60. A pole is 24 meters in the air, which is 3 eighths of its height. What is the length of the pole? **Ans:** 64 meters.

61. A pole is 30 meters in the air, which is 3 fifths of 2 fourths of the length of the pole. What is the length of the pole? **Ans:** 100 meters.

62. A book cost $24, which is 3 fourths of 4 fifths of the cost of the book and a calculator. What was the cost of the calculator?
Ans: One-fourth of 4 fifths is one-fifth, and 3 fourths of 4 fifths is 3 fifths. If 3 fifths of the cost of both is $24, one-fifth of the cost is one-third of $24, or $8, and 5 fifths is 5 times $8, or $40. $40, the cost of both, minus $24, the cost of the book, leaves $16, the cost of the calculator.

63. Anna's new bike cost $200. The special biking outfit she bought cost 4 fifths of the cost of the bike. What did her biking outfit cost? **Ans:** $160.

64. A park has 24 geese, and 3 fourths of the number of geese equals one half the number of ducks. How many ducks are in the park? **Ans:** 36 ducks.

65. A man bought a jacket for $90, which is 5 fourths of 4 times what his shoes cost. What was the cost of shoes?
Ans: Five-fourths of 4 times the cost of the jacket is 5 times the cost of the shoes. The shoes cost one-fifth of $60, or $12.⌣

Lesson 10 – *Relationship of Numbers*

SIX is one-half of what number? **Ans:** 12.

1. Eight is one-half of one-half of what number? **Ans:** 32.

2. Eight is one-half of one-fourth of what number? **Ans:** 64.

3. Eight is one-fifth of two-fifths of what number? **Ans:** Eight is one-fifth of 40. If 40 is two-fifths of a number, then one-fifth of the number is 40 divided by 2 or, 20. The five-fifths of that number is 5 times 20 or, 100.

4. 20 is one-third of one-half of what number?
   Ans: First do the first fraction. 20 is one-third of 60. Now do the second fraction which is one-half. 60 is one-half of 120.

5. 100 is one-third of one-third of what number?
   Ans: 100 is one-third of 300. 300 is one-third of 900.

6. 100 is 4 fifths of one-half of what number?
   Ans: If 100 is 4 fifths of a number, then one-fifth of that number is 25. The number is 5 times 25 or, 125. Then 125 is one-half of 250.

7. 100 is one-third of one-half of what number? **Ans:** 600.

8. 200 is 4 fifths of 5 sixths of what number? **Ans:** 300.

9. 210 is 3 fourths of 2 thirds of what number? **Ans:** 420.

10. 10 is 2 fifths of one-third of what number? **Ans:** 150.

11. 70 is 7 halves of 3 fifths of what number? **Ans:** 105.

12. 40 is 4 thirds of 3 fourths of what number? **Ans:** 40.

13. 400 is 4 fifths of 5 sixths of what number? **Ans:** 600.

14. Jack bought a bookcase for $200, which is 4 fifths of 5 sixths of the cost of the books in it. What did the books cost?
    Ans: If 4 fifths of 5 sixths of the cost is $200, one-fifth of 5 sixths of the cost is one-fourth of $200, or $500. If one-fifth of 5 sixths, or one-sixth, of the cost is $50, 6 sixths, or the cost, is 6 times $50, or $300.

15. Illya sold his car for $700, which is 7 eighths of 4 thirds of its original cost. What was the cost of the car?
    Ans: If 7 eighths of 4 thirds of the cost of the car is $700, one-eighth

of 4 thirds of its cost will be one-seventh of $700, or $100, and 4 thirds of its cost will be 8 times 100, or $800. If 4 thirds of the cost is $800, one-third will be one-fourth of $800, or $200, and 3 thirds, will be 3 times $200, or $600.

16. First set of cables for the computer cost $6, which is 3 fourths of 4 fifths of the cost of the second set. What is the cost of the second set of cables?
Ans: One-fourth of 4 fifths is one-fifth, and 3 fourths of 4 fifths are 3 fifths. If $6 is 3 fifths of the cost of the second set, one-fifth of the cost is one-third of $6, or $2, and 5 fifths are 5 times 2, or $10.

17. Twenty meters of a ship is under the water, which is 2 fifths of 5 sevenths of its height in the air. What is the total height of the ship?
Ans: Two-fifths of 5 sevenths is 2 sevenths. If 2 sevenths of the height in the air is 20 meters, one-seventh of the height is one-half of 20, or 10 meters, and 7 sevenths is 7 times 10 meters, or 70 meters, the height above the water. When added to 20 meters, the height in the water, gives 90 meters, the total height of the ship.

18. A bridge spans 30 meters over the river, which is 3 fifths of 2 fourths of the length of the bridge including the part on the land. What is the length of the bridge? **Ans:** 100 meters.

19. A book cost $12, which is 3 fourths of 4 fifths of the cost of the book and a calculator. What was the cost of the calculator?
Ans: One-fourth of 4 fifths is one-fifth, and 3 fourths of 4 fifths is 3 fifths. If 3 fifths of the cost of both is $12, one-fifth of the cost is one-third of $12, or $4, and 5 fifths is 5 times $4, or $20. $20, the cost of both, minus $12, the cost of the book, leaves $8, the cost of the calculator.

20. Jill has 24 party dresses, and 3 fourths of the number of dresses equals 2 times the number of jackets she has. How many jackets does she have? **Ans:** 9 jackets.

21. Molly has 8 really good friends, and 3 fourths of the number of her good friends equals two times the number of best friends she has. How many best friends does she have? **Ans:** 3 best friends.

22. How far can a camel walk in 20 days if he can walk 32 miles in 4 days?
Ans: In one day camel goes 8 miles, in 20 days, 160 miles.

23. If 6 workers build 10 meters of a castle in a given time, how many meters can 54 workers build in the same time?

Ans: 54 workers, which is 9 times 6 workers, can build 9 times 10 meters of the castle, or 90 meters, in the same time.

24. Kevin bought 6 noise makers for $11. How many could he have bought for $44?

Ans: $44, which is 4 times $11, would have bought 4 times 6 noise makers, or 24 noise makers.

25. Two girls do some work for a family and earn $120 in 3 days. How much could they earn in 27 days?

Ans: In 27 days, which is 9 times 3 days, they could earn 9 times $120, or $1080.

26. If 5 finches weigh same as one parrot, how many parrots weigh same as 30 finches?

Ans: 30 finches, which is 6 times 5 parrots, weigh same as 6 times one parrot, or 6 parrots.

27. If $8 will buy 5 stamps, how many stamps can you buy for $56? **Ans:** 35 stamps.

28. If 6 balloons cost 2 thirds of $12, what will 30 balloons cost?

Ans: 30 balloons, which is 5 times 6 balloons, will cost 5 times 2 thirds of $12; 2 thirds of $12 are $8, and 5 times $8 is $40.

29. Devin paid $600 for rent at the rate of $100 for $3\frac{1}{2}$ days. For how many days did he pay? **Ans:** 21 days.

30. If 4 boys can do a piece of work in 18 days, how long will 12 boys take to do it?

Ans: 12 boys, which is 3 times 4 boys, will need one-third of 18 days, or 6 days.

31. If 6 workers can build a rocket in 10 fourth days, how long will it take 3 workers to build it?

Ans: 3 workers, which is one-half of 6 workers, will require 2 times 10 fourths days, or 20 fourths days, or 5 days.

32. If $150 is 3 eighths of what Julio earns in 5 days, how much will he earn in 15 days?

Ans: If 3 eighths of what Julio earns in 5 days is $150, and one-eighth of what he earns is one-third of $150, or $50. Then 8 eighths, or his earnings for 5 days, is 8 times $50, or $400. In 15 days, which is 3 times 5 days, he will earn 3 times $400, or $1200.

33. 18 gardeners are 3 fifths of the number that can plant a field in 8 days. How many gardeners would be needed to plant it in 24 days?
Ans: If 3 fifths of the number required is 18, then one-fifth of the number will be one-third of 18, or 6 gardeners. 5 fifths, or the number, will be 5 times 6, or 30 gardeners; to plant it in 24 days, which is 3 times 8 days, would require one-third of 30 gardeners, or 10 gardeners.

34. $45 is $12 more than one-third of what number? **Ans:** 99.

35. $30 is $6 more than 2 thirds of what number? **Ans:** 36.

36. $20 is $4 more than 2 fourths of what number? **Ans:** 32.

37. $20 is $4 more than 2 thirds of 4 times what Vergie paid for a lock, and her extra keys cost 5 times as much as the lock. What is the cost of each?
Ans: Since $20 is $4 more than 2 thirds of 4 times the cost of the lock, $20 − $4, or $16, will be 2 thirds of 4 times the cost. Four times the cost is $24, and the cost is one-fourth of $24, or $6. Since the keys cost 5 times as much as the lock, the keys cost $30.

38. If $8 will buy 5 stamps, how many stamps can you buy for $32? **Ans:** 20 stamps.

39. Forty is 8 more than 2 thirds of what number? **Ans:** 48.

40. Martin is 4 years old, and his age is one-third of one-fourth of his father's age. How old is his father?
Ans: If one-third of one-fourth of the father's age is 4 years, then 3 thirds of one-fourth of the father's age is 3 times 4, or 12 years. If one-fourth of the father's age is 12 years, then 4 fourths will be 4 times 12 years, or 48 years.

41. Ella's hat cost $30, which is one-fifth of one-half the cost of her coat. What is the cost of the coat? **Ans:** $300.

42. Philip's notebook cost $4, which is one-half of one-third of the cost of his books. What was the cost of his books?
Ans: If one-half of one-third of the cost of his notebook is $4, then 2 halves of one third of the cost is $8. If one third of the cost is $8, 3 thirds, or the cost of the books, will be 3 times $8, or $24.

43. A farmer paid $100 for the fertilizer, which is one-fifth of one-third of the cost of seeds. What is the cost of the seeds? **Ans:** $1500.

44. The plant's tip is 3 inches long, and its roots are 5 inches long, which is one-half of one-third of the length of its stem. What is the length of the plant?
Ans: If one-half of one-third of the length of the stem is 5 inches, one-third of the length of the stem is 10 inches, so the length of the stem is 30 inches; $30 + 5 + 3$ is 38 inches, the length of the plant.

45. By what number do you divide 60 to get $\frac{1}{3}$ of 12? **Ans:** 15.

46. One-third of 2 dozen is equal to how many twelfths of 2 dozen? **Ans:** 4.

47. How many more minutes in one-tenth of an hour are there than in one-twelfths of an hour? **Ans:** One minute.

48. If $\frac{5}{12}$ of a car costs $10000, then what is the cost of the car?
Ans: One-twelfth of the car costs one-fifth of $10000 or $2000, then the whole car costs 12 times $2000 or $24000. ⌣

Lesson 11 – *Fraction as Part of a Number*

FOUR is what part of 8?
   Ans: Four is one-half of 8.

1. Three and 6 are what parts of 12?
   Ans: Three is one-fourth of 12, since 4 times 3 is 12. 6 is one-half of 12, since 2 times 6 is 12.

2. Four and 8 are what part of 16?
   Ans: One-fourth; one-half.

3. Three and 6 are what part of 24?
   Ans: One-eighth; one-fourth.

4. Seven and 3 are what part of 21?
   Ans: One-third; one-seventh.

5. Four and 9 are what parts of 36?
   Ans: One-ninth; one-fourth.

6. What is the relation of 2 to 6? of 4 to 8?
   Ans: One-third; one-half.

7. What is the relation of 3 to 9? of 5 to 10?
   Ans: One-third; one-half.

8. What is the relation of 3 to 12? of 4 to 16?
   Ans: One-fourth; one-fourth.

9. What is the relation of 5 to 20? of 6 to 36?
   Ans: One-fourth; one-sixth.

10. What is the relation of 7 to 42? of 8 to 40?
    Ans: One sixth; one-fifth.

11. What is the relation of 6 to 54? of 9 to 27?
    Ans: One ninth; one-third.

12. What is the relation of 2 to 14? of 3 to 18?
    Ans: One seventh; one-sixth.

13. What is the relation of 5 to 20? of 10 to 12?
    Ans: One-fourth; five-sixth.

14. What is the relation of 5 to 35? of 48 to 120?
    Ans: One seventh; one-sixth.

15. If 6 crayons cost 100 cents, what will 3 crayons cost?

Ans: Three crayons, which is one-half of 6 crayons, will cost one-half of 100 cents, or 50 cents.

16. How much will 5 notebooks cost if 20 notebooks cost $16?

Ans: If 20 notebooks cost $16, 5 notebooks, or one-fourth of 20 notebooks, will cost one-fourth of $16, or $4.

17. How much will 3 flying carpets cost if 18 of them cost $24?

Ans: If 18 flying carpets cost $24, 3 flying carpets, or one-sixth of 18 flying carpets, will cost one-sixth of $24, or $4.

18. If 14 pencils cost 35 cents, what will 2 pencils cost, at the same rate?

Ans: If 14 pencils cost 35 cents, 2 pencils, or one-seventh of 14 pencils, will cost one-seventh of 35 cents, or 5 cents.

19. If 10 peaches are worth 12 oranges, how many oranges are 5 peaches worth?

Ans: If 10 peaches are worth 12 oranges, 5 peaches, or one-half of 10 peaches, will cost one-half of 12 oranges, or 6 oranges.

20. How much will 4 apples cost if 16 apples cost 240 cents?

Ans: 60 cents.

21. How much will 9 disks cost if 27 disks cost $36? **Ans:** $12.

22. What is the cost of 7 minutes of phone conversation to a foreign country if 49 minutes cost $9? **Ans:** $1.30.

23. If 42 plants cost $108, what is the cost of 7 plants? **Ans:** $18.

24. If 12 plants cost $11, what is the cost of 108 plants? **Ans:** $99.

25. What is the cost of 5 apples if 15 apples cost 2 thirds of 18 dimes?

Ans: 2 thirds of 18 dimes are 12 dimes. If 15 apples cost 12 dimes, 5 apples, or one-third of 15 apples, cost one-third of 12 dimes, or 4 dimes.

26. If 2 boxes of chocolates cost $10, what will 2 thirds of 6 boxes cost?

Ans: 2 thirds of 6 boxes are 4 boxes. If 2 boxes cost $10, then 4 boxes, will cost $20.

27. If 3 fourths of 48 candies cost $40, what will 3 fourths of 12 candies cost?

Ans: If 3 fourths of 48 candies cost $40, 3 fourths of 12 candies, or one-fourth of 3 fourths of 48 candies, will cost one-fourth of $40, or $10.

28. If Ian walked 88 miles in 33 days, how far can he walk in 3 days?
Ans: 8 miles.

29. If Lee rode his bike 84 miles in 6 hours, how far did he walk in 2 hours? **Ans:** 32 miles.

30. James bought 8 pens at the rate of $45 a dozen. How much did 8 pens cost?
Ans: If one dozen pens cost $45, then 8 pens, or 2 thirds of a dozen, will cost 2 thirds of $45, or $30.

31. Geena had 27 roses. She gave one-third to her teacher and one-third to Annie. How many roses does she have left?
Ans: She gave away, one-third + one-third which is 2 thirds. Three-thirds − 2 thirds = one-third what she has left. One-third of 27 is 9.

32. Kim worked 5 weeks for $70 a week, and received 21 sacks of cement worth 10 dollars each plus cash. How much did she receive in cash?
Ans: Kim's wages for 5 weeks, at $70 a week, are $350. Twenty one sacks of cement at $10 each are worth $210. 350 − 210 = 140, the amount she received in cash.

33. A plant researcher exchanged 10 bags of rye seeds, worth 60 cents a bag, for sesame seeds worth $3 a bag. How many bags of sesame seeds did he receive?
Ans: Ten bags of rye, at 60 cents a bags, are worth 600 cents, or $6, for which we can buy as many bags of sesame, at $3 a bag, as 3 is contained in 6, which is 2.

34. Think of a number, multiply by 10, divide by 5, multiply by 3, divide by 6, add 30, subtract the original number, divide by 10, then add 7. What is the result?
Ans: Multiplying by 10 and dividing by 5, we have 2 times the number. Multiplying by 3 and dividing by 6, we have the number; adding 30, we have the number + 30; subtracting the original number, we have 30 dividing by 10 and adding 7, we have 10.

35. A girl exchanged 20 dolls worth $2 each for books worth $5 a box. How many boxes of books did she receive? **Ans:** 8 boxes.

36. If Nan walked 44 miles in 22 days, how far can she walk in 3 days?
Ans: 6 miles.

37. If a train goes 84 miles in 6 hours, how far did it go in 3 hours? **Ans:** 42 miles.

38. James bought 8 shirts at the rate of $45 for 3 shirts. How much did the 8 shirts cost? **Ans:** $120.

39. I planted 27 bushes. One-third of these died. I then planted one-third more of the number that were left. How many bushes are now in my garden?
Ans: 18 are left. One third more makes it 24 bushes.

40. Sharon worked 5 weeks for $250 a week, how much did she get for 3 weeks? **Ans:** $150.

41. A man exchanged 36 parts worth $3 each for parts worth $4 each. How many parts did he receive? **Ans:** 4.

42. A man exchanged 24 nuts worth 2 for $1 for bolts worth 3 for $9. How many bolts did he get?
Ans: 24 nuts cost $12. For $12 he can get, 5 bolts. ☺

Lesson 12 – *Properties of Numbers*

1. NUMBERS which can be created by multiplying together other numbers, each of which is larger than one, are called *composite numbers*. 6 is a composite number because $6 = 2 \times 3$. *Ask child to give example.*

2. Numbers which cannot be produced by multiplying together two or more numbers, each of which is larger than a unit, are called *prime numbers*.
2 is a prime number.
23 is a also prime number because there are no two numbers that when multiplied together will produce 23. *Ask child to give example.*

3. The numbers which, when multiplied together, will produce a composite number, are called *factors* of the composite number.
2 and 3 are factors of 6. *Ask child to give example.*

4. A number which is one or more times another number is called a *multiple* of that number.
6 is a multiple of 3. *Ask child to give example.*

5. When these factors are prime numbers, they are called *prime factors*.
Ans: 46 is a multiple of 23 and 2. Both of these multiples 2 and 23, are prime factors.

6. The square root of a number is one of the two *equal factors* of that number; the cube root, one of the three equal factors; the fourth root, one of the four equal factors.
6 has two equal factors 4×4. 4 is also its square root.
27 has three equal factors $= 3 \times 3 \times 3$. 3 is also its cube root.

7. A divisor common to two or more numbers is called their *common divisor*.
3 is a common divisor to both 12 and 15.

8. The result of the multiplication of two numbers is called their *product*.
6 is a product of 2 and 3.

The greatest divisor common to two or more numbers is called their *greatest common divisor*.
A number which is one or more times another number is called a multiple of that number.

A multiple common to two or more numbers is called their *common multiple*. $21 = 7 \times 3$ and $27 = 9 \times 3$, so 27 and 21 have a common multiple of 3.

The least multiple common to two or more numbers is called their *least common multiple*. Two is the least common multiple of 40 and 50.

1. What numbers multiplied together will produce 4? 8? 10? 16? 12? 18? 24?
   Ans: 2 and 2; 4 and 2; 2 and 5, etc.

2. What numbers multiplied together will produce 15? 21? 28? 35? 36? 39? 48?
   Ans: 3 and 5; 3 and 7; 4 and 7, etc.

3. What numbers multiplied together will produce 40? 42? 45? 49? 50? 51? 52?
   Ans: 4 and 10; 7 and 6; 9 and 5, etc.

4. Which of the following numbers are prime, and which are composite: 4, 5, 6, 7, 8, 9, 10, 11, 12, 13, 14, 15, 16, 17, 18, 19, 20, 21, 22, 23.
   Ans: Primes: 5, 7, 11, 13, 17, 19, 23. The rest are composite.

5. Name the prime and composite numbers in the following list: 24, 25, 26, 27, 28, 29, 30, 31, 32, 33, 34, 35, 36, 37, 38, 39, 40, 41.
   Ans: Primes: 29, 31, 37, 41.

6. What are the factors of 12? 20? 16? 33? 30? 24? 27? 18? 25? 32?
   Ans: 3 and 4, or 6 and 2; 4 and 5, or 2 and 10; 4 and 4, or 2 and 8, etc.

7. What are the factors of 9? 10? 14? 34? 36? 40? 48? 50? 56? 60? 63? 72?
   Ans: 3 and 3; 2 and 5; 2 and 7, etc.

8. What are the prime factors of 4? 6? 9? 12? 15? 18?
   Ans: 2×2; 2×3; 3×3, etc.

9. What are the prime factors of 10? 20? 21? 22? 24? 25? 27? 28? 30?
   Ans: 2×5; $2 \times 2 \times 5$; 3×7, etc.

10. What are the prime factors of 32? 33? 35? 44? 45? 46? 48? 49? 50? **Ans:** $2 \times 2 \times 2 \times 2 \times 2$; 3×11; 7×5, etc.

11. What are the prime factors of 52? 54? 55? 56? 57? 60? 64? 68? 70? 72? 75? 80?
Ans: $2 \times 2 \times 13$; $3 \times 3 \times 3 \times 2$; 5×11, etc.

12. Is it possible to divide a number exactly by any number except its prime factors, or some product of them?
Ans: It is not.
Ask for an example such as 12 divided by all other numbers smaller than it. 1, 2, 3 are prime, the rest are products of these three numbers.

13. Name the divisors of 4; of 6; of 8; of 10; of 12; of 14; of 16; of 20.
Ans: 2; 2 and 3; 2 and 4; 2 and 5, etc.

14. What divisors are common to 4 and 6? to 8 and 12? To 6 and 9?
Ans: 2; 4; 3.

15. What divisors are common to 10 and 30? to 9 and 18? To 8 and 24?
Ans: 2, 5, 10; 3, 9; 2, 4, 8.

16. What divisors are common to 9 and 27? to 10 and 20? To 16 and 24? **Ans:** 3, 9; 2, 5, 10; 2, 4, 8.

17. What is a common divisor of 8 and 24? of 9 and 15? of 15 and 20?
Ans: 4; 3; 5.

18. What is a common divisor of 18 and 80? of 16 and 32? of 32 and 40? **Ans:** 2; 8; 8.

19. What is the greatest common divisor of 4 and 8? of 8 and 24? **Ans:** 4; 8.

20. What is the greatest common divisor of 9 and 27? of 16 and 24? of 24 and 32? **Ans:** 9; 8; 8.

21. What is a multiple of 4? of 3? of 5? of 61 of 11? **Ans:** 8; 9; 15; 24; 55.

22. What is a multiple of 7? of 8? of 9? of 10? of 12? of 20? **Ans:** 22; 14; 32; 27; 50; 72; 30.

23. What is a common multiple of 2 and 3? of 3 and 12? of 4 and 5? of 5 and 6? **Ans:** 6; 12; 20; 30.

24. What is a common multiple of 6 and 7? of 4 and 6? of 5 and 10? of 9 and 12? **Ans:** 84; 24; 50; 108.

25. What is the least common multiple of 4 and 6? of 6 and 8? of 8 and 10? of 10 and 12? **Ans:** 12; 24; 40; 60.

26. What is the least common multiple of 8 and 12?   of 9 and 6?   of 9 and 12?   of 12 and 20? **Ans:** 24;   18;   36;   60.

27. What is the square of 1?   2?   3?   4?   5?   6?   7?   8?   9?   10?   12?   13?
Ans: 1;   4;   9;   16;   25;   36;   49;   64;   81;   100;   121;   144;   169.

28. What is the fourth root of 1?   16?   81?   256?   625?
Ans: 1;   2;   3;   4;   5.

29. Define a prime number and give an example of: composite number; prime factor; common divisor; greatest common divisor; common multiple; least common multiple; square, cube, and fourth power; square, cube, and fourth roots.

Lesson 13 — *Unit Values*

ARITHMETIC analysis is a process of comparing numbers. In comparing, the unit value is considered the basis of the comparison. It is a very important concept.

The following concepts should be explained to the student rather than read by him or her. Create examples as necessary to make sure that the student understands the concept of the unit. Many of the problem solutions show how the unit analysis is done.

Case I—To pass from unit value to value of a group.

If one apple costs 3 cents, what will four apples cost?

Note—Here, 3 cents is the unit value and we want to calculate the value of the group of 4 apples. We use the unit value to figure out the cost of 4 apples. We can do a straight-forward multiplication to solve these problems but it is better for the child when the solution is explained by the unit method.

Ans: If one apple costs 3 cents, 4 apples, which is 4 times one apple, will cost 4 times 3 cents, or 12 cents.

Case II—To pass from a group value to the unit value.

If 4 apples cost 12 cents, what will one apple cost?

Ans: If 4 apples cost 12 cents, one apple, which is one-fourth of 4 apples, will cost one-fourth of 12 cents, or 3 cents.

Note—This is the reverse of the preceding case. We have the group value and we want to figure out the unit value.

Case III—To pass from a number to an another number.

If 3 apples cost 6 cents, what will 4 apples cost?

Ans: If 3 apples cost 6 cents, then one apple will cost $\frac{1}{3}$ of 6 cents, or 2 cents. Four apples will cost 4 times 2 cents, or 8 cents.

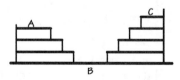

Note—In this case we are to pass from the group of three to the group of four. In comparing three and four, their relationship is not readily seen; but knowing the relationship of three to the unit, and of the unit to four we make the transition from 3 to 4 by passing through the unit. The unit becomes a basis of reference in the comparison, a kind of "stepping-stone" process.

Suppose one is standing at step A, and wishes to get to step C. Unable to go directly from A to C, she first steps down to the starting-point, B, and then go to C. Comparing numbers, when we cannot pass from the one number to the other, we go down to the unit or starting-point of numbers, and then go up to the other number.

In the given problems, we stand three steps above the unit and wish to go four steps above the unit. To do this we first go down three steps, and then up four steps.

Case IV—To pass from a unit to a fraction.

If one box of candies costs \$8, what will $\frac{3}{4}$ of a box cost?

Ans: If one box of candies costs \$8, one-fourth of a box will cost $\frac{1}{4}$ of \$8, or \$2. And three-fourths of a box will cost 3 times \$2, or \$6.

Case V—To pass from a fraction of a group to unit value.

If $\frac{3}{4}$ of a box of candies cost \$6, what will one box cost?

Ans: If three-fourths of a box of candies cost \$6, one-fourth of a box will cost $\frac{1}{3}$ of \$6, or \$2. And if one-fourth of a box cost \$2, four fourths of a box, or one box, will cost 4 times \$2, or \$8.

CASE VI —To pass from a fraction to a fraction.

If three fourths of a pound of fish costs \$15, what will four fifths of a pound cost?

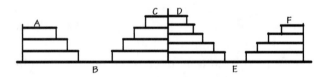

Ans: If three-fourths of a pound cost \$15, one-fourth of a pound will cost $\frac{1}{3}$ of \$15, or \$5. And if one-fourth of a pound costs \$5, four fourths of a pound, or one pound, will cost 4 times 5, or \$20. If one pound cost \$20, one-fifth of a pound will cost $\frac{1}{5}$ of \$20, or \$4, and four fifths of a pound will cost 4 × \$4, or \$16.

Note—In this problem we need to compare two fractions; but since we cannot perceive the relationship between them directly, we must compare them through their relation to the unit. To do this we first go from three fourths to one-fourth, then from one-fourth to the unit, then from the unit to one-fifth, and then to four fifths. ⌣

Lesson 14 – *Numbers to Fractions*

NATURAL Number: a natural number is any whole number bigger than zero, such as 1, 2, 5, 17, etc. (The counting numbers.)

    Proper Fraction: a fraction where the top number (numerator) is smaller than the bottom number (denominator), such as $\frac{2}{3}$.

    Improper Fraction: a fraction where the top number is greater than or equal to the bottom number, such as $\frac{5}{3}$.

    Mixed Number: a number written as a whole number and a fraction, such as $4\frac{2}{3}$.

1. How many thirds are in $4\frac{2}{3}$?
   Ans: In one there are $\frac{3}{3}$ (read as 3 thirds) and in 4 there are 4 times $\frac{3}{3}$, which is $\frac{12}{3}$ and $\frac{12}{3}$ plus $\frac{2}{3}$ is $\frac{14}{3}$. Therefore, in $4\frac{2}{3}$ there are 14 thirds.

2. How many halves are in $3\frac{1}{2}$? $2\frac{1}{2}$? $4\frac{1}{2}$? $6\frac{1}{2}$?
   Ans: In one there are $\frac{2}{2}$ (read as 2 halves), and in 3 there are 3 times $\frac{2}{2}$, which is $\frac{6}{2}$ and $\frac{6}{2}$ plus $\frac{1}{2}$ is $\frac{7}{2}$. Therefore, in $3\frac{1}{2}$ there are 7 halves.
   Ans: $\frac{7}{2}$; $\frac{5}{2}$; $\frac{9}{2}$; $\frac{13}{2}$.

3. How many thirds are in $3\frac{1}{3}$? $2\frac{2}{3}$? $4\frac{1}{3}$? $5\frac{2}{3}$? **Ans:** 10; 8; 13; 19.

4. How many fourths are in $3\frac{1}{4}$? $4\frac{3}{4}$? $2\frac{2}{4}$? $7\frac{3}{4}$? **Ans:** 13; 19; 10; 31.

5. How many fifths are in $1\frac{1}{5}$ $2\frac{2}{5}$? $3\frac{3}{5}$? $4\frac{4}{5}$? **Ans:** 6; 12; 18; 24.

6. How many sixths are in $2\frac{1}{6}$ $3\frac{2}{6}$ $4\frac{3}{6}$ $5\frac{4}{6}$? **Ans:** 13; 20; 27; 34.

7. How many eighths are in $2\frac{3}{8}$ $6\frac{1}{8}$ $7\frac{4}{8}$ $8\frac{5}{8}$? **Ans:** 19; 49; 60; 69.

8. How many sevenths are in of $3\frac{2}{7}$ $5\frac{1}{7}$ $4\frac{3}{7}$ $2\frac{5}{7}$? **Ans:** 23; 36; 31; 19.

9. How many ninths are in $2\frac{2}{9}$ $3\frac{4}{9}$ $7\frac{5}{9}$ $6\frac{7}{9}$? **Ans:** 20; 31; 68; 61.

10. How many tenths are in $5\frac{3}{10}$? $7\frac{5}{10}$? $3\frac{8}{10}$? $6\frac{7}{10}$? **Ans:** 53; 75; 38; 67.

11. Which of these numbers is a proper fraction; $\frac{1}{3}$; $\frac{5}{3}$? **Ans:** $\frac{1}{3}$.

12. Can a mixed number be less than 1? **Ans:** No.

13. Can a natural number be an integer? **Ans:** All natural numbers are integers.

14. Reduce to improper fractions: $2\frac{3}{4}$; $5\frac{2}{3}$; $6\frac{2}{5}$; $4\frac{1}{5}$.
    Ans: $\frac{11}{4}$; $\frac{17}{3}$; $\frac{32}{5}$; $\frac{21}{5}$.

15. Reduce to improper fractions: $5\frac{2}{5}$; $2\frac{5}{6}$; $3\frac{2}{7}$; $8\frac{2}{3}$.
Ans: $\frac{27}{5}$; $\frac{17}{6}$; $\frac{23}{7}$; $\frac{26}{3}$.

16. Reduce to improper fractions: $4\frac{3}{4}$; $6\frac{2}{7}$; $5\frac{1}{8}$; $9\frac{1}{3}$.
Ans: $\frac{10}{4}$; $\frac{44}{7}$; $\frac{41}{8}$; $\frac{28}{3}$.

17. Reduce to improper fractions: $7\frac{2}{3}$; $8\frac{3}{4}$; $6\frac{5}{8}$; $9\frac{4}{5}$.
Ans: $\frac{23}{3}$; $\frac{35}{4}$; $\frac{53}{8}$; $\frac{49}{5}$.

18. If one meter of tape costs $2\frac{1}{3}$ cents, what will 5 meters cost?
Ans: $2\frac{1}{3} = 2 + \frac{1}{3}$. Two is equal to $\frac{6}{3}$, add to that $\frac{1}{3}$, we get $\frac{7}{3}$. If one meter of tape costs $\frac{7}{3}$ cents, 5 meters will cost 5 times $\frac{7}{3}$ cents, which is $\frac{35}{3}$ cents.

19. How many fourths of a dollar will 7 shots cost at the rate of $2\frac{1}{4}$ dollars a shot?
Ans: $2\frac{1}{4}$ equals $\frac{9}{4}$. If one shot costs $\frac{9}{4}$, 7 shots will cost 7 times $\frac{9}{4}$, or $\frac{63}{4}$ dollars.

20. If 4 boys can earn $6\frac{2}{3}$ dollars in a week, how much does each boy earn?
Ans: $6\frac{2}{3}$ equals $\frac{20}{3}$. If 4 boys earn $\frac{20}{3}$ a week, one boy will earn $\frac{1}{4}$ of $\frac{20}{3}$, or $\frac{5}{3}$ dollars.

21. Carrie bought 5 pairs of twinkles for $18\frac{3}{4}$ dollars. How much was each pair?
Ans: $18\frac{3}{4}$ equals $\frac{75}{4}$. If Carrie bought 5 pairs of twinkles for $\frac{75}{4}$, one pair cost $\frac{1}{5}$ of $\frac{75}{4}$, or $\frac{15}{4}$ dollars.

22. How far will a man walk in one hour at the rate of $19\frac{1}{4}$ miles in 7 hours? **Ans:** $\frac{11}{4}$ miles.

23. If 3 children can earn $2\frac{1}{4}$ stars in a day by being good, how many stars can 5 children earn at the same rate?
Ans: $2\frac{1}{4}$ equals $\frac{9}{4}$. If 3 children can earn $\frac{9}{4}$ stars, one child will earn $\frac{1}{3}$ of $\frac{9}{4}$, or $\frac{3}{4}$ of a star, and 5 children will earn 5 times $\frac{3}{4}$, or $\frac{15}{4}$ stars.

24. If a girl helps her mom wrap presents and earn $5\frac{1}{4}$ dollars in 3 hours, how much can she earn in 5 hours?
Ans: $5\frac{1}{4}$ equals $\frac{21}{4}$. In one day she will earn $\frac{1}{3}$ of $\frac{21}{4}$ dollars, and in 5 hours 5 times $\frac{7}{4}$, or $\frac{35}{4}$ dollars.

25. How long will it take a boy to do 8 math problems if it takes him $13\frac{3}{4}$ minutes to do 5 problems?
Ans: $13\frac{3}{4}$ equals $\frac{55}{4}$. To do one problem, it will take $\frac{11}{4}$ minutes, and to do 8 problems, it will take $\frac{88}{4}$, or 22 minutes.

26. How far can Harry walk in 5 hours if he can walk $8\frac{2}{5}$ miles in 2 hours?
Ans: $8\frac{2}{5}$ equals $\frac{42}{5}$. In one hour he can walk $\frac{21}{5}$ miles, and in 5 hours, 21 miles.

27. How much do 9 bags of chips cost if 2 bags cost $\$10\frac{2}{3}$?
Ans: $10\frac{2}{3}$ equals $\frac{32}{3}$. One box will cost $\frac{16}{3}$, and 9 boxes will cost 9 times $\frac{16}{3}$, or $\frac{144}{3}$ or 48 dollars.

28. If $2\frac{2}{3}$ meters of fog cost $\$16$, how much will one meter cost?
Ans: $2\frac{2}{3}$ equals $\frac{8}{3}$. If $\frac{8}{3}$ meters of fog cost $\$16$, $\frac{1}{4}$ of a meter will cost $\frac{1}{8}$ of $\$16$, or $\$2$ and $\frac{3}{3}$, or one meter, will cost 3 times 2, or $\$6$.

29. If $3\frac{1}{2}$ tons of fertilizer cost $\$2100$, how much will one ton cost, at the same rate?
Ans: $3\frac{1}{2}$ equals $\frac{7}{2}$. One half ton will cost $\frac{1}{7}$ of 2100, or $\$300$, and one ton will cost $\$600$.

30. If 5 CD's are on sale for $\$11\frac{1}{4}$, how much will 8 CD's cost?
Ans: $11\frac{1}{4}$ equals $\frac{45}{4}$. One CD will cost $\frac{9}{4}$, and 8 CDs will cost $\frac{72}{4}$ or $\$18$.

31. If $4\frac{1}{2}$ pounds of peppers cost 360 cents, how much would you pay for 7 pounds of peppers?
Ans: $4\frac{1}{2}$ equals $\frac{9}{2}$. One-half of a pound of peppers will cost 40 cents, one pound will cost 80 cents, and 7 pounds will cost 560 cents.

32. How much will 14 pounds of oat bran cost if $3\frac{1}{3}$ pounds can be bought for 50 cents?
Ans: $3\frac{1}{3}$ equals $\frac{10}{3}$. $\frac{1}{3}$ of a pound will cost 5 cents, one pound will cost 15 cents, and 14 pounds will cost 14 times 15 cents, or 210 cents.

33. If $2\frac{1}{7}$ meters of velvet cost $\$30$, how much will 10 meters cost, at the same rate?
Ans: $2\frac{1}{7}$ equals $\frac{15}{7}$. $\frac{1}{7}$ of a meter will cost $\$2$, one meter will cost $\$14$, and 10 meters will cost 10 times $\$14$, or $\$140$.

34. A woman had $\$7$ in coins and gave several children half-dollar coins. How many children were there if each child received one half-dollar coin?
Ans: $\$7$ can be divided in 14 half dollars, so there were 14 children each getting a half-dollar.

35. What fraction of 7 is 3? **Ans:** $\frac{3}{7}$.

36.

37. What fraction of $\frac{1}{2}$ is $\frac{1}{3}$?

Solution one—Since $\frac{1}{2} = \frac{3}{6}$ and $\frac{1}{3} = \frac{2}{6}$, $\frac{2}{6}$ is the same part of $\frac{3}{6}$ that 2 is of 3 or $\frac{2}{3}$.

Solution two—Alternately we can divide, which is harder to do mentally. $\frac{1}{3} \div \frac{1}{2} = \frac{1}{3} \times \frac{2}{1} = \frac{2}{3}$.

38. What fraction of $\frac{1}{2}$ is $\frac{1}{4}$? **Ans:** $\frac{1}{2}$.

39. What fraction of $\frac{1}{3}$ is $\frac{2}{3}$? **Ans:** $\frac{1}{2}$.

40. What fraction of $\frac{1}{4}$ is $\frac{1}{8}$? **Ans:** $\frac{1}{2}$.

41. What fraction of $\frac{1}{8}$ is $\frac{1}{16}$? **Ans:** $\frac{1}{2}$.

42. What fraction of $\frac{1}{4}$ is $\frac{1}{8}$? **Ans:** $\frac{1}{2}$.

43. What fraction of $\frac{2}{3}$ is $\frac{1}{3}$? **Ans:** $\frac{1}{2}$.

44. What fraction of $\frac{2}{4}$ is $\frac{1}{3}$? **Ans:** $\frac{2}{3}$.

45. Reduce mixed number $2\frac{2}{3}$ to a fraction.

Ans: 2 is equal to $\frac{6}{3}$, add to that $\frac{2}{3}$, we get $\frac{6}{3} + \frac{2}{3} = \frac{8}{3}$.

46. Reduce mixed number $4\frac{2}{3}$ to a fraction.

Ans: 4 is equal to $\frac{12}{3}$, add to that $\frac{2}{3}$, we get $\frac{12}{3} + \frac{2}{3} = \frac{14}{3}$.

47. Reduce mixed number $4\frac{1}{3}$ to a fraction.

Ans: 4 is equal to $\frac{12}{3}$, add to that $\frac{1}{3}$, we get $\frac{12}{3} + \frac{1}{3} = \frac{13}{3}$.

48. Reduce mixed number $5\frac{3}{4}$ to a fraction.

Ans: 5 is equal to $\frac{20}{4}$, add to that $\frac{3}{4}$, we get $\frac{20}{4} + \frac{3}{4} = \frac{23}{4}$.

49. Reduce mixed number $10\frac{3}{4}$ to a fraction.

Ans: 10 is equal to $\frac{40}{4}$, add to that $\frac{3}{4}$, we get $\frac{40}{4} + \frac{3}{4} = \frac{43}{4}$.

50. Reduce mixed number $11\frac{1}{4}$ to a fraction. **Ans:** $\frac{45}{4}$.

51. Reduce mixed number $6\frac{3}{4}$ to a fraction. **Ans:** $\frac{27}{4}$.

52. Change $\frac{2}{3}, \frac{3}{4}, \frac{5}{6}$ to twelfths?

Ans: To make twelfths, we need to have a 12 in the denominator. Which means we multiply both the top and the bottom of $\frac{2}{3}$ by 4. $\frac{2\times4}{3\times4} = \frac{8}{12}; \frac{3\times3}{4\times3} = \frac{9}{12}; \frac{5\times2}{6\times2} = \frac{10}{12}.$ ⌣

Lesson 15 – *Fractions to Numbers*

HOW many ones are there in $\frac{14}{3}$?

Ans: There are $\frac{3}{3}$ in 1, and in $\frac{14}{3}$ there are as many 1's as 3 is *contained* in 14, which, is $\frac{14}{3}$ or $4\frac{2}{3}$.

1. How many ones in $\frac{7}{2}$; $\frac{5}{2}$; $\frac{12}{3}$; $\frac{3}{3}$? **Ans:** $3\frac{1}{2}$; $2\frac{1}{2}$; 4; $2\frac{2}{3}$.

2. How many ones in $\frac{5}{3}$; $\frac{9}{3}$; $\frac{10}{3}$; $\frac{12}{3}$? **Ans:** $1\frac{2}{3}$; 3; $3\frac{1}{3}$; $1\frac{4}{8}$.

3. How many ones in $\frac{3}{4}$; $\frac{14}{4}$; $\frac{10}{4}$; $\frac{16}{4}$? **Ans:** $\frac{3}{4}$; $3\frac{2}{4}$; $2\frac{2}{4}$; 4.

4. How many ones in $\frac{7}{5}$; $1\frac{1}{3}$; $\frac{18}{6}$; $2\frac{1}{7}$? **Ans:** $1\frac{2}{5}$; $3\frac{2}{3}$; 3; 3.

5. How many ones in $\frac{5}{4}$; $\frac{18}{9}$; $\frac{14}{6}$; $\frac{28}{14}$? **Ans:** $1\frac{1}{4}$; 2; $2\frac{2}{6}$; 2.

6. How many ones in $\frac{15}{5}$; $\frac{16}{3}$; $\frac{17}{8}$; $\frac{21}{9}$? **Ans:** 3; $5\frac{1}{3}$; $2\frac{1}{8}$; $2\frac{3}{9}$.

7. How many ones in $\frac{16}{9}$; $\frac{15}{7}$; $\frac{11}{4}$; $\frac{10}{6}$? **Ans:** $1\frac{7}{9}$; $2\frac{1}{7}$; $2\frac{3}{4}$; $1\frac{4}{6}$.

8. How many ones in $\frac{18}{7}$; $\frac{25}{8}$; $\frac{24}{10}$; $\frac{27}{7}$? **Ans:** $2\frac{4}{7}$; $4\frac{1}{6}$; $2\frac{4}{10}$; 3.

9. How many ones in $\frac{11}{4}$; $\frac{22}{4}$; $\frac{15}{10}$; $\frac{16}{11}$? **Ans:** $2\frac{3}{4}$; $5\frac{2}{4}$; $1\frac{5}{10}$; $1\frac{5}{11}$.

10. In reducing $\frac{14}{3}$ to a mixed number, by what do we divide the numerator 14? **Ans:** The denominator, 3.

11. In reducing any improper fraction such as $\frac{5}{3}$ to a whole or mixed number, by what do we divide the numerator 5?
Ans: The denominator, 3.

12. Reduce improper fraction $\frac{5}{2}$ to a mixed number. **Ans:** $2\frac{1}{2}$.

13. Reduce to mixed numbers $\frac{16}{5}$; $\frac{15}{2}$; $\frac{19}{6}$; $\frac{25}{3}$.
Ans: $3\frac{1}{5}$; $7\frac{1}{2}$; $2\frac{1}{9}$; $8\frac{1}{3}$.

14. Reduce to mixed numbers $\frac{14}{8}$; $\frac{15}{4}$; $\frac{13}{7}$; $\frac{22}{6}$?
Ans: $1\frac{3}{4}$; $3\frac{3}{4}$; $1\frac{6}{7}$; $3\frac{5}{6}$.

15. Reduce to mixed numbers $\frac{28}{5}$; $\frac{41}{6}$; $\frac{23}{8}$; $\frac{44}{9}$?
Ans: $5\frac{3}{5}$; $6\frac{5}{6}$; $2\frac{7}{8}$; $4\frac{8}{9}$.

16. Reduce to mixed numbers $\frac{24}{7}$; $\frac{25}{8}$; $\frac{26}{9}$; $\frac{27}{10}$?
Ans: $3\frac{3}{7}$; $8\frac{1}{8}$; $2\frac{8}{9}$; $2\frac{7}{10}$.

17. If one kilogram of sugar costs $6\frac{2}{3}$, what will 8 kilograms cost?
Note—*Ask child to estimate the answer first.*
Solution one—If one kilogram of sugar costs $6\frac{2}{3}$ dollars, 8 kilograms will cost 8 times $6\frac{2}{3}$; 8 times 6 dollars are \$48; 8 times $\frac{2}{3}$ are $\frac{16}{3}$, or

$5\frac{1}{3}$; \$48 plus \$$5\frac{1}{3}$ are \$$53\frac{1}{3}$.

Solution two—Another method as taught in schools is to reduce the mixed fraction $6\frac{2}{3}$ to $\frac{20}{3}$, which is the cost of one pound, so 8 pounds cost 8 times that or $\frac{160}{3}$ or \$$53\frac{1}{3}$.

The second method is an algorithmic way of solving problems. Using the first method, the child is able to develop some insight as to why we can solve the problem this way.

18. At $6\frac{4}{5}$ dimes a kilograms, what will 12 kilograms of spinach cost?
  Ans: If one kilogram of spinach costs $6\frac{4}{5}$ dimes, 12 kilograms will cost 12 times $6\frac{4}{5}$ dimes; 12 times 6 dimes is 72 dimes; 12 times $\frac{4}{5}$ of a dime is $\frac{48}{5}$, or $9\frac{3}{5}$ dimes; 72 dimes + $9\frac{3}{5}$ dimes are $81\frac{3}{5}$ dimes.

19. What is the cost of 8 bags of peanuts at the rate of one-eighth of a dollar for a bag?
  Ans: If one bag of peanuts costs $\frac{1}{8}$ dollar, 8 bags will cost 8 times $\frac{1}{8}$, which is one dollar.

20. How much will a man earn in a week at the rate of \$80 a day?
  Ans: If he earns \$80 a day, in a week he will earn 5 times \$80; 5 times \$80 is \$400.

21. At the rate of 180 cents a dozen, what will 3 dozen eggs cost? **Ans:** 3 times 180 cents is 540 cents.

22. If 2 nails cost $4\frac{2}{3}$ cents, how much will 5 nails cost?
  Ans: If 2 nails cost $4\frac{2}{3}$ cents, one nail will cost $\frac{1}{2}$ of $4\frac{2}{3}$, or $2\frac{1}{3}$ cents, and 5 nails will cost 5 times $2\frac{1}{3}$ cents; 5 times 2 cents is 10 cents. Five times $\frac{1}{3}$ of a cent is $\frac{5}{3}$, or $1\frac{2}{3}$ cents; 10 cents + $1\frac{2}{3}$ cents is $11\frac{2}{3}$ cents.

23. If three bags of planting soil costs $5\frac{1}{4}$ dollars, what will 6 bags of soil cost?
  Ans: 6 bags of soil, which is 2 times 3 bags, will cost 2 times $5\frac{1}{4}$, or \$$10\frac{2}{4}$.

24. What is the cost of 5 pounds of sand at the rate of $3\frac{1}{3}$ dollars for 10 pounds?
  Ans: $3\frac{1}{3}$ equals $\frac{10}{3}$. If 10 pounds cost $\frac{10}{3}$, 5 pounds will cost $\frac{1}{2}$ of $\frac{10}{3}$, or $\frac{5}{3}$, or $1\frac{2}{3}$ dollars.

25. What is the cost of 7 bags of okra at the rate of \$9 for $2\frac{1}{4}$ bags?
  Ans: $2\frac{1}{4}$ equals $\frac{9}{4}$. If $\frac{9}{4}$ bag cost \$9, $\frac{1}{4}$ of a bag costs one dollar, one bag costs \$4, and 7 bags cost 7 times 4, or \$28.

26. How many raindrops can I buy for $7 if 14 raindrops cost 3\frac{1}{2}$?

Ans: $3\frac{1}{2}$ equals $\frac{7}{2}$. $7, which is twice $\frac{7}{2}$, will buy twice 14 beads, or 28 raindrops.

27. What is the cost of $5\frac{3}{8}$ pounds of air if 2 pounds cost 320 cents?

Ans: $5\frac{3}{8}$ equals $\frac{43}{8}$. If 2 pounds cost 320 cents, one pound costs 160 cents, $\frac{1}{8}$ of a pound costs 20 cents, and $\frac{43}{8}$ of a pound cost 43 times 20 cents, or 860 cents.

28. How far will a woman drive in $5\frac{1}{3}$ hours at the rate 210 miles in $3\frac{1}{2}$ hours?

Ans: $5\frac{1}{3}$ equals $\frac{16}{3}$; $3\frac{1}{2}$ equals $\frac{7}{2}$. If she drives 210 miles in $\frac{7}{2}$ hours, in $\frac{1}{2}$ of an hour she will drive 30 miles, or 60 miles an hour; in $\frac{1}{3}$ of an hour she will drive 20 miles, and in $\frac{16}{3}$ hours she will drive 16 times 20, or 320 miles.

29. A boat sailed 23 miles in $4\frac{3}{5}$ hours. How far did it sail in 12 hours?

Ans: $4\frac{3}{5}$ equals $\frac{23}{5}$. If it sails 23 miles in $\frac{23}{5}$ hours, it will sail one mile in $\frac{1}{5}$ of an hour, or 5 miles an hour, and in 12 hours it will sail 12 times 5, or 60 miles.

30. A kite rose 48 meters in $3\frac{3}{7}$ minutes. At this rate how far will it rise in 6 minutes?

Ans: $3\frac{3}{7}$ equals $\frac{24}{7}$. If it rises 48 meters in $\frac{24}{7}$ minutes, it will rise 2 meters in $\frac{1}{7}$ of a minute, or 14 meters a minute, and in 6 minutes it will rise 84 meters.

31. What is the cost of 18 pounds of feathers, at the rate of $4\frac{1}{2}$ pounds of feathers for 3\frac{3}{8}$?

Ans: 18 pounds is 4 times $4\frac{1}{2}$ pounds, and will cost 4 times $3\frac{3}{8}$, or $13\frac{4}{8}$ dollars.

32. If $\frac{2}{5}$ of a box is worth 4\frac{4}{5}$, what is the cost $7\frac{2}{3}$ boxes?

Ans: $\frac{2}{5}$ of a box is worth $4\frac{4}{5}$ dollars and one box is worth $\frac{24}{5}$ divided by $\frac{2}{5}$, or $12, 7 bags are worth $84, and $\frac{2}{3}$ of a bag is worth $\frac{2}{3}$ of $12, or $8; $84 + $8 are $92.

33. If a man walks 7 miles in $2\frac{1}{3}$ hours, how far did he walk in 4 hours?

Ans: In $4\frac{2}{3}$ hours, which is twice $2\frac{1}{3}$ hours, he walked twice 7 miles, or 14 miles.

34. A student read $\frac{13}{3}$ stories in $6\frac{1}{2}$ hours. How many stories can she read in $7\frac{1}{2}$ hours?

Ans: In $6\frac{1}{2}$ hours, which is $\frac{13}{2}$ hours, she can read $\frac{13}{3}$ stories. So in half an hour, she can read one-third of a story. In seven hours, she can read 42 sixths plus one-sixth story, or 43 sixths, which is $7\frac{1}{6}$ stories.

35. If 4 puppies can eat $3\frac{1}{2}$ cups of food per day, then how long will 17 cups of food last them? **Ans: 6 days.**

36. If a yacht sails $6\frac{2}{3}$ miles in an hour, how many miles will it sail in $\frac{4}{5}$ of an hour? **Ans:** $\frac{16}{3}$ miles.

37. If some biscuits are divided equally among 7 puppies, what part of all the biscuits will each of the 5 puppies receive? **Ans:** $\frac{5}{7}$ part of all the biscuits.

38. Mr. Beam sold his car for $\frac{2}{3}$ of its original cost and received \$12000. How much did the car cost originally? **Ans:** $\frac{3}{2}$ of \$12000 or \$18000.

39. Sixty is $\frac{4}{5}$ of what number?
Ans: If 60 is $\frac{4}{5}$ of a number, then one-fifth of that number is 60 divided by 4, or 15. The number is 5 times 15, or 75.

40. Forty-two is $\frac{6}{7}$ of what number?
Ans: If 42 is $\frac{6}{7}$ of a number, then one-seventh of that number is 42 divided by 6, or 7. The number is then 7 times 7 or 49.

41. Twenty-two is $\frac{11}{5}$ of what number? **Ans: 10.**

42. If a pound of steak costs $9\frac{3}{4}$ dollars, then what will 2 pounds cost? **Ans:** \$$19\frac{1}{2}$.

43. How many 5-cent coins make $\frac{7}{20}$ of a dollar? **Ans: 7.**

44. If five workers can build a wall in $5\frac{1}{10}$ of a hour. How long would it take one worker?
Ans: $5\frac{1}{10} = \frac{51}{10}$ hours. If 5 workers take $\frac{51}{10}$ hours, then one worker will take $\frac{51}{10}$ multiplied by 5 or $\frac{51}{2}$ or $25\frac{1}{2}$ hours. Note that we could have gotten this number by just multiplying each part of the mixed fraction separately, $(5 \times 5) = 25$ and $\frac{1}{10} \times 5 = \frac{1}{2}$.

45. If four workers can build a wall in $4\frac{1}{10}$ of a hour, how long would it take one worker? **Ans:** $14\frac{2}{5}$ hours. ⌣

Lesson 16 – *Reduction to Higher Terms*

HOW many fourths are in $\frac{1}{2}$?
    Ans: In one there are 4 fourths, and in $\frac{1}{2}$ there are $\frac{1}{2}$ of $\frac{4}{4}$, or $\frac{2}{4}$.

1. How many sixths are in $\frac{1}{2}$? $\frac{1}{3}$? $\frac{2}{3}$? $\frac{3}{2}$?
    Ans: 3; 2; 4; 9.

2. How many eighths are in $\frac{1}{2}$? $\frac{1}{4}$? $\frac{2}{4}$? $\frac{3}{4}$?
    Ans: 4; 2; 4; 6.

3. How many tenths are in $\frac{1}{2}$? $\frac{1}{5}$? $\frac{3}{5}$?
    Ans: 5; 2; 6.

4. How many twelfths are in $\frac{1}{3}$? $\frac{1}{4}$? $\frac{4}{6}$?
    Ans: 4; 3; 8.

5. How many fourteenths are in $\frac{1}{2}$? $\frac{2}{7}$? $\frac{4}{7}$? $\frac{5}{7}$?
    Ans: 7; 4; 8; 10.

6. How many fifteenths are in $\frac{2}{3}$? $\frac{3}{5}$? $\frac{4}{5}$? $\frac{5}{3}$?
    Ans: 10; 9; 12; 25.

7. How many sixteenths are in $\frac{1}{4}$? $\frac{3}{4}$? $\frac{6}{7}$? $\frac{5}{8}$?
    Ans: 4; 12; 4; 10.

8. How many eighteenths are in $\frac{2}{3}$? $\frac{4}{6}$? $\frac{3}{9}$? $\frac{8}{9}$?
    Ans: 12; 12; 6; 16.

9. How many twentieths are in $\frac{4}{5}$? $\frac{3}{4}$? $\frac{7}{10}$? $\frac{3}{10}$?
    Ans: 16; 15; 14; 12.

10. Reduce $\frac{2}{3}$, $\frac{3}{4}$, and $\frac{5}{6}$ to twelfths.
    Ans: $\frac{8}{12}$; $\frac{9}{12}$; $\frac{10}{12}$.

11. Reduce $\frac{1}{2}$, $\frac{3}{4}$, $\frac{4}{5}$ and $\frac{9}{10}$ to twentieths.
    Ans: $\frac{10}{20}$; $\frac{15}{20}$; $\frac{16}{20}$; $\frac{18}{20}$.

12. Reduce $\frac{2}{3}$, $\frac{4}{5}$, $\frac{9}{10}$ and $\frac{14}{15}$ to thirtieths.
    Ans: $\frac{20}{30}$; $\frac{24}{30}$; $\frac{27}{30}$; $\frac{28}{30}$.

13. Since $\frac{2}{3} = \frac{4}{6}$, by what number should you multiply both the numerator and denominator of $\frac{2}{3}$ to get $\frac{4}{6}$? **Ans:** 2.

14. Since $\frac{3}{4} = \frac{9}{12}$, by what number should you multiply both the numerator and denominator of $\frac{3}{4}$ to get $\frac{9}{12}$? **Ans:** 3.

15. By what must you multiply the numerator and denominator of $\frac{3}{5}$ to reduce it to tenths? **Ans:** 2.

16. By what must you multiply both the numerator and denominator of $\frac{3}{4}$ to reduce it to twentieths? **Ans:** 5.

17. Reduce $\frac{1}{2}$, $\frac{3}{4}$, and $\frac{4}{5}$ to twentieths.
Ans: Multiplying both the numerator and denominator of $\frac{1}{2}$ by 10, we have $\frac{1}{2}$ equal to $\frac{10}{20}$; multiplying both numerator and denominator of $\frac{3}{4}$ by 5, we get $\frac{3}{4}$ equal to $\frac{15}{20}$, etc.

18. Reduce $\frac{1}{2}$, $\frac{3}{5}$, and $\frac{4}{6}$ to thirtieths.
Ans: Multiplying both the numerator and denominator of $\frac{1}{2}$ by 15, we have $\frac{1}{2} = \frac{15}{30}$, etc.

19. Reduce $\frac{1}{2}$, $\frac{2}{3}$ and $\frac{3}{4}$ to twelfths.
Ans: $\frac{6}{12}$; $\frac{8}{12}$; $\frac{9}{12}$.

20. Reduce $\frac{1}{2}$, $\frac{2}{3}$, $\frac{5}{6}$, and $\frac{7}{9}$ to eighteenths.
Ans: $\frac{9}{18}$; $\frac{12}{18}$; $\frac{15}{18}$; $\frac{14}{18}$.

21. 22. Reduce $\frac{1}{2}$, $\frac{2}{4}$, $\frac{3}{8}$, and $\frac{5}{8}$ to sixteenths.
Ans: $\frac{8}{16}$; $\frac{8}{16}$; $\frac{6}{16}$; $\frac{10}{16}$.
Note—*When fractions have the same denominator, they are said to have a common denominator.*

22. Reduce $\frac{2}{3}$ and $\frac{3}{4}$ to a common denominator.
Ans: A common denominator for $\frac{2}{3}$ and $\frac{3}{4}$ is $\frac{1}{12}$.

23. Reduce $\frac{2}{3}$ and $\frac{3}{5}$ to a common denominator. **Ans:** $\frac{10}{15}$; $\frac{9}{15}$.

24. Reduce $\frac{1}{4}$ and $\frac{1}{5}$ to a common denominator **Ans:** $\frac{5}{20}$; $\frac{4}{20}$.

25. Reduce $\frac{1}{3}$ and $\frac{1}{5}$ to a common denominator. **Ans:** $\frac{5}{15}$; $\frac{3}{15}$.

26. Reduce $\frac{1}{5}$ and $\frac{1}{6}$ to a common denominator. **Ans:** $\frac{5}{15}$; $\frac{3}{15}$.

27. Reduce $\frac{2}{3}$ and $\frac{3}{6}$ to a common denominator. **Ans:** $\frac{4}{6}$; $\frac{3}{6}$.

28. Reduce $\frac{1}{2}$ and $\frac{1}{7}$ to a common denominator. **Ans:** $\frac{7}{14}$; $\frac{2}{14}$.

29. Reduce $\frac{2}{3}$ and $\frac{3}{8}$ to a common denominator. **Ans:** $\frac{12}{30}$; $\frac{10}{30}$.

30. Reduce $\frac{2}{5}$ and $\frac{2}{6}$ to a common denominator. **Ans:** $\frac{10}{20}$; $\frac{6}{10}$.

31. Reduce $\frac{2}{4}$ and $\frac{3}{10}$ to a common denominator. **Ans:** $\frac{10}{20}$; $\frac{6}{10}$.

32. Reduce $\frac{1}{2}$, $\frac{1}{3}$, and $\frac{1}{4}$ to a common denominator.
Ans: $\frac{6}{12}$; $\frac{4}{12}$; $\frac{3}{12}$.

33. Reduce $\frac{1}{3}$, $\frac{1}{4}$ and $\frac{1}{6}$ to a common denominator.
Ans: $\frac{8}{24}$; $\frac{6}{24}$; $\frac{4}{24}$.

34. Reduce $\frac{1}{2}$, $\frac{1}{4}$, and $\frac{1}{8}$ to a common denominator.
Ans: $\frac{4}{8}$; $\frac{2}{8}$; $\frac{1}{8}$.

35. Reduce $\frac{1}{4}$, $\frac{1}{5}$, and $\frac{1}{10}$ to a common denominator.
Ans: $\frac{10}{40}$; $\frac{8}{40}$; $\frac{4}{40}$.

36. If $2\frac{1}{2}$ meters of vinyl costs \$20, what will 4 meters cost?
Ans: $2\frac{1}{2}$ equals $\frac{5}{2}$, and 4 equals $\frac{8}{2}$. If $\frac{5}{2}$ meters of silk cost \$20, $\frac{1}{2}$ of a meter will cost $\frac{1}{5}$ of \$20, or \$4, and $\frac{8}{2}$ will cost 8 times 4, or \$32.

37. If $2\frac{1}{6}$ meters of tape cost 13 cents, what will 3 meters cost?
Ans: $2\frac{1}{6}$ equals $\frac{13}{6}$, and 3 equals $\frac{18}{6}$. If $\frac{13}{6}$ meters cost 13 cents, $\frac{1}{6}$ of a meter will cost one cent, and $\frac{18}{6}$ meters will cost 18 cents.

38. Kathy gave 20 roses to her friend, which is $\frac{2}{3}$ as many as she then had left. How many did she have at first?
Ans: Since $\frac{2}{3}$ of the number of roses left is 20, $\frac{1}{3}$ of that number is 10 roses, and $\frac{3}{3}$, or the number left, is 30 roses. She has 20, plus 30 she gave away. 30 roses + 20 roses is 50 roses.

39. John found 60 cents, which is $\frac{5}{4}$ of $\frac{1}{2}$ of what he had before. How much did he have at first?
Ans: If 60 cents is $\frac{5}{4}$ of $\frac{1}{2}$ of what he had before, $\frac{1}{4}$ of $\frac{1}{2}$ of what he had is $\frac{1}{5}$ of 60 cents, or 12 cents, and $\frac{4}{4}$ of $\frac{1}{2}$ of what he had before is 4 times 12 cents, or 48 cents. What he had before equals 2 times 48 cents, or 96 cents; then before he found 60 cents he had 96 cents − 60 cents, or 36 cents.

40. What is the cost of $3\frac{1}{5}$ pounds of sugar, if $2\frac{1}{5}$ of sugar costs \$2.20 cents? **Ans:** \$3.20.

41. What is $\frac{5}{4}$ of 60? **Ans:** 72.

42. What is $\frac{5}{4}$ of $\frac{1}{2}$ of 60? **Ans:** 24.

43. Daniel gave his sister 20 cents, which is $\frac{4}{5}$ of what Daniel had at first and $\frac{1}{2}$ of what his sister now has. How much did each have at first?
Ans: If $\frac{4}{5}$ of what Daniel had at first is 20 cents, $\frac{1}{5}$ of what he had is $\frac{1}{4}$ of 20, or 5 cents, and $\frac{5}{5}$, or what he had, is 5 times 5, or 25 cents. If the 20 cents he gave his sister is $\frac{1}{2}$ of what she now has, she must have had 20 cents at first.

44. What is $\frac{5}{3}$ of 90? **Ans:** 150.

45. What is $\frac{2}{5}$ of $\frac{3}{5}$ of 100? **Ans:** 30.

46. What is $\frac{7}{3}$ of $\frac{1}{2}$ of 30? **Ans:** 35.

Lesson 17 – *Reduction to Lower Terms*

HOW many thirds are there in $\frac{4}{6}$?

When a fraction cannot be reduced to an equivalent one having a lesser denominator, it is said to be in its lowest terms.

Solution one—In one there are $\frac{6}{6}$, and in $\frac{1}{3}$ there is $\frac{1}{3}$ of $\frac{6}{6}$, which is $\frac{2}{6}$. If there are $\frac{2}{6}$ in $\frac{1}{3}$, in $\frac{4}{6}$ there are as many thirds as 2 is contained in 4, which is 2. So in $\frac{4}{6}$ there are 2 thirds or, $\frac{2}{3}$.

Solution two—We can write $\frac{4}{6}$ as $\frac{2\times 2}{2\times 3}$, which is same as $\frac{2}{3}$.

1. How many halves are in $\frac{2}{4}$? $\frac{6}{4}$? $\frac{8}{4}$? $\frac{10}{4}$?
   Ans: 1; 3; 4; 5.

2. How many thirds are in $\frac{2}{6}$? $\frac{4}{6}$? $\frac{6}{9}$? $\frac{8}{12}$?
   Ans: 1; 2; 2; 2.

3. How many fourths are in $\frac{1}{2}$? $\frac{6}{8}$? $\frac{9}{12}$? $\frac{10}{8}$?
   Ans: 1; 3; 3; 5.

4. How many sixth are in $\frac{10}{12}$? $\frac{9}{18}$? $\frac{2}{3}$? $\frac{8}{12}$? $\frac{4}{6}$?
   Ans: 5; 3; 4; 4.

5. How many eighths in $\frac{4}{16}$? $\frac{12}{16}$? $\frac{8}{16}$? $\frac{12}{24}$?
   Ans: 2; 6; 4; 4.

6. How many fifths in $\frac{8}{10}$? $\frac{6}{15}$? $\frac{12}{20}$? $\frac{16}{20}$?
   Ans: 4; 2; 3; 4.

7. How many sevenths are in $\frac{10}{14}$? $\frac{9}{21}$? $\frac{12}{21}$? $\frac{12}{21}$?
   Ans: 5; 4; 3; 4.

8. How many ninths are in $\frac{12}{18}$? $\frac{16}{18}$? $\frac{15}{27}$? $\frac{18}{27}$?
   Ans: 6; 8; 5; 6.

9. How many tenths are in $\frac{16}{20}$? $\frac{21}{30}$? $\frac{24}{40}$? $\frac{25}{50}$?
   Ans: 8; 7; 6; 5.

10. Since $\frac{4}{6} = \frac{2}{3}$, by what may we divide both numerator and denominator of $\frac{4}{6}$ to get $\frac{2}{3}$? **Ans:** By 2.

11. By what number must we divide both numerator and denominator of $\frac{4}{8}$ to reduce it to fourths? **Ans:** By 2.

12. By what must we divide both the numerator and denominator of $\frac{5}{10}$ to reduce it to halves? **Ans:** By 5.

13. Reduce $\frac{6}{10}$ to fifths. Reduce $\frac{3}{12}$ to fourths.

Ans: Dividing both the numerator and denominator of $\frac{6}{10}$ by 2, we have $\frac{3}{5}$. And dividing both numerator and denominator of $\frac{3}{12}$ by 3, we have $\frac{1}{4}$.

14. Reduce $\frac{7}{14}$ to halves. Reduce $\frac{9}{12}$ to fourths.

Ans: Dividing both the numerator and denominator of $\frac{7}{14}$ by 7, we have $\frac{1}{2}$. Dividing both numerator and denominator of $\frac{9}{12}$ by 3 we have $\frac{3}{4}$.

15. Reduce $\frac{8}{16}$ to fourths, and reduce $\frac{6}{9}$ to thirds. **Ans:** $\frac{2}{4}$; $\frac{2}{3}$.

16. Reduce $\frac{16}{20}$ to fifths, and reduce $\frac{8}{24}$ to sixths. **Ans:** $\frac{4}{5}$; $\frac{2}{6}$.

17. Reduce $\frac{9}{21}$ to sevenths, and reduce $\frac{16}{36}$ to ninths. **Ans:** $\frac{3}{7}$; $\frac{4}{9}$.

18. Reduce $\frac{25}{24}$ to eighth, and reduce $\frac{24}{30}$ to tenths. **Ans:** $\frac{5}{8}$; $\frac{8}{10}$.

19. Reduce $\frac{28}{40}$ to tenths, and reduce $\frac{35}{60}$ to twelfths. **Ans:** $\frac{7}{10}$; $\frac{7}{12}$.

20. Reduce $\frac{25}{45}$ to ninths, and reduce $\frac{35}{55}$ to elevenths. **Ans:** $\frac{5}{9}$; $\frac{7}{11}$.

21. Reduce $\frac{10}{12}$ and $\frac{9}{15}$ to their lowest terms.

Ans: Dividing both the numerator and denominator of $\frac{10}{12}$ by the greatest number that will divide them both without remainder is 2, so we have $\frac{10}{12} = \frac{5}{6}$; dividing both numerator and denominator of $\frac{9}{15}$ by its greatest common divisor, 3, gives us $\frac{9}{15} = \frac{3}{5}$

22. Reduce $\frac{12}{15}$ and $\frac{8}{12}$ to their lowest terms.

Ans: Dividing both the numerator and denominator of $\frac{12}{15}$ by its greatest common divisor, 3, gives us $\frac{12}{15} = \frac{4}{5}$. Dividing both the numerator and denominator of $\frac{8}{12}$ by its greatest common divisor, 4, gives us $\frac{8}{12} = \frac{2}{3}$.

23. Reduce $\frac{16}{20}$ and $\frac{20}{36}$ to their lowest terms.

Ans: Dividing both the numerator and denominator of $\frac{16}{20}$ by their greatest common divisor, 4, gives us $\frac{16}{20} = \frac{4}{5}$. Dividing both the numerator and denominator of $\frac{20}{36}$ by its greatest common divisor, which is 4, gives us $\frac{20}{36} = \frac{5}{9}$.

24. Reduce $\frac{15}{45}$ and $\frac{24}{36}$ to their lowest terms. **Ans:** $\frac{1}{3}$; $\frac{2}{3}$.

25. Reduce $\frac{21}{42}$ and $\frac{24}{48}$ to their lowest terms. **Ans:** $\frac{1}{2}$; $\frac{1}{2}$.

26. Reduce $\frac{25}{35}$ and $\frac{27}{36}$ to their lowest terms. **Ans:** $\frac{5}{7}$; $\frac{3}{4}$.

27. If 6 is $\frac{2}{3}$ of some number, what is $\frac{1}{3}$ of 3 times the same number?
Ans: If $\frac{2}{3}$ of some number is 6, $\frac{1}{3}$ of that number is $\frac{1}{2}$ of 6, or 3, and $\frac{3}{3}$, or the number, is 3 times 3, or 9; 3 times 9 is 27, and $\frac{1}{3}$ of 27 is 9.

28. If 8 is $\frac{4}{5}$ of some number, what is $\frac{1}{5}$ of 2 times the same number?
Ans: If $\frac{4}{5}$ of some number is 8, $\frac{1}{5}$ of that number is $\frac{1}{4}$ of 8, or 2, and $\frac{5}{5}$, or the number, is 5 times 2, or 10; 2 times 10 is 20, and $\frac{1}{5}$ of 20 is 4.

29. Four times 50 is 10 years less than 10 times the age of James. How old is James?
Ans: 4 times 50 years is 200 years. If 200 years is 10 years less than 10 times the age of James, 10 times his age will be 200 years plus 10 years, or 210 years, and his age will be $\frac{1}{10}$ of 210 years, or 21 years.

30. If 4 dogs need 2 bags of food for 8 weeks, how long will it take 5 dogs to eat the same amount?
Ans: If 4 dogs eat 2 bags of food in 8 weeks, one dog would eat that in 4 times 8 weeks, or 32 weeks, and 5 dogs would require $\frac{1}{5}$ of 32 weeks, or $6\frac{2}{5}$ weeks.

31. If 2 men can build a boat in 16 days, how long will it take 8 men to build it?
Ans: If 2 men can build a boat in 16 days, 8 men, which is 4 times 2 men, will require $\frac{1}{4}$ of 16 days, or 4 days.

32. If $8\frac{2}{3}$ meters of cloth is needed to make 2 tents, how much will be needed to make 9 tents?
Ans: One tent will require $\frac{1}{2}$ of $8\frac{2}{3}$ meters, or $4\frac{1}{3}$ meters, and 9 tents will require 9 times $4\frac{1}{3}$ meters, or 39 meters.

33. $42 is $\frac{6}{7}$ of all the money Anna has and Bill has 3 times as much as Anna, then how much money does Bill have?
Ans: If $\frac{6}{7}$ of Anna's money is $42, $\frac{1}{7}$ of her money is $\frac{1}{6}$ of $42, or $7, and $\frac{7}{7}$ is $49; Bill has 3 times 49, or $147.

34. Anna gave Bill $48, and $\frac{5}{6}$ of this is 4 times as much as she had left. How much did she have at first?
Ans: $\frac{5}{6}$ of $48 is $40. If $40 is 4 times what is left, $\frac{1}{4}$ of $40, or $10, is what is left; $48 + $10 = $58, what she had at first.

35. Amanda collected 50 flowers, threw away $\frac{4}{5}$ of them, then picked $\frac{2}{5}$ as many flowers as she had left. How many does she have now?

Ans: $\frac{5}{5} - \frac{4}{5}$ leaves $\frac{1}{5}$, what remained; $\frac{1}{5}$ of 50 flowers is 10 flowers; $\frac{2}{5}$ of 10 is 4 flowers; $10 + 4 = 14$ flowers, what she then had.

36. The food for a party cost $90, which is $\frac{3}{9}$ of 10 times what the drinks cost. What is the cost of both?
Ans: $\frac{3}{9} = \frac{1}{3}$. If $90 is $\frac{1}{3}$ of 10 times the cost, then 10 times the cost is 3 times $90, or $270. And if $270 is 10 times the cost of the food, then the drinks cost $27.

37. How many mangoes will pay for 7 melons if 6 mangoes are worth $4\frac{4}{5}$ melons?
Ans: $4\frac{4}{5}$ melons $= \frac{24}{5}$ melons; $\frac{1}{5}$ of a melon is worth $\frac{1}{24}$ of 6 mangoes, which is $\frac{6}{24}$, or $\frac{1}{4}$ of a mango. A $\frac{5}{5}$ of a melon is worth $\frac{5}{4}$ of a mango, and 7 melons are worth $\frac{35}{4}$, or $8\frac{3}{4}$ mangoes.

38. Mary gave Lily 24 flowers, which is $\frac{3}{5}$ of what Lily then had, and $\frac{3}{5}$ of what Mary had left. How many does each of them have now?
Ans: 24 flowers is $\frac{3}{5}$ of what each had. If 24 flowers is $\frac{3}{5}$, then $\frac{1}{5}$ is $\frac{1}{3}$ of 24, or 8, and $\frac{5}{5}$ is 5 times 8, or 40 flowers.

39. If the numerator and the denominator of $\frac{3}{4}$ is multiplied by 6, what is the result? **Ans:** $\frac{3\times6}{4\times6} = \frac{18}{24}$.

40. Reduce $\frac{18}{24}$ to a simple fraction. **Ans:** $\frac{18}{24} = \frac{3\times6}{4\times6} = \frac{3}{4} \times \frac{6}{6} = \frac{3}{4}.\smile$

Lesson 18 – *Simple and Mixed Fractions*

A MIXED number is also called a compound fraction. Mixed numbers can be easily converted to a fractions.

Convert $2\frac{1}{2}$ to a fraction.

Ans: $2\frac{1}{2} = 2 + \frac{1}{2}$; $2 \times \frac{2}{2} + \frac{1}{2} = \frac{4}{2} + \frac{1}{2} = \frac{5}{2}$.

Convert these compound fractions to simple fractions.

1. $2\frac{1}{2} = ?$ **Ans:** $\frac{5}{2}$.

2. $3\frac{1}{2} = ?$ **Ans:** $\frac{7}{2}$.

3. $4\frac{1}{2} = ?$ **Ans:** $\frac{9}{2}$.

4. $5\frac{1}{2} = ?$ **Ans:** $\frac{11}{2}$.

5. $7\frac{1}{2} = ?$ **Ans:** $\frac{15}{2}$.

6. $2\frac{1}{3} = ?$ **Ans:** $\frac{7}{3}$.

7. $4\frac{1}{3} = ?$ **Ans:** $\frac{13}{3}$.

8. $5\frac{1}{3} = ?$ **Ans:** $\frac{16}{3}$.

9. $7\frac{1}{3} = ?$ **Ans:** $\frac{22}{3}$.

10. $10\frac{1}{4} = ?$ **Ans:** $\frac{45}{4}$.

11. $11\frac{1}{2} = ?$ **Ans:** $\frac{23}{2}$.

12. $12\frac{1}{3} = ?$ **Ans:** $\frac{37}{3}$.

13. $15\frac{1}{2} = ?$ **Ans:** $\frac{31}{2}$.

14. $7\frac{1}{5} = ?$ **Ans:** $\frac{36}{5}$.

15. $2\frac{1}{5} = ?$ **Ans:** $\frac{11}{2}$.

16. $7\frac{2}{3} = ?$ **Ans:** $\frac{23}{3}$.

17. $3\frac{2}{3} = ?$ **Ans:** $\frac{11}{3}$.

18. $7\frac{2}{3} = ?$ **Ans:** $\frac{23}{3}$.

19. $5\frac{2}{3} = ?$ **Ans:** $\frac{17}{3}$.

20. $7\frac{3}{4} = ?$ **Ans:** $\frac{31}{4}$.

Simple method: Let's take compound number $7\frac{3}{4}$. Multiply the denominator 4 by the whole number 7 and then add the numerator to the result. We get $7 \times 4 = 28, +3 = 31$. Write this as the numerator with the same denominator as in the original compound fraction, $\frac{31}{4}$.

Convert these compound fractions to simple fractions using the second method.

1. $2\frac{2}{2} = ?$ **Ans:** 3.

2. $4\frac{1}{2} = ?$ **Ans:** $\frac{9}{2}$.

3. $6\frac{2}{4} = ?$ **Ans:** $\frac{13}{2}$.

4. $8\frac{1}{2} = ?$ **Ans:** $\frac{17}{2}$.

5. $9\frac{1}{2} = ?$ **Ans:** $\frac{19}{2}$.

6. $11\frac{1}{3} = ?$ **Ans:** $\frac{34}{3}$.

7. $10\frac{1}{3} = ?$ **Ans:** $\frac{31}{3}$.

8. $5\frac{2}{5} = ?$ **Ans:** $\frac{27}{5}$.

9. $7\frac{1}{3} = ?$ **Ans:** $\frac{22}{3}$.

10. $10\frac{7}{8} = ?$ **Ans:** $\frac{87}{8}$.

11. $11\frac{5}{7} = ?$ **Ans:** $\frac{82}{7}$.

12. $12\frac{5}{6} = ?$ **Ans:** $\frac{77}{6}$.

Lesson 19 – *Addition of Fractions*

WHAT is the sum of $\frac{1}{3}$ and $\frac{2}{3}$?
   Ans: $\frac{1}{3} + \frac{2}{3} = \frac{3}{3}$, or 1.

1. What is the sum of $\frac{2}{4}$ and $\frac{3}{4}$? **Ans:** $\frac{2}{4} + \frac{3}{4} = \frac{5}{4}$, or $1\frac{1}{4}$.

2. What is the sum of $\frac{4}{6}$ and $\frac{3}{6}$? **Ans:** $\frac{4}{6} + \frac{3}{6} = \frac{7}{6}$, or $1\frac{1}{6}$.

3. What is the sum of $\frac{2}{5}$ and $\frac{4}{5}$? **Ans:** $\frac{6}{5}$, or $1\frac{1}{5}$.

4. How many fourths are in $\frac{1}{2}$ and $\frac{3}{4}$? **Ans:** $\frac{5}{4}$.

5. How many eighths are in $\frac{3}{4}$ and $\frac{3}{8}$? **Ans:** $\frac{9}{8}$.

6. How many tenths are in $\frac{1}{2}$ and $\frac{1}{5}$? **Ans:** $\frac{7}{10}$.

7. How many twelfths are in $\frac{1}{4}$ and $\frac{1}{6}$? **Ans:** $\frac{5}{12}$.

8. How many fifteenths are in $\frac{2}{3}$ and $\frac{3}{5}$? **Ans:** $\frac{19}{25}$.

9. How many sixteenths are in $\frac{3}{4}$ and $\frac{5}{8}$? **Ans:** $\frac{22}{16}$.

10. How many eighteenths are in $\frac{2}{3}$ and $\frac{5}{6}$? **Ans:** $\frac{27}{18}$.

11. What is the sum of $\frac{2}{3}$ and $\frac{3}{4}$?
   Ans: $\frac{2}{3}$ equals $\frac{8}{12}$, and $\frac{3}{4}$ equals $\frac{9}{12}$; plus $\frac{9}{12}$ is $\frac{17}{12}$, equals $1\frac{5}{12}$.

   What is the sum of:

12. $\frac{1}{2}$ and $\frac{1}{3}$? **Ans:** $\frac{1}{2} = \frac{3}{6}$ and $\frac{1}{3} = \frac{2}{6}$; $\frac{3}{6} + \frac{2}{6}$ is $\frac{5}{6}$.

13. $\frac{1}{3}$ and $\frac{1}{4}$? **Ans:** $\frac{1}{3} = \frac{4}{12}$ and $\frac{1}{4} = \frac{3}{12}$; $\frac{4}{12} + \frac{3}{12} = \frac{7}{12}$.

14. $\frac{1}{4}$ and $\frac{1}{5}$? **Ans:** $\frac{9}{20}$.

15. $\frac{2}{3}$ and $\frac{3}{4}$? **Ans:** $1\frac{5}{12}$.

16. $\frac{2}{3}$ and $\frac{2}{5}$? **Ans:** $1\frac{1}{15}$.

17. $\frac{2}{5}$ and $\frac{3}{4}$? **Ans:** $1\frac{3}{20}$.

18. $\frac{3}{4}$ and $\frac{3}{6}$? **Ans:** $1\frac{1}{4}$.

19. $\frac{2}{4}$ and $\frac{2}{7}$? **Ans:** $\frac{11}{14}$.

20. $\frac{5}{6}$ and $\frac{4}{5}$? **Ans:** $1\frac{19}{20}$.

21. $\frac{1}{4}$ and $\frac{1}{9}$? **Ans:** $\frac{13}{36}$.

22. $\frac{2}{5}$ and $\frac{3}{7}$? **Ans:** $\frac{29}{35}$.

23. $\frac{6}{7}$ and $\frac{3}{5}$? **Ans:** $\frac{17}{20}$.

24. $\frac{5}{6}$ and $\frac{4}{7}$? **Ans:** $1\frac{17}{42}$.

25. $\frac{3}{7}$ and $\frac{3}{8}$? **Ans:** $\frac{45}{56}$.

26. $2\frac{1}{2}$ and $3\frac{1}{3}$? **Ans:** $5\frac{5}{6}$.

27. $3\frac{1}{3}$ and $4\frac{1}{4}$? **Ans:** $7\frac{7}{12}$.

28. $2\frac{2}{3}$ and $1\frac{3}{4}$? **Ans:** $4\frac{5}{12}$.

29. $3\frac{1}{4}$ and $2\frac{3}{5}$? **Ans:** $5\frac{17}{20}$.

30. $6\frac{2}{5}$ and $5\frac{3}{6}$? **Ans:** $11\frac{9}{10}$.

31. $4\frac{1}{6}$ and $5\frac{1}{7}$? **Ans:** $9\frac{13}{42}$.

32. $6\frac{1}{5}$ and $5\frac{1}{8}$? **Ans:** $11\frac{13}{40}$.

33. $7\frac{2}{3}$ and $8\frac{3}{7}$? **Ans:** $6\frac{2}{21}$.

34. Arun received $\frac{1}{4}$ of a dollar on Monday, and $\frac{1}{5}$ of a dollar on Tuesday. How much did he get in total?

    Ans: In 2 days he will receive $\frac{1}{4}$ of a dollar plus $\frac{1}{5}$ of a dollar; $\frac{1}{4} = \frac{5}{20}$ and $\frac{1}{5} = \frac{4}{20}$; $\frac{5}{20} + \frac{4}{20} = \frac{9}{20}$ of a dollar.

35. Jane bought one stamp for $\frac{1}{4}$ of a dollar, and an another stamp for $\frac{5}{8}$ of a dollar. What was the cost of both stamps? **Ans:** $\frac{7}{8}$ of a dollar.

36. There was $\frac{2}{5}$ of a bucket of paint left when a $\frac{3}{4}$ of bucket of paint was found. How much paint is now available?

    Ans: $\frac{2}{5} = \frac{8}{20}$. And $\frac{3}{4} = \frac{15}{20}$; $\frac{8}{20} + \frac{15}{20} = \frac{23}{20}$, or $1\frac{3}{20}$ buckets.

37. Rachel had $\frac{1}{2}$ dozen socks and found $\frac{5}{6}$ of a dozen more. How many socks did she have?

    Ans: $\frac{1}{2} = \frac{3}{6}$; $\frac{3}{6}$ of a dozen + $\frac{5}{6}$ of a dozen = $\frac{8}{6}$, or $1\frac{1}{3}$ dozens, or 16 socks.

38. Jane had some money and she received another $\frac{3}{4}$ as much. What part of the starting money does she have now?

    Ans: She had $\frac{4}{4}$ of the sum at first. She received $\frac{4}{4}$ of the sum, the total is $\frac{4}{4} + \frac{3}{4} = \frac{7}{4}$ of the sum she had before.

39. Sarah had 48 daisies and gave $\frac{1}{2}$ of them to her sister and $\frac{1}{3}$ of them to her mother. How many daisies does she have left?

    Ans: $\frac{1}{2} = \frac{3}{6}$ and $\frac{1}{3} = \frac{2}{6}$; $\frac{3}{6} + \frac{2}{6} = \frac{5}{6}$; $\frac{6}{6} - \frac{5}{6} = \frac{1}{6}$; $\frac{1}{6}$ of 48 is 8.

40. James' money increased by $\frac{4}{5}$, equals 90 cents. How much money did James have?

    Ans: $\frac{5}{5}$ of James's money + $\frac{4}{5}$ of his money = $\frac{9}{5}$ of his money, which is 90 cents. So he had 50 cents.

41. $\frac{2}{3}$ of a certain number increased by $\frac{3}{4}$ of the same number, equals 84. What is the number?

    Ans: $\frac{2}{3} = \frac{8}{12}$ and $\frac{3}{4} = \frac{9}{12}$; $\frac{8}{12} + \frac{9}{12} = \frac{17}{12}$. If $\frac{17}{12}$ of the number equals 34, the number is 24.

42. Danny's number of stickers increased by $\frac{1}{2}$ and $\frac{1}{3}$ of his number, equals 55. How many stickers did he have?

    Ans: $\frac{1}{2} + \frac{1}{3} = \frac{5}{6}$; $\frac{6}{6} + \frac{5}{6} = \frac{11}{6}$. If $\frac{11}{6}$ of his number equals 55, the number is 30.

43. $\frac{2}{5}$ of Ahmad's money increased by $\frac{3}{4}$ of his money, equals $69. How much money did Ahmad have?

    Ans: $\frac{2}{5} + \frac{3}{4} = \frac{8}{20} + \frac{15}{20} = \frac{23}{20}$. If $\frac{23}{20}$ of his money equals 69, then his money is $60.

44. Peter had $\frac{3}{8}$ of a certain sum of money, and then was given $\frac{1}{2}$ of the same sum, and then had $21. How much did have at the beginning?
Ans: $\frac{3}{8} + \frac{1}{2} = \frac{3}{8} + \frac{4}{8} = \frac{7}{8}$. If $\frac{7}{8}$ of the sum is $21, the sum is $24.

45. Ann paid $24 for a ring, and $\frac{1}{2} + \frac{2}{3}$ of this is 4 times what she paid for the chain. What is the cost of the chain?
Ans: $\frac{1}{2} + \frac{2}{3} = \frac{7}{6}$; $\frac{7}{6}$ of $24, or $28, equals 4 times the cost of the chain, therefore the chain cost $\frac{1}{4}$ of $28, or $7.

46. What is the sum of: $\frac{1}{3}$ and $\frac{1}{2}$; $\frac{1}{3}$ and $\frac{1}{4}$; $\frac{1}{3}$ and $\frac{1}{5}$; $\frac{1}{3}$ and $\frac{1}{6}$; $\frac{1}{3}$ and $\frac{1}{7}$; $\frac{1}{3}$ and $\frac{1}{9}$.
Ans: $\frac{5}{6}$; $\frac{7}{12}$; $\frac{8}{15}$; $\frac{1}{2}$; $\frac{10}{21}$; $\frac{4}{9}$.

47. What is the sum of: $\frac{1}{4}$ and $\frac{1}{2}$; $\frac{1}{4}$ and $\frac{1}{5}$; $\frac{1}{3}$ and $\frac{1}{5}$; $\frac{1}{6}$ and $\frac{1}{5}$; $\frac{1}{7}$ and $\frac{1}{5}$; $\frac{1}{5}$ and $\frac{1}{9}$.
Ans: $\frac{3}{4}$; $\frac{9}{20}$; $\frac{8}{15}$; $\frac{11}{30}$; $\frac{12}{35}$; $\frac{14}{45}$.

48. What is the sum of: $\frac{1}{5}$ and $\frac{1}{2}$; $\frac{1}{3}$ and $\frac{1}{5}$; $\frac{1}{4}$ and $\frac{1}{5}$; $\frac{1}{5}$ and $\frac{1}{6}$; $\frac{1}{4}$ and $\frac{1}{7}$; $\frac{1}{2}$ and $\frac{1}{9}$.
Ans: $\frac{3}{10}$; $\frac{8}{15}$; $\frac{9}{20}$; $\frac{11}{30}$; $\frac{11}{28}$; $\frac{11}{18}$.

49. What is the sum of: $\frac{1}{6}$ and $\frac{1}{2}$; $\frac{1}{6}$ and $\frac{1}{4}$; $\frac{1}{6}$ and $\frac{1}{5}$; $\frac{1}{6}$ and $\frac{1}{6}$; $\frac{1}{6}$ and $\frac{1}{7}$; $\frac{1}{6}$ and $\frac{1}{9}$.
Ans: $\frac{2}{3}$; $\frac{10}{24}$; $\frac{11}{30}$; $\frac{1}{3}$; $\frac{13}{42}$; $\frac{1}{5}$.

50. What is the sum of: $\frac{1}{10}$ and $\frac{1}{2}$; $\frac{1}{10}$ and $\frac{1}{3}$; $\frac{1}{10}$ and $\frac{1}{4}$; $\frac{1}{10}$ and $\frac{1}{5}$; $\frac{1}{10}$ and $\frac{1}{6}$; $\frac{1}{10}$ and $\frac{1}{10}$.
Ans: $\frac{6}{10}$; $\frac{13}{30}$; $\frac{7}{20}$; $\frac{8}{30}$; $\frac{1}{5}$.

51. What is the sum of: $\frac{1}{2}$ and $\frac{1}{2}$; $\frac{1}{3}$ and $\frac{1}{3}$; $\frac{1}{4}$ and $\frac{1}{4}$; $\frac{1}{5}$ and $\frac{1}{5}$; $\frac{1}{6}$ and $\frac{1}{6}$; $\frac{1}{10}$ and $\frac{1}{10}$.
Ans: 1; $\frac{2}{3}$; $\frac{1}{2}$; $\frac{2}{5}$; $\frac{1}{3}$; $\frac{1}{5}$.

52. If $\frac{1}{2}$ of a number increased by $\frac{1}{3}$ of the number equals 50, what is the number?
Ans: The number is $\frac{6}{6}$ then one-half of the number is $\frac{3}{6}$. One-third of $\frac{3}{6}$ is $\frac{1}{6}$. If $\frac{3}{6} + \frac{1}{6} = \frac{4}{6}$ of the number equals 50 then the number is 75. ⌣

Lesson 20 – *Subtraction of Fractions*

WHAT is the difference between $\frac{6}{7}$ and $\frac{3}{7}$?
   Ans: $\frac{6}{7} - \frac{3}{7} = \frac{4}{7}$.

1. What is the difference between $\frac{7}{8}$ and $\frac{3}{8}$?
   Ans: $\frac{7}{8} - \frac{3}{8} = \frac{4}{8}$, or $\frac{1}{2}$.

2. What is the difference between $\frac{8}{9}$ and $\frac{5}{9}$?
   Ans: $\frac{8}{9} - \frac{5}{9} = \frac{3}{9}$, or $\frac{1}{3}$.

3. What is the difference between $2\frac{3}{4}$ and $1\frac{1}{4}$?
   Ans: $2 - 1 = 1$; $\frac{3}{4} - \frac{1}{4} = \frac{2}{4}$, or $\frac{1}{2}$. The whole number difference is $1\frac{1}{2}$.
   Note—*Of course we could have done this problem by first reducing the mixed fraction to an improper fraction and then doing the subtraction. But often you can skip that step and do the addition or the subtraction by first carefully looking at the mixed fraction to see if they can be added or subtracted directly as in this case.*

4. What is the difference between $3\frac{2}{3}$ and $2\frac{1}{3}$? **Ans:** $1\frac{1}{3}$.

5. What is the difference between $5\frac{3}{5}$ and $2\frac{2}{5}$? **Ans:** $3\frac{1}{5}$.

6. Subtract $\frac{1}{3}$ from $\frac{1}{2}$.
   Ans: 1 is equal to $\frac{3}{6}$, and $\frac{1}{3}$ to $\frac{2}{6}$; $\frac{3}{6} - \frac{2}{6} = \frac{1}{6}$.

7. Subtract $\frac{1}{5}$ from $\frac{1}{4}$.
   Ans: $\frac{1}{5}$ is equal to $\frac{4}{20}$, and $\frac{1}{4}$ to $\frac{5}{20}$; $\frac{5}{20} - \frac{4}{20} = \frac{1}{20}$.

8. Subtract $\frac{2}{3}$ from $\frac{3}{4}$.
   Ans: $\frac{2}{3}$ is equal to $\frac{8}{12}$, and $\frac{3}{4}$ to $\frac{9}{12}$; $\frac{9}{12} - \frac{8}{12} = \frac{1}{12}$.

9. What is $\frac{1}{2}$ minus $\frac{1}{4}$? **Ans:** $\frac{1}{4}$.

10. What is $\frac{7}{8}$ minus $\frac{3}{4}$? **Ans:** $\frac{1}{8}$.

11. What is $\frac{1}{2}$ minus $\frac{1}{3}$? **Ans:** $\frac{1}{6}$.

12. What is $\frac{5}{6}$ minus $\frac{3}{4}$? **Ans:** $\frac{1}{12}$.

   Subtract

13. $\frac{1}{2} - \frac{1}{3} = ?$ **Ans:** $\frac{1}{6}$.

14. $\frac{1}{2} - \frac{1}{4} = ?$ **Ans:** $\frac{1}{4}$.

15. $\frac{1}{2} - \frac{1}{5} = ?$ **Ans:** $\frac{3}{10}$.

16. $\frac{1}{2} - \frac{1}{8} = ?$ **Ans:** $\frac{3}{8}$.

17. $\frac{1}{2} - \frac{1}{6} = ?$ **Ans:** $\frac{1}{3}$.

18. $\frac{1}{2} - \frac{1}{7} = ?$ **Ans:** $\frac{5}{14}$.

19. $\frac{1}{2} - \frac{1}{10} = ?$ **Ans:** $\frac{2}{5}$.

20. $\frac{1}{2} - \frac{1}{20} = ?$ **Ans:** $\frac{9}{20}$.

21. $\frac{1}{3} - \frac{1}{3} = ?$ **Ans:** 0.

22. $\frac{1}{3} - \frac{1}{4} = ?$ **Ans:** $\frac{1}{12}$.

23. $\frac{1}{3} - \frac{1}{5} = ?$ **Ans:** $\frac{2}{15}$.

24. $\frac{1}{3} - \frac{1}{8} = ?$ **Ans:** $\frac{5}{24}$

25. $\frac{1}{3} - \frac{1}{6} = ?$ **Ans:** $\frac{1}{6}$.

26. $\frac{1}{3} - \frac{1}{7} = ?$ **Ans:** $\frac{4}{21}$.

27. $\frac{1}{3} - \frac{1}{10} = ?$ **Ans:** $\frac{7}{30}$.

28. $\frac{1}{3} - \frac{1}{20} = ?$ **Ans:** $\frac{17}{60}$.

29. $\frac{1}{4} - \frac{1}{5} = ?$ **Ans:** $\frac{1}{20}$.

30. $\frac{1}{4} - \frac{1}{6} = ?$ **Ans:** $\frac{1}{12}$.

31. $\frac{1}{4} - \frac{1}{8} = ?$ **Ans:** $\frac{1}{8}$.

32. $\frac{1}{4} - \frac{1}{6} = ?$ **Ans:** $\frac{1}{12}$.

33. $\frac{1}{4} - \frac{1}{7} = ?$ **Ans:** $\frac{3}{28}$.

34. $\frac{1}{4} - \frac{1}{10} = ?$ **Ans:** $\frac{3}{20}$.

35. $\frac{1}{4} - \frac{1}{40} = ?$ **Ans:** $\frac{9}{40}$.

36. $\frac{1}{5} - \frac{1}{6} = ?$ **Ans:** $\frac{1}{30}$.

37. $\frac{1}{5} - \frac{1}{7} = ?$ **Ans:** $\frac{2}{35}$.

38. $\frac{1}{5} - \frac{1}{8} = ?$ **Ans:** $\frac{3}{40}$.

39. $\frac{1}{5} - \frac{1}{9} = ?$ **Ans:** $\frac{4}{45}$.

40. $\frac{1}{5} - \frac{1}{7} = ?$ **Ans:** $\frac{2}{35}$.

41. $\frac{1}{5} - \frac{1}{10} = ?$ **Ans:** $\frac{1}{10}$.

42. $\frac{1}{5} - \frac{1}{20} = ?$ **Ans:** $\frac{3}{20}$.

43. $\frac{1}{4} - \frac{1}{5} = ?$ **Ans:** $\frac{1}{20}$.

44. $\frac{1}{5} - \frac{1}{10} = ?$ **Ans:** $\frac{1}{10}$.

45. A man owned $\frac{3}{4}$ of a boat, and sold $\frac{1}{3}$ of his share. What part of the boat does he still own?

Ans: If he sold $\frac{1}{3}$ of his share then he has left $\frac{2}{3}$ of his share; $\frac{3}{4} \times \frac{2}{3} = \frac{1}{2}$.

46. A pole is in the mud, air, and water. If $\frac{3}{5}$ of it is in the mud and water, how much is in the air? **Ans:** $\frac{2}{5}$.

47. If $\frac{1}{2}$ of a pole is in the air, $\frac{1}{3}$ in the water, and the rest in the mud, how much is in the mud?

Ans: $\frac{1}{2} + \frac{1}{3} = \frac{5}{6}$, the part in the air and water; $\frac{6}{6} - \frac{5}{6} = \frac{1}{6}$, the part in the mud.

48. Michael Wilson's age reduced by $\frac{1}{4}$ is 15 years. How old is he?

Ans: $\frac{4}{4} - \frac{1}{4} = \frac{3}{4}$. If $\frac{3}{4}$ of his age is 15 years, his age is 20 years.

49. The difference between $\frac{2}{3}$ of my money and $\frac{3}{4}$ of my money is $90. How much money do I have?

Ans: $\frac{3}{4} - \frac{2}{3} = \frac{1}{12}$. If $\frac{1}{12}$ of my money is $9, I have $108.

50. Mr. Singh bought 50 meters of a sailcloth for his sailboat, and used just $\frac{3}{5}$ of it. How many meters does he have left?

Ans: $\frac{5}{5} - \frac{3}{5} = \frac{2}{5}$; $\frac{2}{5}$ of 50 meters is 20 meters, the amount left.

51. Nina owes $\frac{3}{5}$ of a dollar for a purchase. If she hands the clerk $\frac{3}{4}$ of a dollar, how much change would she receive?

Ans: $\frac{3}{4}$ of a dollar, minus $\frac{3}{5}$ of a dollar, equals $\frac{3}{20}$ of a dollar, or 15 cents.

52. In an orchard, $\frac{1}{2}$ of the trees are apples, $\frac{1}{3}$ are peaches, and the rest are pear trees. What part of the whole are pear trees?

Ans: $\frac{1}{2} + \frac{1}{3} = \frac{5}{6}$; $\frac{6}{6} - \frac{5}{6} = \frac{1}{6}$, the number of pear trees.

53. A boy had 36 model cars, broke $\frac{3}{4}$ of them, and then bought $\frac{5}{6}$ as many as he had at first. How many did he have then?

Ans: $\frac{4}{4} - \frac{3}{4} = \frac{1}{4}$; $\frac{1}{4}$ of 36 model cars is 9 model cars, the number left; $\frac{5}{6}$ of 36 is 30; 30 + 9 = 39 model cars.

54. $40 is 4 times what Aron paid for parking, and the cost of the show is 8 times the cost of parking. What is the cost of the show?

Ans: The cost of the parking is $\frac{1}{4}$ of $40, or $10, which is $\frac{1}{8}$ of the cost of the show. So the show costs 8 times $10, or $80.

55. $600 is $\frac{3}{5}$ of what Ron paid for a computer. The cost of the computer, if increased by 3 fifths, is 5 times what he paid for the software. What is the cost of the software?

Ans: If $\frac{3}{5}$ of the cost of the computer is $600, the whole cost of the computer is $1000. $1000 + $600 = $1600, which is 5 times the cost of the software. So the cost of the software is $\frac{1}{5}$ of $1600, or $320.

Subtract these fractions.

1. $\frac{1}{4} - \frac{1}{6} = ?$ **Ans:** $\frac{1}{12}$.

2. $\frac{2}{4} - \frac{2}{5} = ?$ **Ans:** $\frac{1}{10}$.

3. $\frac{4}{5} - \frac{2}{3} = ?$ **Ans:** $\frac{2}{15}$.

4. $\frac{1}{10} - \frac{2}{5} = ?$ **Ans:** $\frac{3}{10}$

5. $\frac{3}{4} - \frac{3}{5} = ?$ **Ans:** $\frac{3}{20}$.

6. $\frac{8}{9} - \frac{3}{4} = ?$ **Ans:** $\frac{5}{36}$.

7. $\frac{1}{5} - \frac{1}{6} = ?$ **Ans:** $\frac{1}{20}$.

8. $\frac{1}{6} - \frac{1}{7} = ?$ **Ans:** $\frac{1}{42}$.

9. $\frac{5}{8} - \frac{1}{3} = ?$ **Ans:** $\frac{7}{24}$.

10. $\frac{2}{3} - \frac{2}{5} = ?$ **Ans:** $\frac{4}{15}$.

11. $\frac{5}{7} - \frac{1}{2} = ?$ **Ans:** $\frac{3}{14}$.

12. $\frac{1}{7} - \frac{1}{8} = ?$ **Ans:** $\frac{1}{56}$.

13. $\frac{1}{2} - \frac{1}{9} = ?$ **Ans:** $\frac{7}{18}$.

14. $\frac{2}{3} - \frac{2}{7} = ?$ **Ans:** $\frac{8}{21}$.

15. $\frac{6}{8} - \frac{3}{7} = ?$ **Ans:** $\frac{9}{28}$.

Lesson 21 – *Product of Fractions and Numbers*

WHAT is $\frac{1}{3}$ of 4?

Ans: $\frac{1}{3}$ of one is $\frac{1}{3}$, and if $\frac{1}{3}$ of one is $\frac{1}{3}$, then $\frac{1}{3}$ of 4 is 4 times $\frac{1}{3}$, which is $\frac{4}{3}$. Therefore $\frac{1}{3}$ of 4 is $\frac{4}{3}$ of one.

Note—*This may seem like a convoluted way of solving a simple problem, but it shows the consistency and reason of using unit values.*

1. What is $\frac{1}{3}$ of 5? $\frac{1}{4}$ of 6? **Ans:** $\frac{5}{3}$; $\frac{6}{4}$.

2. What is $\frac{1}{5}$ of 7? $\frac{1}{6}$ of 9? **Ans:** $\frac{7}{5}$; $\frac{9}{6}$.

3. What is $\frac{1}{2}$ of 5? $\frac{1}{4}$ of 10? **Ans:** $\frac{5}{2}$; $\frac{10}{4}$.

4. What is $\frac{1}{7}$ of 9? $\frac{1}{8}$ of 20? **Ans:** $\frac{9}{7}$; $\frac{20}{8}$.

5. What is $\frac{2}{4}$ of 6? $\frac{3}{4}$ of 10? **Ans:** $\frac{12}{4}$ or 3; $\frac{30}{4}$ or $\frac{15}{2}$.

6. What is $\frac{3}{4}$ of 3? $\frac{5}{6}$ of 14? **Ans:** $\frac{9}{5}$; $\frac{70}{6}$.

7. What is $\frac{2}{7}$ of 4? $\frac{3}{9}$ of 15? **Ans:** $\frac{8}{7}$; $\frac{45}{9}$.

8. Mary has \$6, and her brother has $\frac{3}{5}$ as much. How much does her brother have?

    Ans: $\frac{1}{5}$ of 6 is $\frac{6}{5}$, and $\frac{3}{5}$ is 3 times $\frac{6}{5}$, or $\frac{18}{5}$, or \$3$\frac{3}{5}$.

9. Asha has \$20, and $\frac{1}{3}$ of her money equals 4 times Bina's money. How much money does Bina have?

    Ans: $\frac{1}{3}$ of 20 is $\frac{20}{3}$. If $\frac{20}{3}$ is 4 times Bina's money, then Bina's money is $\frac{1}{4}$ of $\frac{20}{3}$, or $\frac{5}{3}$ of \$20.

10. Kevin is 7 years old, and $\frac{4}{9}$ of his age equals $\frac{7}{9}$ of Ashley's age. How old is Ashley?

    Ans: $\frac{4}{9}$ of 7 years is $\frac{28}{9}$ years, which is $\frac{7}{9}$ of Ashley' age. So $\frac{1}{9}$ of Ashley's age equals $\frac{1}{7}$ of $\frac{28}{9}$ and $\frac{4}{9}$ years and her age equals 9 times $\frac{4}{9}$ years, or 4 years.

11. A family paid \$21 for the movie tickets. $\frac{4}{5}$ of the ticket's cost is $\frac{7}{10}$ of the cost of the snacks they bought. What is the cost of both tickets and the snacks?

    Ans: $\frac{4}{5}$ of \$21 is \$$\frac{84}{5}$. If $\frac{84}{5}$ is $\frac{7}{10}$ of the cost of the movie, then $\frac{1}{10}$ of the cost is $\frac{1}{7}$ of $\frac{84}{5}$ or $\frac{12}{5}$. 10 times $\frac{12}{5}$ is \$24.

12. A jug contains 5 gallons, and $\frac{6}{7}$ of its contents is $\frac{10}{14}$ the contents of an another jug. What is the content, in gallons, of the second jug?

    Ans: $\frac{6}{7}$ of 5 gallons is $\frac{30}{7}$ gallons. If $\frac{30}{7}$ gallons is $\frac{10}{14}$ of the second jug, $\frac{1}{14}$ of the $\frac{10}{14}$ is $\frac{1}{10}$ of $\frac{30}{7}$ or $\frac{3}{7}$ of a gallon and $1\frac{4}{14}$ is 6 gallons.

13. What is $\frac{2}{3}$ of $\frac{6}{8}$?
Ans: $\frac{1}{3}$ of $\frac{6}{8}$ is $\frac{6}{24}$, and if $\frac{1}{3}$ of $\frac{5}{8}$ is $\frac{6}{24}$, then $\frac{2}{3}$ of $\frac{6}{8}$ is 2 times $\frac{6}{7}$, which is $\frac{4}{8}$, or $\frac{1}{2}$.

14. What is $\frac{2}{3}$ of 42? **Ans:** 24.

15. What is $\frac{5}{4}$ of 36? **Ans:** 45.

16. What is $\frac{4}{5}$ of 60? **Ans:** 49.

17. What is $\frac{1}{2}$ of $\frac{6}{9}$? **Ans:** $\frac{1}{3}$.

18. What is $\frac{1}{3}$ of $\frac{4}{5}$? **Ans:** $\frac{4}{15}$.

19. What is $\frac{1}{4}$ of $4\frac{1}{2}$? **Ans:** $1\frac{1}{8}$.

20. What is $\frac{1}{5}$ of $2\frac{1}{2}$? **Ans:** $\frac{1}{2}$.

21. What is $\frac{1}{3}$ of $3\frac{1}{3}$? **Ans:** $1\frac{1}{9}$.

Note—*The term "of" between two numbers means the product of, or multiplication. So if we say "what is $\frac{2}{3}$ of 3?", then it often means we multiply the first term with the second one.*

22. What is $\frac{2}{3}$ of $\frac{6}{7}$?
Ans: $\frac{1}{3}$ of $\frac{6}{7}$ is $\frac{2}{7}$, and $\frac{2}{3}$ of $\frac{6}{7}$ is 2 times $\frac{2}{7}$, or $\frac{4}{7}$. Or we could have multiplied $\frac{2}{3}$ with $\frac{6}{7}$, canceling 3 with 6, $\frac{2}{1}$ with $\frac{2}{7}$, and we get $\frac{4}{7}$.

23. What is $\frac{2}{7}$ of $\frac{7}{8}$? **Ans:** $\frac{1}{7}$ of $\frac{7}{8}$ is $\frac{1}{8}$, and $\frac{2}{7}$ of $\frac{7}{8}$ is $\frac{2}{8}$, or $\frac{1}{4}$.

24. $\frac{3}{6}$ of $\frac{6}{9}$? **Ans:** $\frac{1}{3}$.

25. $\frac{4}{9}$ of $\frac{18}{20}$? **Ans:** $\frac{2}{5}$.

26. $\frac{3}{5}$ of $\frac{15}{18}$? **Ans:** $\frac{1}{2}$.

27. $\frac{2}{7}$ of $\frac{14}{16}$? **Ans:** $\frac{1}{4}$.

28. $\frac{3}{5}$ of $2\frac{1}{2}$? **Ans:** $\frac{3}{2}$.

29. $\frac{5}{6}$ of $2\frac{2}{5}$? **Ans:** 2.

30. $\frac{3}{5}$ of 6? **Ans:** $2\frac{3}{5}$.

31. $\frac{2}{5}$ of $3\frac{3}{4}$? **Ans:** $\frac{3}{2}$.

32. $\frac{3}{2}$ of 11? **Ans:** $16\frac{1}{2}$.

33. $\frac{3}{5}$ of $40 is 2 times what was paid for a calendar. What was the cost of the calendar? **Ans:** $12.

34. $\frac{5}{7}$ of $\frac{14}{25}$ of $100 is $\frac{1}{10}$ the cost of a watch. How much did the watch cost? **Ans:** $400.

35. Lim got 27 points on his test, and $\frac{2}{3}$ of what Lim got equals $\frac{2}{5}$ of Chee's points. How many points did Chee get? **Ans:** 45 points.

36. Ivan's cap cost $\frac{4}{5}$ of \$20, which is $\frac{5}{3}$ of $\frac{3}{5}$ of the cost of his muffler. What is the cost of his muffler? **Ans:** \$16.

37. If Asher receives $\frac{6}{8}$ of 48 Jordon almonds and Ben receives $\frac{2}{3}$ as many as Asher, how many Jordon almonds does each boy receive? **Ans:** Asher, 36 Jordon almonds; Ben, 24.

38. Hanah bought $\frac{4}{6}$ of a box of gummy bears, which is $\frac{8}{3}$ of what Sarah bought. How many gummy bears did each purchase, if there were 24 gummy bears in box? **Ans:** Hanah, 16; Sarah, 2.

39. Alan has 40 fruit trees in his orchard; $\frac{4}{10}$ are apples, $\frac{1}{2}$ of the rest are pears, and the rest are peaches. How many trees are there of each kind? **Ans:** 16 apple, 12 pear, 12 peach.

40. Jenson's age reduced by $\frac{1}{4}$ and $\frac{1}{5}$ is 20 years, and his age is $\frac{4}{5}$ of his uncle's age. What is the age of each?
Ans: $\frac{1}{4} + \frac{1}{5} = \frac{9}{20}$; $\frac{20}{20} - \frac{9}{20} = 1\frac{1}{20}$. If $\frac{11}{20}$ of his age is 22 years, $\frac{20}{20}$ is 40 years. If $\frac{4}{5}$ of his uncle's age is 40 years, his uncle's age is 50 years.

41. Solve these by multiplying the numerators and denominators and then reducing to lowest terms.

42. $\frac{1}{2} \times \frac{1}{3} =$? **Ans:** $\frac{1}{6}$.

43. $\frac{1}{2} \times \frac{1}{4} =$? **Ans:** $\frac{1}{8}$.

44. $\frac{1}{2} \times \frac{1}{6} =$? **Ans:** $\frac{1}{12}$.

45. $\frac{1}{3} \times \frac{1}{6} =$? **Ans:** $\frac{1}{18}$.

46. $\frac{1}{3} \times \frac{1}{4} =$? **Ans:** $\frac{7}{12}$.

47. $\frac{1}{4} \times \frac{1}{8} =$? **Ans:** $\frac{1}{24}$.

48. $\frac{1}{4} \times \frac{1}{5} =$? **Ans:** $\frac{1}{20}$.

49. $\frac{1}{4} \times \frac{2}{3} =$? **Ans:** $\frac{1}{6}$.

50. $\frac{2}{3} \times \frac{1}{2} =$? **Ans:** $\frac{1}{3}$.

51. $\frac{3}{4} \times \frac{2}{3} =$? **Ans:** $\frac{1}{2}$.

52. $\frac{1}{3} \times \frac{1}{5} =$? **Ans:** $\frac{1}{15}$.

53. $\frac{1}{4} \times \frac{2}{4} =$? **Ans:** $\frac{1}{8}$.

54. $\frac{2}{3} \times \frac{1}{4} =$? **Ans:** $\frac{1}{6}$.

Lesson 22 – *Multiplication of Fractions*

WHAT is $\frac{1}{3}$ of $\frac{1}{4}$?

Ans: $\frac{1}{3}$ of $\frac{1}{4}$ is one of the three equal parts into which $\frac{1}{4}$ may be divided. If each fourth is divided into three equal parts, 4 fourths or the unit, will be divided into 4 times 3, or 12 equal parts. So, each part is $\frac{1}{12}$ of a unit. Therefore, $\frac{1}{3}$ of $\frac{1}{4}$ is $\frac{1}{12}$.

1. What is $\frac{1}{2}$ of $\frac{1}{4}$? $\frac{1}{2}$ of $\frac{1}{8}$? $\frac{1}{2}$ of $\frac{1}{10}$?
   Ans: $\frac{1}{8}$; $\frac{1}{16}$; $\frac{1}{20}$.

2. What is $\frac{1}{3}$ of $\frac{1}{5}$? $\frac{1}{3}$ of $\frac{1}{2}$? $\frac{1}{3}$ of $\frac{1}{6}$?
   Ans: $\frac{1}{15}$; $\frac{1}{6}$; $\frac{1}{18}$.

3. What is $\frac{1}{4}$ of $\frac{1}{6}$? $\frac{1}{6}$ of $\frac{1}{5}$? $\frac{1}{7}$ of $\frac{1}{6}$?
   Ans: $\frac{1}{24}$; $\frac{1}{30}$; $\frac{1}{42}$.

4. What is $\frac{1}{5}$ of $\frac{1}{3}$? $\frac{1}{7}$ of $\frac{1}{2}$? $\frac{1}{7}$ of $\frac{1}{3}$?
   Ans: $\frac{1}{15}$; $\frac{1}{14}$; $\frac{1}{21}$.

5. What is $\frac{1}{4}$ of $\frac{1}{8}$? $\frac{1}{6}$ of $\frac{1}{8}$? $\frac{1}{7}$ of $\frac{1}{9}$?
   Ans: $\frac{1}{32}$; $\frac{1}{48}$; $\frac{1}{63}$.

6. What is $\frac{1}{6}$ of $\frac{1}{12}$? $\frac{1}{3}$ of $\frac{1}{12}$? $\frac{1}{35}$ of $\frac{1}{2}$?
   Ans: $\frac{1}{72}$; $\frac{1}{36}$; $\frac{1}{70}$.

7. Marta had $\frac{1}{5}$ of a pie. She gave $\frac{1}{3}$ of it to Hannah. What part of the pie did Hannah receive?
   Ans: If Marta had $\frac{1}{5}$ of a pie, and gave $\frac{1}{3}$ of it to Hannah, then Hannah received $\frac{1}{3}$ of $\frac{1}{5}$ of a pie. $\frac{1}{3}$ of $\frac{1}{5}$ is $\frac{1}{15}$ of the pie.

8. Philip, had $\frac{1}{4}$ of an orange, and gave $\frac{1}{5}$ of it to Peter. What part of the orange did Peter receive? **Ans:** $\frac{1}{20}$ of an orange.

9. Anisah had $\frac{1}{2}$ of a dollar, and gave $\frac{1}{5}$ of it to Serena. What part of a dollar did Serena receive? **Ans:** $\frac{1}{10}$ of a dollar.

10. What is $\frac{1}{3}$ of $\frac{1}{4}$? **Ans:** $\frac{1}{12}$.

11. What is $\frac{1}{4}$ of $\frac{1}{5}$? **Ans:** $\frac{1}{20}$.

12. What is $\frac{1}{2}$ of $\frac{1}{3}$? $\frac{1}{3}$ of $\frac{1}{6}$? $\frac{1}{5}$ of $\frac{1}{6}$? $\frac{1}{5}$ of $\frac{1}{7}$?
    Ans: $\frac{1}{6}$; $\frac{1}{18}$; $\frac{1}{30}$; $\frac{1}{35}$.

13. What is $\frac{1}{3}$ of $\frac{1}{6}$? $\frac{1}{5}$ of $\frac{1}{8}$? $\frac{1}{7}$ of $\frac{1}{3}$? $\frac{1}{8}$ of $\frac{1}{9}$?
    Ans: $\frac{1}{18}$; $\frac{1}{40}$; $\frac{1}{21}$; $\frac{1}{72}$.

14. What is $\frac{1}{6}$ of $\frac{1}{4}$? $\frac{1}{7}$ of $\frac{1}{7}$? $\frac{1}{9}$ of $\frac{1}{5}$? $\frac{1}{10}$ of $\frac{1}{11}$?

Ans: $\frac{1}{24}$; $\frac{1}{49}$; $\frac{1}{45}$; $\frac{1}{110}$.

15. A man owned $\frac{1}{8}$ of a farm and sold $\frac{1}{6}$ of it to his neighbor. What part of the farm did he sell?

Ans: If he sold $\frac{1}{6}$ of his farm to his neighbor, he sold $\frac{1}{6}$ of $\frac{1}{8}$ of the whole farm; multiplying the denominators together, we have 48; therefore $\frac{1}{6}$ of $\frac{1}{8}$ is $\frac{1}{48}$.

16. Susan took $\frac{1}{6}$ of a cake, and gave Elizabeth $\frac{1}{3}$ of her piece. How much did Elizabeth receive?

Ans: If Susan gave Elizabeth $\frac{1}{3}$, she must have given her $\frac{1}{3}$ of $\frac{1}{6}$ of the cake, and multiplying the denominators together, we have 18; therefore $\frac{1}{3}$ of $\frac{1}{6}$ is $\frac{1}{18}$.

17. Lindy is 8 years old, and her age is $\frac{1}{2}$ of $\frac{1}{3}$ of her mother's age. How old is her mother?

Ans: $\frac{1}{2}$ of $\frac{1}{3}$ of her mother's age is $\frac{1}{6}$ of her mother's age. If 8 years is $\frac{1}{6}$ of her mother's age, then $\frac{6}{6}$ is 6 times 8, or 48 years, is her mother's age.

18. A man had $\frac{1}{7}$ of the stock in a company and sold $\frac{1}{4}$ of it. What part of his stock did he keep?

Ans: If he sold $\frac{1}{4}$, he kept $\frac{4}{4} - \frac{1}{4}$, or $\frac{3}{4}$ of his stock. He had $\frac{1}{7}$ of the stock, so he still has $\frac{3}{4}$ of $\frac{1}{7}$ or $\frac{3}{28}$.

19. Carlo bought $\frac{1}{5}$ of a ton of peanuts and let his pet elephant, Momo, take $\frac{1}{4}$ of it. What part of the peanuts did Carlo keep?

Ans: If Momo took $\frac{1}{4}$, Carlo kept $\frac{4}{4} - \frac{1}{4}$, or $\frac{3}{4}$; $\frac{1}{4}$ of $\frac{1}{5}$ is $\frac{1}{20}$, and $\frac{3}{4}$ is $\frac{3}{20}$, the part of the ton which Carlo has left.

20. An envelope cost 12 cents, and $\frac{2}{3}$ of its cost is $\frac{1}{3}$ of $\frac{1}{4}$ of the cost of the stamp. What is the cost of the stamp.

Ans: $\frac{2}{3}$ of 12 cents is 8 cents; $\frac{1}{3}$ of $\frac{1}{4}$ is $\frac{1}{12}$. If $\frac{1}{12}$ of the cost of the stamp is 8 cents, $\frac{12}{12}$ is 12 times 8 cents, or 96 cents.

21. What is $\frac{2}{3}$ of $\frac{4}{5}$?

Ans: $\frac{1}{3}$ of $\frac{1}{5}$ is $\frac{1}{15}$ and if $\frac{1}{3}$ of $\frac{1}{5}$ is $\frac{1}{15}$, $\frac{1}{3}$ of $\frac{4}{5}$ is 4 times $\frac{1}{15}$ which is $\frac{4}{15}$, and $\frac{2}{3}$ of $\frac{4}{5}$ is 2 times $\frac{4}{15}$, or $\frac{8}{15}$.

22. What is $\frac{1}{3}$ of $\frac{2}{3}$? $\frac{1}{4}$ of $\frac{3}{5}$? $\frac{1}{5}$ of $\frac{4}{6}$?

Ans: $\frac{2}{9}$; $\frac{3}{20}$; $\frac{2}{15}$.

23. What is $\frac{1}{4}$ of $\frac{5}{7}$? $\frac{1}{6}$ of $\frac{5}{8}$? $\frac{1}{7}$ of $\frac{5}{6}$?

Ans: $\frac{5}{28}$; $\frac{5}{48}$; $\frac{5}{42}$.

24. What is $\frac{1}{5}$ of $\frac{6}{7}$?; $\frac{1}{8}$ of $\frac{7}{9}$? $\frac{1}{6}$ of $\frac{4}{12}$?
Ans: $\frac{6}{35}$; $\frac{7}{42}$; $\frac{1}{15}$.

25. What is $\frac{2}{3}$ of $\frac{5}{6}$? $\frac{3}{4}$ of $\frac{5}{6}$? $\frac{4}{5}$ of $\frac{6}{8}$?
Ans: $\frac{5}{9}$; $\frac{5}{8}$; $\frac{3}{5}$.

26. What is $\frac{3}{5}$ of $\frac{4}{6}$? $\frac{5}{6}$ of $\frac{5}{7}$? $\frac{3}{4}$ of $\frac{3}{6}$?
Ans: $\frac{2}{5}$; $\frac{25}{42}$; $\frac{3}{8}$.

27. What is $\frac{2}{5}$ of $\frac{4}{7}$? $\frac{7}{10}$ of $\frac{5}{8}$? $\frac{5}{9}$ of $\frac{7}{10}$?
Ans: $\frac{8}{35}$; $\frac{7}{16}$; $\frac{7}{18}$.

28. What is $\frac{3}{8}$ of $\frac{3}{9}$? $\frac{2}{5}$ of $\frac{2}{7}$? $\frac{3}{4}$ of $\frac{3}{5}$?
Ans: $\frac{1}{8}$; $\frac{4}{35}$; $\frac{9}{20}$.

29. What is $\frac{5}{7}$ of $\frac{2}{3}$? $\frac{6}{8}$ of $\frac{3}{4}$? $\frac{7}{6}$ of $\frac{3}{7}$?
Ans: $\frac{10}{21}$; $\frac{9}{16}$; $\frac{1}{2}$.

30. What is $\frac{3}{4}$ of $\frac{8}{6}$? $\frac{4}{5}$ of $\frac{10}{8}$? $\frac{3}{7}$ of $\frac{14}{9}$?
Ans: 1; 1; $\frac{2}{3}$.

31. A boy had $\frac{3}{4}$ of a dollar and gave $\frac{2}{5}$ of it to his sister. How much did he give to his sister? **Ans:** $\frac{3}{10}$ of a dollar.

32. A man had $\frac{2}{5}$ of the stock in a bank and sold $\frac{3}{8}$ of it. How much of his stock did he sell?
Ans: He sold $\frac{3}{8}$ of $\frac{2}{5}$; therefore he sold $\frac{6}{40}$, or $\frac{3}{20}$ of the stock.

33. Chin had $\frac{2}{7}$ of a melon and gave $\frac{2}{3}$ of it to Cho. What part of the melon remained?
Ans: If she gave away $\frac{2}{3}$ of $\frac{2}{7}$, she had left $\frac{3}{3} - \frac{2}{3}$, or $\frac{1}{3}$ of $\frac{2}{7}$.

34. I had $\frac{3}{4}$ of a kingdom. I gave $\frac{3}{5}$ of it to my sister Elizabeth. What part of the kilogram did I keep for myself? **Ans:** $\frac{4}{4} - \frac{3}{4} = \frac{1}{4}$; $\frac{3}{5}$ of $\frac{1}{4}$ is $\frac{3}{20}$ of the kingdom.

35. Eva withdrew $\frac{4}{5}$ of her money from her bank account, and spent $\frac{5}{6}$ of it. How much does she have left in her account?
Ans: $\frac{6}{6} - \frac{5}{6} = \frac{1}{6}$, what is left; $\frac{1}{6}$ of $\frac{4}{5} = \frac{4}{30}$, or $\frac{2}{15}$ of the money is left.

36. I lost $\frac{1}{4}$ of my money and later found $\frac{1}{2}$ of what I lost. I now have $70. How much did I have at first?
Ans: After I lost $\frac{1}{4}$, I had left $\frac{4}{4} - \frac{1}{4} = \frac{3}{4}$. I found $\frac{1}{2}$ of $\frac{1}{4}$, or $\frac{1}{8}$; add this to what I had left, $\frac{3}{4} + \frac{1}{8} = \frac{7}{8}$. If $\frac{7}{8}$ of my money is $70, then $\frac{8}{8}$ is $80, which is what I had at first.

37. The general lost $\frac{8}{9}$ of his army and then found $\frac{1}{6}$ of the rest. What part of his his army did he have then?

Ans: $\frac{9}{9} - \frac{8}{9} = \frac{1}{9}$, what was left. He found $\frac{1}{6}$ of $\frac{1}{9}$, or $\frac{1}{54}$ and then had $\frac{1}{9} + \frac{1}{54}$, or $\frac{7}{54}$ of his army.

38. Annie had $\frac{2}{5}$ of a pound of candies, and shared them equally with 5 of her school mates. What part of a pound did each receive?

Ans: If she shared them with 5 school mates, there were 6 among whom to divide, and each received $\frac{1}{6}$ of $\frac{2}{5}$, or $\frac{1}{15}$ of a pound.

39. A squirrel fell $\frac{5}{6}$ of the distance from the top of a tree to the ground, and then climbed $\frac{1}{4}$ of the distance he was from the ground. What part of the whole distance is he from the ground?

Ans: $\frac{1}{6}$ of the whole distance equals the distance he was from the ground. He climbed $\frac{1}{4}$ of $\frac{1}{6}$, or $\frac{1}{24}$, of the whole distance; $\frac{1}{6} + \frac{1}{24}$, or $\frac{5}{24}$, of the whole distance equals the distance he was from the ground.

Lesson 23 – *Multiplication of Numbers and Fractions*

WHAT is 4 times $\frac{3}{8}$?
  Ans: 4 times $\frac{3}{8}$ is $\frac{4 \times 3}{8} = \frac{12}{8}$, which equals $\frac{3}{2}$, or $1\frac{1}{2}$.

1. What is the product:

2. 3 times $\frac{3}{6}$? **Ans:** $1\frac{1}{2}$.

3. 3 times $\frac{2}{9}$? **Ans:** $\frac{2}{3}$.

4. 4 times $\frac{6}{8}$? **Ans:** 3.

5. 3 times $\frac{2}{6}$? **Ans:** 1.

6. 7 times $\frac{3}{14}$? **Ans:** $1\frac{1}{2}$.

7. 5 times $\frac{4}{10}$? **Ans:** 2.

8. 4 times $\frac{6}{12}$? **Ans:** 2.

9. 6 times $\frac{7}{12}$? **Ans:** $3\frac{1}{2}$.

10. 3 times $\frac{6}{9}$? **Ans:** 2.

11. 4 times $\frac{2}{6}$? **Ans:** $1\frac{1}{3}$.

12. 8 times $\frac{2}{4}$? **Ans:** 6.

13. 8 times $\frac{3}{6}$? **Ans:** 4.

14. 5 times $\frac{3}{6}$? **Ans:** $\frac{1}{2}$.

15. 5 times $\frac{7}{6}$? **Ans:** $5\frac{5}{6}$.

16. 3 times $\frac{7}{9}$? **Ans:** $2\frac{4}{9}$.

17. 4 times $\frac{3}{8}$? **Ans:** $1\frac{1}{2}$.

18. 3 times $\frac{8}{9}$? **Ans:** $\frac{8}{9}$.

19. 5 times $\frac{11}{15}$? **Ans:** $3\frac{2}{3}$.

20. 5 times $\frac{9}{10}$? **Ans:** $4\frac{1}{2}$.

21. 6 times $\frac{18}{24}$? **Ans:** $4\frac{1}{2}$.

22. 7 times $\frac{18}{21}$? **Ans:** 6.

23. 6 times $\frac{11}{18}$? **Ans:** $3\frac{2}{3}$.

24. 7 times $\frac{12}{21}$? **Ans:** 4.

25. 8 times $\frac{12}{24}$? **Ans:** 4.

26. 9 times $\frac{24}{27}$? **Ans:** 8.

27. 6 times $\frac{5}{6}$? **Ans:** 5.

28. 7 times $\frac{3}{14}$? **Ans:** $1\frac{1}{2}$.

29. 5 times $1\frac{9}{10}$? **Ans:** $9\frac{1}{2}$.

30. 8 times $\frac{10}{16}$? **Ans:** 5.

31. 9 times $\frac{15}{27}$? **Ans:** 5.

32. 8 times $\frac{24}{32}$? **Ans:** 6.

33. 6 times $\frac{18}{36}$? **Ans:** 3.

34. 4 times $\frac{15}{16}$? **Ans:** $3\frac{3}{4}$.

35. 3 times $2\frac{4}{6}$? **Ans:** 8.

36. 5 times $2\frac{2}{5}$? **Ans:** 12.

37. 7 times $3\frac{1}{7}$? **Ans:** 22.

38. How much will $4\frac{2}{3}$ meters of curtains cost, at the rate of $6 a meter?
  Ans: If one meter costs $6, 4 meters will cost 4 times 6, or $24, and $\frac{2}{3}$ of a meter will cost $\frac{2}{3}$ of $6, or $4. Altogether the curtains will cost $24 + $4 = $28.

39. If to 8 boys you give to $2\frac{3}{4}$ sticks each, how many sticks will you need?

Ans: If one boy receives $2\frac{3}{4}$ sticks, 8 boys will receive 8 times $2\frac{3}{4}$ sticks; 8 times 2 is 16 and 8 times $\frac{3}{4}$ is 6; 16 + 6 is 22 sticks.

40. How many chocolates does a woman give if she gives $\frac{4}{5}$ of a chocolate to each of 10 kids ?

Ans: 10 times $\frac{4}{5}$ of a chocolate are 8 chocolates.

41. Debbie gave to each of 12 children $\frac{5}{6}$ of a pie and had 3 pies left. How many pies did she have?

Ans: 12 times $\frac{5}{6}$ of a pie is 10 pies. She had 10 pies + 3 pies, or 13 pies.

42. How much does 10 pounds of pepper cost, at the rate of $\frac{4}{5}$ of a dollar per pound? **Ans:** 10 times $\frac{4}{5}$ of a dollar is $8.

43. How much will 9 hot dogs cost at the rate of 2 for $\frac{4}{6}$ of a dollar?

Ans: If 2 hot dogs cost $\frac{4}{6}$, or $\frac{2}{3}$ of a dollar, one will cost $\frac{1}{3}$ of a dollar, and 9 will cost 9 times $\frac{1}{3}$ of a dollar, or $3.

44. If 4 Jordan almonds cost $\frac{3}{4}$ of a coin, what will 16 Jordan almonds cost at the same rate?

Ans: 16 Jordan almonds, which is 4 times 4 Jordan almonds, will cost 4 times $\frac{3}{4}$ of a coin, or 3 coins.

45. What will 7 quarts of a milk cost, if 4 quarts cost $\frac{4}{7}$ of a dollar?

Ans: One quart will cost $\frac{1}{7}$ of a dollar; 7 quarts, one dollar.

46. If a man walks $3\frac{1}{5}$ miles in 2 hours, how far can he walk in 10 hours?

Ans: In 10 hours, which is 5 times 2 hours, he will walk 5 times $3\frac{1}{5}$ miles, or 16 miles.

47. 5 times $4\frac{4}{5}$ miles is 3 times the distance from San Jose to Fremont. What is the distance between the cities?

Ans: 5 times $4\frac{4}{5}$ miles, or 24 miles, is 3 times the distance. So the distance is $\frac{1}{3}$ of 24, or 8 miles.

48. 6 times $2\frac{2}{6}$ miles is $\frac{7}{10}$ of the distance from Oakland to Walnut Creek. What is the distance between the two cities?

Ans: 6 times $2\frac{2}{6}$ miles, or 14 miles, is $\frac{7}{10}$ of the distance. So the distance is 20 miles. Another way is to multiply 2 with 6. which is 12. The multiply 6 with $\frac{3}{6}$ which which is 2. The total is 14 which is $\frac{7}{10}$ of the distance. So $\frac{1}{10}$ of the distance is 2 and the whole distance is 2 times 10 or 20 miles. ⌣

Lesson 24 – *Division of Fractions*

HOW many times is 2 *contained in* $\frac{4}{5}$?

  Ans: 1 is *contained in* $\frac{4}{5}$, $\frac{4}{5}$ times, and if one is contained in $\frac{4}{5}$, $\frac{4}{5}$ times, then 2 is contained in $\frac{4}{5}$, $\frac{1}{2}$ times, or $\frac{2}{5}$ times.

1. How many times is 2 contained in 6? In 8? **Ans:** 3; 4.

2. How many times is $\frac{1}{2}$ contained in 1? In 2? **Ans:** 2; 4.

3. How many times is $\frac{1}{2}$ contained in $\frac{1}{2}$? In $\frac{1}{4}$? **Ans:** 1; 2.

4. How many times is $\frac{1}{2}$ contained in $\frac{1}{2}$? In $\frac{1}{4}$? **Ans:** 1; 2.

5. How many times is one contained in $\frac{1}{2}$? In $\frac{1}{4}$? **Ans:** $\frac{1}{2}$; $\frac{1}{4}$.

6. How many times is 2 contained in $\frac{1}{2}$? In $\frac{3}{2}$?
   Ans: One is *contained in* $\frac{1}{2}$ $\frac{1}{2}$ times, and if one is contained in $\frac{1}{2}$, $\frac{1}{2}$ times, then 2 is contained in $\frac{1}{2}$, $\frac{1}{2}$ of $\frac{1}{2}$ times, or $\frac{1}{4}$ times.
   1 is *contained in* $\frac{3}{2}$ $\frac{3}{2}$ times. If one is contained in $\frac{3}{2}$, $\frac{3}{2}$ times, then 2 is contained in $\frac{3}{2}$, $\frac{1}{2}$ of $\frac{3}{2}$ times, or $\frac{3}{4}$ times.

7. How many times is 2 contained in $\frac{1}{5}$? In $\frac{1}{6}$? **Ans:** $\frac{1}{10}$; $\frac{1}{12}$.

8. How many times is 3 contained in $\frac{3}{4}$? In $\frac{4}{5}$? **Ans:** $\frac{1}{4}$; $\frac{4}{15}$.
   Ans: One is *contained in* $\frac{3}{4}$, $\frac{3}{4}$ times. If one is contained in $\frac{3}{4}$, $\frac{3}{4}$ times, then 3 is contained in $\frac{3}{4}$ $\frac{1}{3}$ of $\frac{3}{4}$ times, or $\frac{1}{4}$ times.

9. How many times is 4 contained in $\frac{8}{9}$? In $\frac{5}{6}$? **Ans:** $\frac{2}{9}$; $\frac{5}{24}$.

10. How many times is 5 contained in $\frac{5}{3}$? In $\frac{2}{3}$? **Ans:** $\frac{1}{6}$; $\frac{2}{15}$.

11. How many times is 6 contained in $\frac{6}{7}$? In $\frac{3}{5}$? **Ans:** $\frac{1}{7}$; $\frac{1}{10}$.

12. How many times is 7 contained in $\frac{7}{8}$? In $\frac{5}{8}$? **Ans:** $\frac{1}{8}$; $\frac{5}{56}$.

13. How many times is $2\frac{1}{2}$ contained in 4? In $4\frac{3}{8}$?.
    Ans: One is *contained in* 4, 4 times. If one is contained in 4, 4 times, then $\frac{5}{2}$ is contained in 4, $\frac{2}{5}$ of 4 times, or $\frac{8}{5}$ times.
    One is *contained in* $\frac{35}{8}$, $\frac{35}{8}$ times. Then $\frac{5}{2}$ is contained in $\frac{35}{8}$, $\frac{35}{8}$ of $\frac{2}{5}$ times, or $\frac{7}{4}$ times.

14. Since $\frac{4}{5} \div 2$ equals $\frac{2}{5}$, how can we divide a fraction by a number which will divide the numerator?
    Ans: Divide the numerator by the number.

15. Since $\frac{5}{6} \div 2$ equals $\frac{5}{12}$, how can we divide a fraction by a number which will not divide the numerator?
    Ans: Multiply the denominator by the number.

16. If a meter-long shelf costs \$4, how long a shelf can you buy for $\frac{3}{4}$ of a dollar?

Ans: If a meter-long shelf costs \$4, for $\frac{3}{4}$ of a dollar you can buy as many meters as 4 is contained in $\frac{3}{4}$; one is contained in $\frac{3}{4}$, $\frac{3}{4}$ times, and 4 is contained in $\frac{3}{4}$, $\frac{1}{4}$ of $\frac{3}{4}$, or $\frac{3}{16}$ times.

17. Susan paid $2\frac{1}{2}$ dollars for wrapping paper at the rate of \$5 a meter. How many meters did she buy?

Ans: If one meter costs \$5, for $\$2\frac{1}{2}$ she can buy as many meters as 5 is contained in $2\frac{1}{2}$; one is contained in $2\frac{1}{2}$, $2\frac{1}{2}$ times, and 5 is contained in $2\frac{1}{2}$, $\frac{1}{5}$ times, or $\frac{1}{2}$ times.

18. How long will it take to skip along $\frac{6}{7}$ of a mile at the rate of 3 miles an hour?

Ans: Three is contained in $\frac{6}{7}$ $\frac{2}{7}$ times. So it will take $\frac{2}{7}$ of an hour.

19. How long will it take to hop $4\frac{1}{2}$ miles at the rate of 6 miles per hour?

Ans: Six is contained in $4\frac{1}{2}$, or $\frac{9}{2}$, $\frac{3}{4}$ times. So it will take $\frac{3}{4}$ of a hour.

20. How many times is $\frac{2}{3}$ contained in 4?

Ans: One is contained in 4, 4 times. If one is contained in 4, 4 times, $\frac{1}{3}$ is contained in 4, 3 times 4 times, which is 12 times, and 2 thirds is contained in 4, $\frac{1}{2}$ of 12 times, or 6 times.

21. How many times is $\frac{3}{4}$ contained in 2? In 3? **Ans:** $2\frac{2}{3}$; 4.

22. How many times is $\frac{2}{5}$ contained in 3? In 5? **Ans:** $7\frac{1}{2}$; $12\frac{1}{2}$.

23. How many times is $\frac{3}{7}$ contained in 2? In 4? **Ans:** $4\frac{2}{3}$; $9\frac{1}{3}$.

24. How many times is $\frac{2}{3}$ contained in 5? In 7? **Ans:** $7\frac{1}{2}$; $10\frac{1}{2}$.

25. How many times is $\frac{5}{6}$ contained in 4? In 5? **Ans:** $4\frac{4}{5}$; 6.

26. How many times is $\frac{6}{8}$ contained in 2? In 4? **Ans:** $2\frac{2}{3}$; $5\frac{1}{3}$.

27. If a meter of ray costs $\frac{3}{5}$ of a dollar, how many meters can you buy for \$12?

Ans: If a meter of ray cost $\frac{3}{5}$ of a dollar, for \$12 you can buy as many meters as $\frac{3}{5}$ is contained in 12, which is $12 \times \frac{5}{3} = \frac{60}{3}$, or 20 meters.

28. If a meter of rainbow costs $\frac{2}{5}$ of a dollar, how many meters can you see for \$10? **Ans:** 25 meters.

29. If one bag of nuts costs $\frac{4}{5}$ of 10 cents, how many bags can be bought for one dollar?

Ans: If one bag of nuts cost $\frac{4}{5}$ of 10 cents, for one dollar, as many bags can be bought as $\frac{4}{5}$ is contained in 10, which is $10 \times \frac{5}{4} = \frac{500}{4}$, or $12\frac{1}{2}$ bags.

30. How many photos can be printed for 11 dollars, if 3 photos cost $2\frac{1}{5}$ dollars?
    Ans: $2\frac{1}{5} = \frac{11}{5}$; 11 dollars, which is 5 times $\frac{11}{5}$ dollars, will print 5 times 3 photos, or 15 photos.

31. How much will 7 joojoos cost if 3 of them cost $4\frac{1}{2}$ dollars?
    Ans: $4\frac{1}{2} = \frac{9}{2}$. If 3 joojoos cost $\frac{9}{2}$ dollars, one joojoo will cost $\frac{3}{2}$ of a dollar, and 7 joojoos cost $\frac{21}{2}$, or $10\frac{1}{2}$ dollars.

32. If 5 pints of carrot juice cost 120 cents, how many pints can you purchase for 250 cents?
    Ans: One pint costs $\frac{120}{5}$ cents, and for 250 cents you can purchase as many pints as $\frac{120}{5}$ is contained in 250, or $\frac{250 \times 5}{120} = 12$ pints.

33. If $2\frac{1}{2}$ bags of magic dust cost \$15, how many bags can be bought for \$12?
    Ans: $2\frac{1}{2} = \frac{5}{2}$; since $\frac{5}{2}$ of a bag cost \$15, one bag will cost \$6, and for \$12, 2 bags can be bought.

34. How much will $2\frac{2}{5}$ bubblegums cost, at the rate of 4 bubblegums for $5\frac{1}{3}$ coins?
    Ans: $5\frac{1}{3} = \frac{16}{3}$. If 4 bubblegums cost $\frac{16}{3}$ coins, one bubblegum will cost $\frac{4}{3}$ of a coin, and $2\frac{2}{5}$, or $\frac{12}{5}$ bubblegums, will cost $\frac{12}{5} \times \frac{4}{3}$ of a coin $= \frac{16}{5}$ or $3\frac{1}{5}$ coins.

35. If $3\frac{1}{3}$ boxes of crackers costs \$$5\frac{1}{4}$, what will 10 boxes cost, at the same rate?
    Ans: $3\frac{1}{3} = \frac{10}{3}$; 10 boxes of crackers, which is 3 times $\frac{10}{3}$ boxes, will cost 3 times $5\frac{1}{4}$, or $15\frac{3}{4}$ dollars.

36. If 3 women can do a piece of work in $6\frac{2}{3}$ days, how long will it take 12 women to do the same work?
    Ans: 12 women, which is 4 times 3 women, will require $\frac{1}{4}$ of $6\frac{2}{3}$ days, which is $1\frac{2}{3}$ days.

37. How many times is $\frac{2}{3}$ contained in $\frac{3}{4}$?
    Ans: One is contained in $\frac{3}{4}$, $\frac{3}{4}$ times. And if one is contained in $\frac{3}{4}$, $\frac{3}{4}$ times, then $\frac{1}{3}$ is contained in $\frac{3}{4}$, 3 times $\frac{3}{4}$ times, or $\frac{9}{4}$ times. And $\frac{2}{3}$ is contained in $\frac{3}{4}$, $\frac{1}{2}$ of $\frac{9}{4}$ times, or $\frac{9}{8}$ times.

38. How many times is $\frac{2}{4}$ contained in $\frac{3}{5}$? In $\frac{3}{8}$?
Ans: One is contained in $\frac{3}{5}$, $\frac{3}{5}$ times, and $\frac{1}{4}$ is contained in $\frac{3}{5}$, 4 times $\frac{3}{5}$ times, or $\frac{12}{5}$ times.

39. How many times is $\frac{3}{4}$ contained in $\frac{2}{7}$? In $\frac{5}{6}$? **Ans:** $\frac{8}{21}$; $1\frac{1}{9}$.

40. How many times is $\frac{5}{6}$ contained in $\frac{3}{4}$ In $\frac{4}{6}$? **Ans:** $\frac{9}{10}$; $\frac{4}{5}$.

41. How many times is $\frac{2}{3}$ contained in $\frac{5}{8}$? In $\frac{7}{9}$? **Ans:** $\frac{15}{16}$; $1\frac{1}{6}$.

42. How many times is $\frac{4}{7}$ contained in $\frac{5}{6}$? In $\frac{6}{8}$? **Ans:** $1\frac{11}{24}$; $1\frac{5}{16}$.

43. How many times is $\frac{4}{5}$ contained in $\frac{3}{9}$? In $\frac{7}{10}$? **Ans:** $1\frac{1}{9}$; $\frac{7}{8}$.

44. How many times is $\frac{3}{8}$ contained in $\frac{3}{7}$? In $\frac{5}{6}$? **Ans:** $1\frac{1}{7}$; $2\frac{2}{9}$.

45. How many times is $\frac{5}{6}$ contained in $\frac{10}{12}$? In $\frac{15}{18}$? **Ans:** 1; 1.

46. How many times is $\frac{2}{4}$ contained $\frac{3}{5}$?
Ans: $\frac{2}{4}$ is equal to $\frac{10}{20}$ and $\frac{3}{5}$ is equal to $\frac{12}{20}$; $\frac{10}{20}$ is contained as many times in $\frac{12}{20}$ as 10 is contained in 12 which is $\frac{12}{20}$, or $\frac{6}{5}$ times.

47. How many times is $\frac{2}{3}$ contained in $\frac{2}{4}$? **Ans:** $\frac{3}{4}$; $\frac{9}{14}$.

48. How many times is $\frac{3}{4}$ contained in $\frac{2}{5}$? **Ans:** $\frac{8}{15}$; $\frac{16}{21}$.

49. How many times is $\frac{2}{5}$ contained in $\frac{3}{4}$? **Ans:** $1\frac{7}{8}$; $1\frac{2}{3}$.

50. How many times is $\frac{5}{6}$ contained in $\frac{2}{4}$? **Ans:** $\frac{3}{5}$; $\frac{18}{35}$.

51. How many times $\frac{3}{4}$ is $\frac{3}{2}$? In $\frac{3}{7}$? In $\frac{4}{7}$? In $\frac{2}{3}$? In $\frac{3}{7}$?
Ans: 2; $1\frac{1}{9}$; $\frac{4}{7}$; $\frac{10}{21}$; $\frac{5}{8}$; $1\frac{1}{2}$.

52. To divide one fraction by an another, what rule can we use?
Ans: Invert the divisor fraction, and then multiply the two fractions.

53. If you can buy a meter of laserbeam for $\frac{3}{5}$ of a token, how many meters can you get for $\frac{7}{8}$ of a token?
Ans: You can get as many meters as $\frac{3}{5}$ is contained in $\frac{7}{8}$, or $1\frac{11}{24}$.

54. If a pint of ice cream costs $\frac{2}{5}$ of a dollar, how many pints can you buy for $2\frac{1}{2}$?
Ans: You can buy as many pints as $\frac{2}{5}$ is contained in $2\frac{1}{2}$; $2\frac{1}{2} = \frac{5}{2}$; $\frac{5}{2} \times \frac{5}{2} = 61$.

55. A boy divided 14 snowballs equally among his friends, giving $3\frac{1}{2}$ snowballs to each. What is the number of his friends?
Ans: He had as many friends as $3\frac{1}{2}$ is contained in 14, or 4.

56. Mrs. Brown exchanged 20 pounds of old books at 15 cents a pound, for rope worth 12 cents a meter. How many meters of rope did she receive?

Ans: 20 pounds of books, at 15 cents a pound, is worth 300 cents, for which she received as many meters of rope as $12\frac{1}{2}$ is contained in 300, or 24.

57. A teacher distributed 29 cookies equally among some children, giving $5\frac{4}{5}$ cookies to each. How many children were there?

Ans: There were as many children as $5\frac{4}{5}$, or $\frac{29}{5}$ is contained in 29, or 5.

58. Becky bought 6 meters of purple ribbon, worth $5\frac{1}{3}$ cents a meter. How many coupons, worth $1\frac{1}{3}$ cents each, are needed to pay for it?

Ans: 6 meters of ribbon, at $5\frac{1}{3}$ cents a meter, is worth 32 cents; it would require as many coupons to pay for the ribbon as $1\frac{1}{3}$, or $\frac{4}{3}$, is contained in 32, or 24 coupons.

59. At the Farmers Market, Harry exchanged 8 kilograms of tomatoes, worth $\frac{5}{8}$ of a dollar per kilograms, with eggs from his hen, worth $\frac{2}{5}$ dollar a dozen. How many eggs did it take to make the exchange?

Ans: 8 kilograms of potatoes at $\frac{5}{8}$ of a dollar per kilograms cost $5, and it will require as many dozen eggs, as $\frac{2}{5}$ is contained in 5, or $12\frac{1}{2}$ dozens.

60. $\frac{3}{5} \div \frac{4}{5} =$? **Ans:** $\frac{3}{4}$.

61. $\frac{7}{8} \div \frac{1}{2} =$? **Ans:** $\frac{7}{4}$.

62. $\frac{3}{7} \div \frac{3}{4} =$? **Ans:** $\frac{4}{7}$.

63. $\frac{8}{5} \div \frac{4}{5} =$? **Ans:** 2.

64. $\frac{9}{8} \div 3 =$? **Ans:** $\frac{3}{8}$.

65. $\frac{4}{11} \div \frac{3}{11} =$? **Ans:** $\frac{4}{3}$.

Lesson 25 — *Proportions and Fractions*

WHAT part of 5 is 3?

Ans: 1 is $\frac{1}{5}$ of 5, and if one is $\frac{1}{5}$ of 5, 3 is 3 times $\frac{1}{5}$, or $\frac{3}{5}$ of 5.

1. What part of 4 is 3? of 6 is 3? **Ans:** $\frac{3}{4}$; $\frac{1}{2}$.

2. What part of 5 is 2? of 8 is 2? **Ans:** $\frac{2}{5}$; $\frac{1}{4}$.

3. What part of 6 is 4? of 5 is 6? **Ans:** $\frac{2}{3}$; $\frac{6}{5}$.

4. What part of 7 is 8? of 6 is 9? **Ans:** $\frac{8}{7}$; $\frac{9}{6}$.

5. What part of 8 is 4? of 4 is 8? **Ans:** $\frac{1}{2}$; 2.

6. If 8 apples cost 12 cents, what will 6 apples cost at the same rate?
   Ans: If 8 bananas cost 12 cents, 6 bananas, which is $\frac{6}{8}$ or $\frac{3}{4}$ of 8 apples, will cost $\frac{3}{4}$ of 12 cents, which is 9 cents.
   Note—*The alternate and less efficient method of solving this problem would be to compute the unit cost and then go from there to cost of 6 apples. But if we can see a relationship between some of the numbers, then the problem can solved without going to the unit cost.*

7. If 9 happy face buttons cost \$21, what will 12 happy face buttons cost at the same rate?
   Ans: Here we can see that the new number of happy face buttons, 12 is related to 9 by $\frac{4}{3}$. So the new cost will be bigger by the same amount and will be $\frac{4}{3}$ of \$21, or \$28.

8. James has \$8 and Rebecca has \$6. What part of James's money equals Rebecca's money?
   Ans: \$6 is $\frac{6}{8}$, or $\frac{3}{4}$ of James's money.

9. A watch cost \$40 and a calculator cost \$12. What part of the cost of the watch equals the cost of the calculator? **Ans:** $\frac{3}{10}$.

10. Brandon has \$20 and Alan has $\frac{3}{5}$ as much plus \$3. What part of Brandon's money equals Alan's money? **Ans:** $\frac{3}{4}$.

11. What part of 2 is $\frac{3}{4}$?
    Ans: 2 is $\frac{8}{4}$. $\frac{3}{4}$ has 3 fourths. So $\frac{3}{4}$ is $\frac{3}{8}$ of 2.
    Its really a division problem. We take the first part which is 2 and divide it by the second part which is $\frac{3}{4}$. What we get is $2 \div \frac{3}{4} = \frac{8}{3}$.

12. What part of 3 is $\frac{2}{3}$? of 2 is $\frac{3}{4}$? **Ans:** $\frac{2}{9}$; $\frac{3}{8}$.

---

13. What part of 4 is $\frac{2}{5}$? of 5 is $\frac{3}{5}$?
Ans: The number of fifths 4 has $= 20$. The number of fifths 2 has is 10, and the number of fifths in $\frac{2}{5}$ is 10 divided by 5 or 2. The ratio 2 and 20 is $\frac{1}{10}$.

14. What part of 4 is $\frac{4}{6}$? of 7 is $\frac{5}{8}$? **Ans:** $\frac{1}{6}$; $\frac{5}{56}$.

15. What part of 9 is $\frac{3}{7}$? of 5 is $\frac{1}{2}$ of $\frac{3}{4}$? **Ans:** $\frac{1}{21}$; $\frac{3}{40}$.

16. What part of 6 is $\frac{2}{3}$? of 7 is $\frac{2}{5}$ of $\frac{3}{2}$? **Ans:** 20.

17. What part of 2 is $\frac{3}{5}$? of 5 is $\frac{4}{5}$ of $\frac{5}{6}$? **Ans:** $\frac{3}{10}$; $\frac{2}{15}$.

18. A notebook cost \$4 and a pen cost $\frac{3}{4}$ of a dollar. What part of the cost of the book equals the cost of the pen? **Ans:** $\frac{3}{16}$.

19. Mark has \$5 and David has \$$2\frac{1}{2}$. What part of Mark's money equals David's money?
Ans: $2\frac{1}{2} = \frac{5}{2}$; one is $\frac{1}{5}$ of 5, and $\frac{5}{2}$ times $\frac{1}{5}$ of 5 is equal to $\frac{1}{2}$ of 5.

20. A stock was bought for \$2 and sold at a gain of \$$\frac{3}{4}$. What part of the cost equals the gain?
Ans: Gain was $\frac{3}{8}$ of the cost. $\frac{3}{4} \div 2 = \frac{3}{8}$.

21. A fox ran a certain distance in 6 hours. What part of the distance can he run in $2\frac{1}{2}$ hours? **Ans:** $\frac{5}{12}$.

22. Sarah bought 5 meters of wrapping paper and used $3\frac{1}{3}$ meters. She then needed $\frac{2}{3}$ meters to wrap an another present. Does she have enough paper? **Ans:** $\frac{2}{3}$ left, yes.

23. Rena bought 6 oranges and Rich bought 4. What did Rich pay for his oranges if Rena paid 30 cents for hers? **Ans:** 20 cents.

24. What part of $\frac{2}{3}$ is $\frac{4}{5}$?
Ans: The best way to do this problem is to make the denominator of both parts equal so we can compare them directly. We multiply the first fraction, $\frac{2}{3}$ with $\frac{5}{5}$. That gives us $\frac{10}{15}$. Multiply the second fraction, $\frac{4}{5}$ with $\frac{3}{3}$ to get $\frac{12}{15}$. $\frac{12}{15}$ is the same part of $\frac{10}{15}$ that 12 is of 10, and 12 is $\frac{12}{10}$ or $\frac{6}{5}$ of 10.

25. What part of $\frac{3}{4}$ is $\frac{2}{5}$?
Ans: $\frac{3}{4}$ is equal to $\frac{15}{20}$. $\frac{2}{5}$ is equal to $\frac{8}{20}$. $\frac{15}{20}$ is the same part of $\frac{8}{20}$ that 15 is of 8, or $\frac{15}{8}$.

26. What part of $\frac{3}{6}$ is $\frac{2}{3}$? **Ans:** $\frac{4}{3}$.

27. What part of $\frac{4}{5}$ is $\frac{5}{6}$? **Ans:** $\frac{25}{24}$.

28. What part of $\frac{6}{7}$ is $\frac{3}{8}$? **Ans:** $\frac{7}{16}$.

29. What part of $\frac{2}{5}$ is $\frac{3}{4}$? **Ans:** $1\frac{5}{8}$.

30. What part of $\frac{3}{5}$ is $\frac{3}{4}$? **Ans:** $\frac{5}{4}$.

31. What part of $\frac{3}{4}$ is $\frac{5}{6}$? **Ans:** $\frac{10}{9}$.

32. What part of $\frac{5}{6}$ of $\frac{3}{4}$? **Ans:** $\frac{9}{10}$.

33. What part of $\frac{5}{7}$ is $2\frac{1}{2}$? **Ans:** $\frac{7}{2}$.

34. What part of $\frac{6}{7}$ is $\frac{2}{3}$ of $\frac{6}{7}$? **Ans:** $\frac{2}{3}$.

35. What part of $\frac{7}{8}$ is $\frac{3}{4}$ of $\frac{5}{6}$? **Ans:** $\frac{5}{7}$.

36. What part of $\frac{9}{10}$ is $\frac{4}{5}$ of $\frac{7}{8}$? **Ans:** $\frac{7}{9}$.

37. A man owned $\frac{2}{3}$ of a factory and sold $\frac{1}{4}$ of it. What part of his share did he sell?
Ans: $\frac{1}{3}$ is $\frac{1}{2}$ of $\frac{2}{3}$, and $\frac{3}{3}$ is $\frac{3}{2}$ of $\frac{2}{3}$; $\frac{1}{4}$ of the vessel is $\frac{1}{4}$ of $\frac{3}{2}$, or $\frac{3}{8}$ of $\frac{2}{3}$.

38. Amin had $\frac{3}{4}$ of a dollar and spent $\frac{2}{5}$ of a dollar. What part of his money did he spend?
Ans: To compare these numbers, we need to put them in a form so that they have the same denominator. $\frac{3}{4}$ is same as $\frac{15}{20}$. $\frac{2}{5}$ is same as $\frac{8}{20}$. He spent $\frac{8}{15}$ of $\frac{3}{4}$.

39. $\frac{5}{6}$ of the trees in the forest were oak trees. Due to the draught $\frac{3}{4}$ of the oak tress died last year. What part of the oak trees are left?
Ans: $\frac{3}{4}$ of $\frac{5}{6} = \frac{3}{4} \times \frac{5}{6} = \frac{15}{24} = \frac{5}{8}$.

40. Francis has 40 cents, Evie has 60 cents, and 20 cents is the same part of Eddie's money that Francis's money is of Evie's. How many cents does Eddie have?
Ans: 40 cents is $\frac{40}{60}$, or $\frac{2}{3}$ of 60 cents. If 20 cents is $\frac{2}{3}$ of Eddie's money, his whole amount is 30 cents.

41. Max and Emma each had \$2; Max spent $\frac{1}{4}$ of his, and Emma spent $\frac{1}{5}$ of hers. What part of Emma's money then equals Max's?
Ans: If Max spent $\frac{1}{4}$ of his money, he had $\frac{3}{4}$ left, and if Emma spent $\frac{1}{5}$ of her money, she had $\frac{4}{5}$ left. $\frac{1}{5}$ is $\frac{1}{4}$ of $\frac{4}{5}$, and $\frac{5}{5}$ are $\frac{5}{4}$ of $\frac{4}{5}$; $\frac{3}{4}$ of Max's money is $\frac{3}{4}$ of $\frac{5}{4}$, or $\frac{15}{16}$ of $\frac{4}{5}$; therefore $\frac{15}{16}$ of Emma's money equals Max's.

42. 3 is $\frac{1}{5}$ of $\frac{1}{4}$ of what number? **Ans:** 60.

43. 2 is $\frac{1}{8}$ of $\frac{1}{4}$ of what number? **Ans:** 64.

44. 2 is $\frac{1}{7}$ of $\frac{1}{6}$ of what number? **Ans:** 84.

45. 4 is $\frac{1}{10}$ of $\frac{1}{5}$ of what number? **Ans:** 200.

46. 12 is $\frac{1}{3}$ of $\frac{1}{2}$ of what number? **Ans:** 72.

47. 6 is $\frac{2}{3}$ of $\frac{1}{3}$ of what number? **Ans:** 27.

48. 4 is $\frac{2}{5}$ of $\frac{1}{3}$ of what number? **Ans:** 30.

49. 5 is $\frac{1}{2}$ of $\frac{1}{7}$ of what number? **Ans:** 70.

50. One half of 30 is equal to how many $\frac{1}{6}$ of 30? **Ans:** 3 times.

51. What part of anything is 2 times $\frac{1}{6}$ of it? **Ans:** $\frac{1}{3}$.

52. What part of anything is 3 times $\frac{1}{6}$ of it? **Ans:** $\frac{1}{2}$.

53. What is $\frac{1}{3}$ of $\frac{6}{6}$? **Ans:** $\frac{2}{7}$.

54. What is $\frac{2}{3}$ of $\frac{9}{10}$? **Ans:** $\frac{6}{10}$.

55. What is $\frac{3}{5}$ of $\frac{10}{12}$? **Ans:** $\frac{1}{2}$.

56. What is $\frac{1}{5}$ of $\frac{10}{13}$? **Ans:** $\frac{2}{13}$.

57. What is $\frac{4}{5}$ of $\frac{10}{15}$? **Ans:** $\frac{8}{15}$.

58. What is $\frac{1}{8}$ of $\frac{2}{3}$ of 12? **Ans:** 1.

59. What is $\frac{3}{2}$ of $\frac{3}{10}$ of 4? **Ans:** $\frac{9}{5}$.

60. What is $\frac{4}{3}$ of $\frac{1}{5}$ of 15? **Ans:** 4.

61. What is $\frac{6}{3}$ of $\frac{1}{3}$ of 9? **Ans:** 6.

62. What part of anything is 4 times $\frac{1}{6}$ of it? **Ans:** Two-thirds.

63. If Henry has $\frac{1}{3}$ of \$45 and John has $\frac{1}{6}$ of \$30. How much money do they have together? **Ans:** \$20.

64. $\frac{7}{12} \div \frac{1}{4} =$? **Ans:** $\frac{7}{3}$.

65. $\frac{7}{12} \div \frac{2}{3} =$? **Ans:** $\frac{7}{2}$.

66. $\frac{7}{12} \div \frac{1}{4} =$? **Ans:** $\frac{7}{3}$.

67. $\frac{7}{12} \div \frac{2}{3} =$? **Ans:** $\frac{7}{2}$.

68. $\frac{7}{12} \div \frac{7}{8} =$? **Ans:** $\frac{2}{3}$.

69. $\frac{1}{3} \div 1\frac{3}{10} =$? **Ans:** $\frac{1}{13}$.

70. $\frac{1}{5} \div \frac{3}{10} =$? **Ans:** $\frac{2}{3}$.

71. $\frac{5}{4} \div \frac{3}{10} =$? **Ans:** $\frac{25}{6}$.

Lesson 26 – *Fraction Operations*

JIMMY bought a guitar for \$240. He signed up to take lessons and $\frac{4}{3}$ of the cost of the guitar was $\frac{2}{9}$ of the cost of his guitar lessons. What was the cost of the lessons?

Ans: $\frac{4}{3}$ of \$240 is \$320. If \$320 is $\frac{2}{9}$ of the cost of lessons, the lessons cost \$144.

1. A purse cost \$150, and $\frac{1}{2}$ of its cost is $\frac{3}{4}$ of the cost of a wallet. What is the cost of the wallet?
   Ans: $\frac{1}{2}$ of 150 is $\frac{150}{2}$. If $\frac{150}{2}$ is $\frac{3}{4}$ of the cost of a purse, then $\frac{1}{4}$ of the cost of a purse is $\frac{1}{3}$ of $\frac{150}{2}$, or $\frac{150}{6}$, and 4 times that is $\frac{150\times4}{6}$, or \$100.

2. How many apples does a teacher give away when she gives $\frac{5}{6}$ of an apple each to 5 kids? **Ans:** 5 times $\frac{5}{6} = \frac{25}{6}$, or $4\frac{1}{6}$ apples.

3. If two bottles of soda cost $\frac{3}{4}$ of a dollar, how many bottles can be bought for \$9?
   Ans: As many bottles as $\frac{3}{4}$ is contained in 9, or 12.

4. How many cans of juice can be bought for \$6 if 2 cans cost $\frac{3}{4}$ of a dollar?
   Ans: One can will cost $\frac{1}{2}$ of $\frac{3}{4}$, or $\frac{3}{8}$. The cans that can be bought for \$6 is the number of times $\frac{3}{8}$ is contained in 6, or 16 cans.

5. If $\frac{1}{2}$ of a mango costs $\frac{1}{3}$ of a dollar, how much does $\frac{1}{5}$ of a mango cost?
   Ans: If $\frac{1}{2}$ of a mango costs $\frac{1}{3}$ of a dollar, one mango is $\frac{2}{3}$ of a dollar, and $\frac{1}{5}$ of an mango will cost $\frac{1}{5}$ of $\frac{2}{3}$, or $\frac{2}{15}$ of a dollar.

6. Francis, after losing $\frac{2}{3}$ of his friends because he ignored them, found that 12 was $\frac{3}{4}$ of the number of friends he had left. How many friends did he have?
   Ans: After losing $\frac{2}{3}$ of his friends, he had $\frac{1}{3}$ left. $\frac{3}{4}$ of $\frac{1}{3}$, or $\frac{1}{4}$ of his number of friends, is 12. So he had at first 48 friends.

7. If 3 elephants can do a piece of work in $3\frac{1}{2}$ days, how long will it take 5 elephants to do it?
   Ans: It will take one elephant 3 times $3\frac{1}{3}$, or 10 days, and it will take 5 elephants $\frac{1}{5}$ of 10, or 2 days.

8. If 7 donkeys can do a piece of work in $2\frac{1}{3}$ days, how long will 6 donkeys need to finish it?
   Ans: It will take one donkeys 7 times $2\frac{1}{3}$, or $\frac{49}{3}$ days, and it will take 6 donkeys $\frac{1}{6}$ of $\frac{49}{3}$, or $2\frac{13}{18}$ days.

9. If a meter of tarp costs $\frac{2}{3}$ of a dollar, how much can you buy for $\frac{5}{6}$ of a dollar?

   Ans: As many meters as $\frac{2}{3}$ is contained in $\frac{5}{6}$, or $\frac{5}{4}$ of a meter.

10. Andrew shared 8 candy bars with his friends, giving to each of his friends $\frac{4}{5}$ of a candy bar. What is the number of his friends?

    Ans: There were as many friends as $\frac{4}{5}$ is contained in 8, or 10 friends. Since he shared the candies, and this included himself, there were 9 friends.

11. How many boxes of popcorn priced at $5\frac{2}{3}$ dollars a box, can be bought for $34?

    Ans: $5\frac{2}{3} = \frac{17}{3}$; as many boxes can be bought for 34 dollars as $\frac{17}{3}$ is contained in 34, or 6 boxes.

12. How many apples are priced same as 10 peaches, if 5 apples cost the same as $8\frac{1}{3}$ peaches?

    Ans: Since $8\frac{1}{3} = \frac{25}{3}$; then $\frac{25}{3}$ peaches are worth 5 apples, $\frac{1}{3}$ of a peach is worth $\frac{1}{25}$ of 5 apples, or $\frac{1}{5}$ of an apple. $\frac{3}{3}$ of a peach is worth 3 times $\frac{1}{5}$, or $\frac{3}{5}$ of an apple, and 10 peaches are worth 10 times $\frac{3}{5}$ of an apple, or 6 apples.

13. Liz shared 21 cupcakes with her schoolmates, giving $2\frac{1}{3}$ cupcakes to each student. How many schoolmates does she have?

    Ans: There were as many schoolmates as $2\frac{1}{3}$, or $\frac{7}{3}$, is contained in 21, or 9 people. Since shared number included herself, she had 8 schoolmates.

14. 7 times $3\frac{1}{7}$ miles is $5\frac{1}{2}$ times the distance from Columbia to Marietta. What is the distance between the two cities?

    Ans: 7 times $3\frac{1}{7}$ miles, or 22 miles, is $5\frac{1}{2}$, or $1\frac{1}{2}$ times the distance. So $\frac{1}{2}$ of the distance is $\frac{1}{11}$ of 22 miles, or 2 miles. The distance is 4 miles.

15. Pedro gave $\frac{1}{5}$ of his collection of rocks to Sam, and 2 times to Andy. How many did he have at first, if he gave away total of 14 rocks?

    Ans: 2 times $\frac{1}{4}$ equals $\frac{1}{2}$ of the rocks; $\frac{1}{2} + \frac{1}{5} = \frac{7}{10}$. If 14 is $\frac{7}{10}$ of his number, $\frac{10}{10}$ is 20 rocks.

16. Sixteen is $\frac{4}{5}$ of how many times 5? **Ans:** 4.

17. Eighteen is $\frac{3}{4}$ of how many times 8? **Ans:** 3.

18. Twenty five is $\frac{5}{8}$ of how many times 10? **Ans:** 4.

19. Fifteen is $\frac{5}{9}$ of how many times 3? **Ans:** 9.

20. Twenty is $\frac{4}{5}$ of how many times $\frac{1}{2}$ of 10? **Ans:** 5.

21. Twenty four is $\frac{3}{4}$ of how many times $\frac{2}{3}$ of 12? **Ans:** 4.

22. Twenty eight is $\frac{4}{7}$ of how many times $\frac{1}{3}$ of 21? **Ans:** 7.

23. Thirty is $\frac{5}{6}$ of how many times $\frac{3}{4}$ of 12? **Ans:** 4.

24. Eighteen is $\frac{6}{8}$ of how many times $\frac{6}{7}$ of 14? **Ans:** 2.

25. Forty is $\frac{4}{5}$ of how many times $\frac{5}{6}$ of 30? **Ans:** 2.

26. Thirty six is $\frac{4}{6}$ of how many times $\frac{3}{5}$ of 15? **Ans:** 6.

27. Sixty is $\frac{6}{5}$ of how many times $\frac{5}{7}$ of 14? **Ans:** 5.

28. $\frac{1}{2}$ of 16 is how many times $\frac{1}{3}$ of 12? **Ans:** 2.

29. $\frac{2}{3}$ of 30 is how many times $\frac{2}{5}$ of 10? **Ans:** 5.

30. $\frac{3}{4}$ of 40 is how many times $\frac{5}{7}$ of 21? **Ans:** 2.

31. $\frac{4}{5}$ of 45 is how many times $\frac{3}{5}$ of 15? **Ans:** 4.

32. $\frac{6}{7}$ of 42 is how many times $\frac{6}{7}$ of 14? **Ans:** 3.

33. $\frac{7}{8}$ of 48 is how many times $\frac{3}{8}$ of 16? **Ans:** 7.

34. $\frac{5}{8}$ of 80 is how many times $\frac{2}{5}$ of 25? **Ans:** 5.

35. $\frac{5}{6}$ of 72 is how many times $\frac{5}{4}$ of 16? **Ans:** 3.

36. Atul's ski boots cost $200. $\frac{4}{5}$ of this is twice the cost of his skis, and the skis cost 2 times as much as his jacket. What is the cost of each? **Ans:** $\frac{4}{5}$ of $200 is $160, or twice the cost of the skis. So the skis cost $80, which is 2 times the cost of the jacket. So the jacket cost $40.

37. Betty's wedding dress cost $400. $\frac{3}{4}$ of this is twice the cost of her veil, and also 3 times the cost of her shoes. What was the cost of each and of all? **Ans:** $\frac{3}{4}$ of $400 is $300; $\frac{1}{2}$ of $300, or $150, which is the price of the veil, and $\frac{1}{3}$ of $300, or $100, is the price of the shoes. $400 + $150 + $100 = $650, the price of all.

38. Margie bought 4 big bulbs at $\frac{2}{3}$ of a dollar per pound. She paid for it by exchanging it with a smaller bulbs, one of which is worth 1\frac{1}{3}$. How many smaller bulbs did she give in exchange for the 4 big bulbs? **Ans:** 2 bulbs.

39. The distance from Paoli to Christiana is 24 miles, and $\frac{2}{3}$ of this distance is $\frac{4}{5}$ of the distance from Christiana to Lancaster. What is the distance to Lancaster? **Ans:** 20 miles.

40. The distance from Columbia to Rockville is 30 miles, and $\frac{2}{3}$ of this distance is $\frac{2}{5}$ of the distance from Columbia to Newport. What is the distance to Newport? **Ans:** 50 miles.

41. The distance from San Ramon to Danville is 3 miles, and $\frac{2}{3}$ of this distance is $\frac{1}{3}$ of the distance from Danville to Walnut Creek. What is the distance to Walnut Creek? **Ans:** 6 miles.

42. Hannah's prom-dress cost $500, and $\frac{4}{5}$ of this is 4 times the cost of her shoes and also $\frac{2}{3}$ of the cost of her new ring. What is the cost of the shoes and ring respectively? **Ans:** Shoes, $100; ring, $200.

What is the sum of

43. $\frac{1}{2} + \frac{1}{3} =$? **Ans:** $\frac{5}{6}$.

44. $\frac{1}{3} + \frac{1}{5} =$? **Ans:** $\frac{8}{15}$.

45. $\frac{2}{3} + \frac{1}{4} =$? **Ans:** $\frac{11}{12}$.

46. $\frac{2}{3} + \frac{1}{5} =$? **Ans:** $\frac{13}{15}$.

47. $\frac{2}{3} + \frac{5}{8} =$? **Ans:** $\frac{31}{24}$.

48. $\frac{1}{2} + \frac{7}{8} =$? **Ans:** $\frac{11}{8}$.

49. $\frac{1}{2} + \frac{1}{5} =$? **Ans:** $\frac{7}{10}$.

50. $\frac{1}{4} + \frac{1}{5} =$? **Ans:** $\frac{9}{20}$.

51. $\frac{3}{4} + \frac{2}{5} =$? **Ans:** $\frac{23}{20}$.

52. $\frac{3}{4} + \frac{2}{3} =$? **Ans:** $\frac{17}{12}$.

53. $\frac{1}{2} + \frac{5}{10} =$? **Ans:** 1.

54. $\frac{1}{2} + \frac{3}{3} + \frac{1}{4} =$? **Ans:** $\frac{7}{4}$.

55. $\frac{1}{4} + \frac{1}{3} + \frac{5}{6} =$? **Ans:** $\frac{17}{12}$.

56. $\frac{1}{2} + \frac{1}{5} + \frac{7}{10} =$? **Ans:** $\frac{7}{5}$.

57. $\frac{1}{2} + \frac{3}{7} + \frac{3}{14} =$? **Ans:** $\frac{8}{7}$.

58. $\frac{1}{2} + \frac{1}{3} + \frac{1}{3} =$? **Ans:** $\frac{7}{6}$.

59. $\frac{3}{8} + \frac{1}{2} + \frac{5}{16} =$? **Ans:** $\frac{19}{16}$.

60. $\frac{3}{8} + \frac{2}{4} + \frac{5}{16} =$? **Ans:** $\frac{19}{16}$.

Lesson 27 – *Given the Sum of Parts*

JERRY'S age plus $\frac{1}{2}$ of his age, equals 24 years. What is his age?

Ans: $\frac{2}{2}$ of Jerry's age, plus $\frac{1}{2}$ of his age, which is then $\frac{3}{2}$ of his age, equals 24 years. Dividing 24 in three parts, we get 8. So $\frac{2}{2}$ of his age is twice 8, or 16 years.

1. What number is that to which, if its $\frac{1}{3}$ is added, the sum is equal to 36? .
   Ans: $\frac{3}{3}$ of the number, plus $\frac{1}{3}$ of itself is equal to $\frac{4}{3}$, and this equals 36. Dividing 36 in four equal parts, we get 9. The starting number is 3 times 9, or 27.

2. A number increased by $\frac{2}{3}$ of itself is equal to 40. What is the number? **Ans:** 24.

3. What number increased by $\frac{3}{7}$ of itself is equal to 80? **Ans:** 56.

4. What number increased by $\frac{3}{5}$ of itself is equal to 20? **Ans:** 15.

5. What number increased by $\frac{3}{5}$ of itself is equal to 80? **Ans:** 50.

6. What number increased by $\frac{5}{7}$ of itself is equal to 24? **Ans:** 14.

7. What number increased by $\frac{3}{5}$ of itself is equal to 40? **Ans:** 25.

8. What number increased by $\frac{1}{3}$ is equal to 36? **Ans:** 24.

9. What number increased by $\frac{1}{4}$ of itself is equal to 50? **Ans:** 40.

10. What number increased by $\frac{1}{5}$ of itself is equal to 15? **Ans:** 15.

11. Three times a certain number, equals 22 when increased by $\frac{2}{3}$ of itself. What is the number? **Ans:** 6.

12. Reuben's age, when doubled and increased by $\frac{3}{4}$ of his age, equals 55 years. How old is he? **Ans:** 20 years.

13. Three and $\frac{1}{2}$ times a number, plus $\frac{2}{3}$ of the number equals 50. What is the number? **Ans:** 12.

14. Two-fifths of a number increased by $\frac{1}{2}$, equals 27. What is the number? **Ans:** 30.

15. Two-fifths of a number increased by $\frac{2}{3}$, equals 40. What is the number? **Ans:** 60.

16. What number is that which increased by the difference between its $\frac{1}{4}$ and $\frac{1}{5}$, equals 42? **Ans:** 40.

17. A boy was asked his age and replied that his age, increased by its $\frac{1}{2}$ and $\frac{2}{3}$, equals 39 years. What is his age? **Ans:** 18 years.

18. Alex has $\frac{2}{5}$ of a dollar, of which he gave $\frac{1}{2}$ to Bill. Bill gave $\frac{1}{3}$ of his to Cal. What part of the dollar did each then have? **Ans:** Alex, $\frac{1}{5}$; Bill, $\frac{3}{20}$, Cal, $\frac{1}{20}$.

19. When Lind graduated from the university, he was 25 years old. $\frac{3}{5}$ of his age was 3 years more than $\frac{2}{3}$ of his younger sister's age. What is the age of his sister?
Ans: $\frac{3}{5}$ of 25 years is 15 years. If 15 years was 3 years more than $\frac{2}{3}$ of his sister's age, $\frac{2}{3}$ of her age was 12 years, and so her age was 18 years.

20. The distance from Medway to Columbia is 42 miles, and $\frac{4}{7}$ of this distance is $\frac{1}{3}$ of the distance from Medway to Rockville. How far is Medway from Rockville? **Ans:** 72 miles.

21. A fishing-rod is 4 meters long. $\frac{3}{4}$ of its length less half a meter is equal to $\frac{2}{3}$ the length of the line. What is the length of the line?
Ans: $\frac{3}{4}$ of 16 meters is 12 meters, which is 2 meters less than $\frac{2}{3}$ the length of the line; $12 + 2$, or 14 meters, is $\frac{2}{3}$ of the length, $\frac{1}{3}$ of the length is 7 meters, and the length is 21 meters.

22. A remote-controlled car cost \$40. This is $\frac{2}{3}$ of $\frac{3}{4}$ of the cost of the car and the battery together. What is the cost of the battery?
Ans: $\frac{2}{3}$ of $\frac{3}{4} = \frac{1}{2}$. If \$40 is half the cost of both, the whole cost was \$80, and the battery cost \$80 − \$40, or \$40.

23. Susan has 7 hats, and $\frac{4}{5}$ of what Susan has, minus $\frac{3}{5}$ of a hat, is $\frac{5}{8}$ of what Elizabeth has. How many hats does Elizabeth have?
Ans: $\frac{4}{5}$ of $7 = \frac{28}{5} = 5\frac{3}{5}$; $5\frac{3}{5} - \frac{3}{5} = 5$ hats, which is $\frac{5}{8}$ of what Elizabeth has. So she has 8 hats.

24. If there are 50 chestnuts in a basket, how many do A and B get respectively, if A gets $\frac{4}{5}$ of a basket, and B gets $\frac{3}{4}$ as many as A? **Ans:** A, 40 chestnuts; B, 30 chestnuts.

25. A garden has 60 fruit trees, $\frac{2}{5}$ of which are peaches, $\frac{2}{3}$ of the remainder pears, and the rest of which are apples. How many are there of each type?
Ans: $\frac{2}{5}$ of $60 = 24$, the number of peach trees; $\frac{5}{5} - \frac{2}{5} = \frac{3}{5}$; $\frac{2}{3}$ of $\frac{3}{5} = \frac{2}{5}$; $\frac{2}{5}$ of $60 = 24$, the number of pear trees; $24 + 24 = 48$; $60 - 48 = 12$, the number of apple trees.

26. Tien lost $\frac{4}{5}$ of his money in an investment and then made $\frac{3}{4}$ as much as he lost, and then had $12000. How much money did he have to start with? **Ans: $15000.**

27. Consuela gave $\frac{3}{4}$ of her money to the charity, and then found that she had $\frac{2}{3}$ as much as she gave away. She found she had $3000. How much did she have at first?
Ans: She had left $\frac{4}{4} - \frac{3}{4}$, or $\frac{1}{4}$ of her money; she found $\frac{2}{3}$ of $\frac{3}{4}$, or $\frac{1}{2}$; she then had $\frac{1}{4} + \frac{1}{2}$, or $\frac{3}{4}$ of her money, which equaled $3000. So she had at first $4000.

28. Andre borrowed $\frac{2}{3}$ of Emily's money and after spending $\frac{3}{4}$ of it returned the rest, which was $20 to Emily. How much did Emily have?
Ans: After spending $\frac{3}{4}$ of what he borrowed, there was $\frac{1}{4}$ of what he borrowed left, or $\frac{1}{4}$ of $\frac{2}{3}$, or $\frac{1}{6}$ of Emily's money, which was $20. So she had $120.

29. A RC car cost $40. This is $\frac{2}{3}$ of $\frac{3}{4}$ of the cost of the car and the battery together. What is the cost of the battery?
Ans: $\frac{2}{3}$ of $\frac{3}{4} = \frac{1}{2}$. If $40 is half the cost of both, the whole cost was $80, and the battery cost $80 − $40, or $40.

30. Jackie has gone on 20 hikes, and $\frac{4}{5}$ of that, minus 2, is $\frac{3}{7}$ of the number of hikes Sammy has been on. How many hikes has Sammy been on?
Ans: $\frac{4}{5}$ of 20 = 16; 16 − 2 = 14 hikes, which is $\frac{3}{7}$ Sammy's number. So he has done 6 hikes.

31. There are $50 in the piggy bank. How will Alex and Bryan divide the money if Alex put in $\frac{4}{5}$ and Bryan put in $\frac{3}{4}$ as much as Alex? **Ans:** Alex, 40 dollars; Bryan, 30 dollars.

32. A garden has 60 rose bushes, $\frac{2}{5}$ of which are red, $\frac{2}{3}$ of the remainder are white, and the rest of which are pink. How many are there of each type?
Ans: $\frac{2}{5}$ of 60 = 24, the number of red roses; $\frac{5}{5} - \frac{2}{5} = \frac{3}{5}$; $\frac{2}{3}$ of $\frac{3}{5} = \frac{2}{5}$; $\frac{2}{5}$ of 60 = 24, the number of white roses; 24 + 24 = 48; 60 − 48 = 12, the number of pink roses.

33. A little girl lost $\frac{4}{5}$ of the money her mom gave her, but then received $\frac{3}{4}$ as much as she lost from her dad, and then had $12. How much money did she start with?
Ans: She had left $\frac{5}{5} - \frac{4}{5}$, or $\frac{1}{5}$ of the money. She received $\frac{3}{4}$ of $\frac{4}{5}$, or $\frac{3}{5}$. She then had $\frac{3}{5} + \frac{1}{5} = \frac{4}{5}$, which equals $12. She had at first $15.

Lesson 28 – *Difference of Parts*

A BOY spent $\frac{3}{5}$ of his budget on a new computer. After spending the money on the computer, he had $600 left. What was his budget?

Ans: After spending $\frac{3}{5}$, he still had $\frac{2}{5}$ left which is equal to $600. Then $\frac{1}{5}$ is $300, and five times that gives all the money he had budgeted, which is $1500.

1. A girl, after spending $\frac{1}{3}$ of her money, had only $40 left. How much money did she have to begin with? **Ans:** $60.

2. A girl invited $\frac{3}{8}$ of her class mates for her birthday party and then had 25 who did not get invited. How many class mates did she have? **Ans:** 40 class mates.

3. Terry spent $\frac{1}{2}$ of her savings on gifts for her family and $\frac{1}{8}$ on books for herself, and had $100 left. How much did she start with? **Ans:** $160.

4. Ivan's money, reduced first by $\frac{1}{5}$ and then by $\frac{1}{6}$, equals $60. How much did he start with?
   Ans: First reduction by $\frac{1}{5}$ leaves $\frac{4}{5}$. This reduced by $\frac{1}{6}$ leaves $\frac{5}{6}$ of $\frac{4}{5}$ or $\frac{20}{30}$ or $\frac{2}{3}$. If $\frac{2}{3}$ is $60, then the number is $90.

5. David's money, increased by $\frac{1}{2}$ and then by $\frac{1}{6}$, equals $30. How much did he start with? **Ans:** $18.

6. $\frac{3}{5}$ of my age reduced by $\frac{2}{6}$, equals 24 years. How old am I? **Ans:** 90 years.

7. Michael paid four dollars for a piece pie, which was $\frac{2}{3}$ of $\frac{1}{2}$ of the cost of his dinner. What was the cost of his dinner? **Ans:** $12.

8. Mr. Kim's hat cost $16, which was $3 less than $\frac{3}{8}$ of the cost of his coat. What's the cost of the coat? **Ans:** $24.

9. What number is that which, when doubled and then reduced by its $\frac{3}{4}$, equals 60? **Ans:** 48.

10. A boy lost 4 coins and found 10, and then had $\frac{3}{2}$ as many as at first. How much did he start with? **Ans:** 12 coins.

11. $\frac{1}{3}$ of the length of a pole is in the air, $\frac{1}{4}$ in the water, and 10 meters in the ground. What's the length of the pole?
    Ans: $\frac{1}{3} + \frac{1}{4} = \frac{7}{12}$; $\frac{12}{12} - \frac{7}{12} = \frac{5}{12}$, the part in the ground, which equals 10 meters. If $\frac{5}{12}$ of the length is 10 meters, $\frac{12}{12}$ is 24 meters.

12. When asked for her age, a woman replied that her daughter's age is 8 years, which is $\frac{4}{5}$ of $\frac{1}{4}$ of her age. How old is she?
Ans: $\frac{4}{5}$ of $\frac{1}{4} = \frac{1}{5}$ of her age; since $\frac{1}{5}$ of her age is 8 years, her age is 40 years.

13. The sergeant found that 16 was $\frac{2}{3}$ of the soldiers who were left after $\frac{2}{5}$ of them went home for the weekend. How many soldiers were there at first?
Ans: $\frac{5}{5} - \frac{2}{5} = \frac{3}{5}$ of the soldiers who stayed; $\frac{2}{3}$ of $\frac{3}{5}$, or $\frac{2}{5}$, equals 16, and $\frac{5}{5}$ equals 40.

14. If $\frac{2}{5}$ of the people of a town were men, $\frac{2}{6}$ were women, and 800 children, of how many people lived in the town? **Ans:** 3000.

15. Evan married when he was 27 years old. $\frac{2}{3}$ of his age then was 4 years more than $\frac{2}{3}$ of his wife's age. What is the age of his wife?
Ans: $\frac{2}{3}$ of 27 years, or 18 years, is 4 years more than $\frac{2}{3}$ of his wife's age; $\frac{2}{3}$ of her age was 14 years, and her age was 21 years.

16. Gina, after spending $\frac{1}{4}$ of her money for candies and $\frac{1}{6}$ for bubblegum, found that $1 was $\frac{2}{7}$ of what she has left. How much money did she have?
Ans: $\frac{1}{4} + \frac{1}{6} = \frac{5}{12}$ of her money, or what she spent; $\frac{12}{12} - \frac{5}{12} = \frac{7}{12}$ of her money, or what remained; $\frac{2}{7}$ of $\frac{7}{12}$, or $\frac{1}{6}$ of her money is 20 cents. So her money is 120 cents or $1.20.

17. A number plus $\frac{1}{2}$ of the number minus $\frac{2}{3}$ of the number, equals 50. What is the number?
Ans: $\frac{2}{2} + \frac{1}{2} = \frac{3}{2}$; $\frac{3}{2} - \frac{2}{3} = \frac{5}{6}$. If $\frac{5}{6}$ of the number is 50, the number is 60.

18. A thief stole $\frac{3}{5}$ of Jindal's money, and before he was caught he spent $\frac{2}{3}$ of it; the rest, which was $20 less than what he stole, was given back. How much money did Jindal have?
Solution one—If the thief spent $\frac{2}{3}$ of what he stole, there remained $\frac{1}{3}$ of what he stole that is, $\frac{1}{3}$ of $\frac{3}{5}$ of Jindal's money, or $\frac{1}{5}$ of Jindal's; then $\frac{3}{5}$ of Jindal's money, what was stolen, minus $\frac{1}{5}$ of his money, what was given back, equals $\frac{2}{5}$ of Jindal's money, which equals $20. So he had $50.
Solution two—The thief spent $\frac{2}{3}$ of $\frac{3}{5}$, or $\frac{2}{5}$ of Jindal's money. What was given back was $20 less than what he stole. Then $20 equals what he spent, or $\frac{2}{5}$ of Jindal's money. So Jindal had $50.

19. A kite in the air dropped $\frac{1}{2}$ of the distance to the ground, then rose $\frac{1}{3}$ of the distance it was from the ground, and then dropped again $\frac{1}{4}$ of the distance it arose. What part of the whole distance is it from the ground now?

Ans: It arose $\frac{1}{3}$ of $\frac{1}{2} = \frac{1}{6}$, and then was $\frac{1}{2} + \frac{1}{6} = \frac{2}{3}$ of the first distance from the ground; it fell $\frac{1}{4}$ of $\frac{1}{6} = \frac{1}{24}$, and then was $\frac{2}{3} - \frac{1}{24} = \frac{5}{8}$ of the whole distance from the ground.

20. Lee put $\frac{3}{4}$ of his money in a little box, and then found that he had $\frac{2}{3}$ as much more in coins as he put in the box. He found $30. How much did he have at first?

Ans: He had left $\frac{4}{4} - \frac{3}{4}$, or $\frac{1}{4}$ of his money; he found $\frac{2}{3}$ of $\frac{3}{4}$, or $\frac{1}{2}$; he then had $\frac{1}{4} + \frac{1}{2}$, or $\frac{3}{4}$ of his money, which equaled $30. So he had at first $40.

21. Andre borrowed $\frac{2}{3}$ of Emily's money, and after spending $\frac{1}{4}$ of it he returned the rest, which was $45, to Emily. How much did Emily have?

Ans: After spending $\frac{1}{4}$ of what he borrowed, there was $\frac{3}{4}$ left of what he borrowed, or $\frac{3}{4}$ of $\frac{2}{3}$, or $\frac{6}{12}$ of Emily's money, which was $45. So she had $90. ⌣

Lesson 29 – *Increasing or Reducing by a Fraction*

MARTA'S age, when increased by 6 years equals 20 years. How old is Marta?

Ans: If Martha's age increased by 6 years, equals 20 years, Martha's age is 20 years minus 6 years, or 14 years.

Note—*Although these problems can be done easily using algebra, we are trying to help your child think out the elementary steps to solving problems using arithmetic only. For mental operations, if division can be transformed into multiplication, the task gets much easier.*

1. What number is that which, when increased by 12, equals 26? **Ans:** 14.

2. What number is that which, when increased by $\frac{1}{2}$ of itself, equals 21? **Ans:** 14.

3. What number is that which, when increased by $\frac{1}{3}$ of itself, equals 63? **Ans:** 21.

4. What number is that which, when increased by $\frac{2}{3}$ of itself, equals 30? **Ans:** 18.

5. What number is that which, when increased by $\frac{7}{5}$ of itself, plus 6 equals 30? **Ans:** 10.

6. Two-thirds of big apes in the zoo, increased by 8, equals 32. How many apes are in the zoo now? **Ans:** 36.

7. Sarah has 25 roses, which is 4 more than $\frac{1}{2}$ of Jennifer's number. How many roses does Jennifer have? **Ans:** 42 roses.

8. A student earned a certain sum of money, and then received $100 more from his family, and now has $480. How much did she earn? **Ans:** $380.

9. Peter's age reduced by 6 years equals 14 years. How old is Peter? **Ans:** 20 years.

10. How heavy is Sarah if her weight reduced by 20 pounds, equals 60 pounds? **Ans:** 80 pounds.

11. How much does Nina weigh if her weight decreased by $\frac{2}{3}$ of itself plus 20 pounds equals 50 pounds? **Ans:** 90 pounds.

12. What is the height of a tree if 4 meters equals the height reduced by 2 meters? **Ans:** 6 meters.

13. What is the height of a tree if 6 meters equals the tree's height reduced by $2\frac{2}{3}$ meters? **Ans:** $8\frac{2}{3}$ meters.

14. How much money does Natasha have if twice her money reduced by $12, equals $38. **Ans:** $25.

15. What is Mohsen's age, if $\frac{3}{4}$ of his age increased by 8 years, equals 35 years? **Ans:** 36 years.

16. A certain number increased by 5 times itself and 15 equals 55. What is the number? **Ans:** 8.

17. A sum of money reduced by $\frac{3}{7}$ of itself and $6 equals $12. How much is the money? **Ans:** $31\frac{1}{2}$.

18. The cost of a bike reduced by $\frac{1}{3}$ of the cost and $200 equals $800. What did the bike cost? **Ans:** $150.

19. A fishing-pole which is 4 meters long equals $\frac{3}{4}$ of the length of the line, minus one meter. What's the length of the line?
Ans: 4 meters + one meter = 5 meters, or $\frac{3}{4}$ of the length of the line; $\frac{4}{4}$, or the length, equals $6\frac{1}{4}$ meters.

20. I sold $\frac{1}{3}$ of my books, and afterward bought 24 more, and now have 56. How many did had I at first?
Ans: $56 - 24 = 32$ books, what I had before buying; $\frac{3}{3} - \frac{1}{3} = \frac{2}{3}$, the part of the books I had left, which was 32. So I had 48 books.

21. Ming spent $\frac{1}{4}$ of her money for magazines and $25 for CD's, and now has $5 left. How much did she start with?
Ans: $\frac{4}{4} - \frac{1}{4} = \frac{3}{4}$ of her money, which equals 25 + 50 or $75. So her money at first was $100.

22. Hua had twice as much money as John and lost $\frac{1}{3}$ of it, but then earned $150 more. Now he has $450. How much money did each of them have?
Ans: $450 - $150 = $300, or Hua's money after his loss; $\frac{3}{3} - \frac{1}{3} = \frac{2}{3}$ of his original money, or $300. He had at first $450, and John had $225.

23. Jason had half as much money as Sam. He then received $\frac{1}{4}$ more, then earned $200 more, and now has $300. How much money did each of them have?

Ans: \$100 = Jason's money plus $\frac{1}{4}$ more, or $\frac{5}{4}$. $\frac{1}{4}$ of what he had is $\frac{1}{5}$ of 100 is 20, so 5 times that is \$80, the money he started with. So Sam must have had twice that, or \$160.

24. If twice my weight is reduced by $\frac{1}{3}$ of my weight and 80 pounds, it will equal 180 pounds. What is my weight?
    Ans: Twice my weight, or $\frac{6}{3} - \frac{1}{3} = \frac{5}{3}$ of my weight; 180 pounds + 30 pounds = 210 pounds, which equals $\frac{5}{3}$ of my weight; since $\frac{5}{3}$ of my weight is 210 pounds, my weight is 126 pounds.

25. Amita baked 3 times as many cookies as Hemma; she then ate $\frac{1}{6}$ of them, and baked 10 more, and then had 30. How many did each bake?
    Ans: $30 - 10 = 20$; $\frac{6}{6} - \frac{1}{6} = \frac{5}{6}$ of the original number $= 20$; Amita's number was 24, and Hemma's, $\frac{1}{3}$ of 24, or 8.

26. A pearl pendant and a chain cost \$150, and $\frac{2}{3}$ of the cost of the pendant plus \$15 equals \$95. What is the cost of each?
    Ans: $\$95 - \$15 = \$80$, or $\frac{2}{3}$ of the cost of the pendant, the pendant cost \$120, and the chain $\$150 - \$120$, or \$30.

27. Another pendant and a chain cost \$100, and $\frac{1}{3}$ of the cost of the pendant equals \$25. What is the cost of each? **Ans:** The pendant cost \$75, and the chain \$25.

28. A fishing rod is 15 meters long. $\frac{3}{5}$ of its length is 3 meters short of being $\frac{6}{7}$ of the length of the line. What is the length of the line?
    Ans: $\frac{3}{5}$ of 15 meters is 9 meters, which lacks 3 meters of $\frac{6}{7}$ the length of the line; $9 + 3$, or 12 ft. $= \frac{6}{7}$ of the length. So the length is 14 meters.

29. A tree is 60 meters high, which is $\frac{5}{6}$ of $\frac{6}{7}$ of the length of its shadow, reduced by 20 meters. What is the length of the shadow?
    Ans: $\frac{5}{6}$ of $\frac{6}{7}$ equals $\frac{5}{7}$. If 60 meters is $\frac{5}{7}$ of the length of the shadow, diminished by 20 meters, 60 meters + 20 meters, or 80 meters, is $\frac{5}{7}$ of the length of the shadow, and the length of the shadow is 112 meters.

30. How much money does Natasha have if half her money reduced by \$15, equals \$50. **Ans:** \$130.

31. How much money does Natasha have if twice her money increased by \$15, equals \$33. **Ans:** \$9.

32. How much money does Natasha have if three times her money reduced by \$40, equals \$20. **Ans:** \$20.

33. How much money does Natasha have if one third her money reduced by \$25, equals \$75. **Ans:** \$300.

34. How much money does Natasha have if one-fifth her money increased by \$35, equals \$45. **Ans:** \$50.

35. If twice my weight is reduced by $\frac{1}{2}$ of my weight less 40 pounds, it will equal 110 pounds. What is my weight?
Ans: $\frac{3}{2}$ of my weight; 110 pounds + 40 pounds = 150 pounds. So my weight is 100 pounds.

36. A baker baked one-third as times as many cookies as the day before; he sold $\frac{1}{3}$ of them, and baked 30 more, and then had 50. How many did he bake the day before?
Ans: $50 - 30 = 20$; this is equal to 2 thirds of what he baked today, so he baked 30 cookies. He must have baked 90 cookies the day before. ◡

Lesson 30 – *One Part More or Less Than Another*

IF two times a number increased by 8 equals 3 times the number, what is the number?

Ans: If 2 times a number increased by 8 equals 3 times the number, then 8 must be the difference between 3 times the number and 2 times the number, which is once the number. So, the number is 8.

1. Alan's money increased by $18 equals 3 times his money. How much money does he have? **Ans:** $18 must equal 2 times his money or $9.

2. Francois's age increased by 42 years equals 4 times his age. What is his age? **Ans:** 14 years.

3. Amie's age increased by 25 years equals 6 times her age. What is her age? **Ans:** 5 years.

4. Three times the length of a rocket reduced by 20 meters, equals the length of the rocket. What is the length of the rocket? **Ans:** 10 meters.

5. If 4 times a number reduced by 8 equals 2 times the number, what is the number?
   Ans: 8 must equal the difference between 2 times and 4 times the number, or just two times the number. So the number is 4.

6. One-third of Brigit's score reduced by 5 equals $\frac{1}{4}$ of her score. What is her score? **Ans:** $\frac{1}{3}$ minus $\frac{1}{4}$ equals $\frac{1}{12}$, which is equal to 5. So her score is 12 times 5, or 60.

7. One-half of Brigit's score, reduced by 12, equals $\frac{1}{4}$ of her score. What is her score?
   Ans: $\frac{1}{2}$ minus $\frac{1}{4}$ equals $\frac{1}{4}$, which is equal to 12. So her score is 12 times 4, or 48.

8. Two-thirds of Ada's score, reduced by 10, equals $\frac{1}{4}$ of her score. What is her score? Hint: What is the difference between $\frac{2}{3}$ and $\frac{1}{4}$? **Ans:** 24.

9. Ben lost $6 more than $\frac{1}{3}$ of his money, and then got back $\frac{3}{5}$ of his money so he now has as much as he had before. How much money did he have? **Ans:** $90.

10. A storm broke off 10 meters less than $\frac{1}{3}$ of a tree, so $\frac{3}{4}$ of the tree remains. What is the length of the tree? **Ans:** 24 meters.

11. Three times the number of sheep a farmer has equals $2\frac{1}{2}$ times the number increased by 8. How many sheep does he have? **Ans:** 16 sheep.

12. Mary spent \$12 more than $\frac{1}{2}$ of her money for a book, and then had $\frac{1}{3}$ of her money left. How much did she have?
Ans: If she had $\frac{1}{3}$ of her money left, she spent $\frac{2}{3}$, which equals \$12 more than $\frac{1}{2}$. So the difference between $\frac{2}{3}$ and $\frac{1}{2}$ of her money, or $\frac{1}{6}$, is \$12, and her money was 6 times 12, or \$72.

13. Three times a number plus 4 equals 2 times the same number, plus 12. What is the number? **Ans:** 8.

14. Three times a number plus 2 equals 2 times the number, plus 6. What is the number? **Ans:** 4.

15. Two times a number plus 6 equals one time the number, plus 12. What is the number? **Ans:** 6.

16. Three times a number plus 8 equals 4 times the same number, plus 3. What is the number?
Ans: If 3 times a number plus 8 = 4 times the same number, plus 3, 3 times the number, plus 8 = 4 times the number, or once the number equals 5.

17. One-half of a number increased by 10 equals $\frac{2}{3}$ of the same number, plus 8. What is the number?
Ans: $\frac{1}{2}$ of a number $+ 10 = \frac{2}{3}$ of the number plus 8, then $\frac{1}{2}$ of the number, plus $2 = \frac{2}{3}$ of the number, and $\frac{2}{3} - \frac{1}{2}$, or $\frac{1}{6}$ of the number $= 2$, and the number is 12.

18. Four times Eliot's age reduced by 10 years equals 3 times his age, increased by 10 years. What is his age?
Ans: If 4 times Eliot's age minus 10 years equals 3 times his age, plus 10 years, 4 times his age equals 3 times his age, plus 20 years. And if 4 times his age equals 3 times his age, plus 20 years, 4 times his age, minus 3 times his age, or once his age, equals 20 years.

19. If a giant grew by $\frac{5}{3}$ plus 10 meters, he will be twice his height. How tall is the giant?
Ans: $\frac{5}{3}$ of the height $+ 10$ meters equals $\frac{6}{3}$ of the height; then $\frac{6}{3}$ of

the height, $-\frac{5}{3}$ of the height, or $\frac{1}{3}$ of the height $= 10$ meters. So his height is 30 meters.

20. If twice the length of a room is increased by $\frac{3}{5}$ plus 2 meters more, the sum will equal 3 times the length of the room. What is its length?
Ans: $\frac{10}{5} + \frac{3}{5} = \frac{13}{5}$; $\frac{13}{5}$ of the length, $+$ 2 meters, equals $\frac{15}{5}$ of the length; then $\frac{15}{5}$ of the length minus $\frac{13}{5}$ of the length, or $\frac{2}{5}$ of the length, equals 2 meters. So the room is 5 meters long.

21. If $3\frac{5}{6}$ times Harry's age is increased by 2 years, the sum will equal 4 times his age. What is his age?
Ans: $3\frac{5}{6}$ times Harry's age $+$ 2 years $=$ 4 times his age; then 4 times his age minus $3\frac{5}{6}$ times his age, or $\frac{1}{6}$ of his age, is 2 years. So his age is 12 years.

22. Two-thirds of Morton's classmates increased by 2 equals $\frac{3}{4}$ what he has, reduced by one. How many classmates does he have?
Ans: $\frac{2}{3}$ of his number $+ 2 = \frac{3}{4}$ of his number minus 1; then $\frac{2}{3}$ of his number $+ 3 = \frac{3}{4}$ of his number; $\frac{3}{4} - \frac{2}{3}$, or $\frac{1}{12}$ of his number, is 3. So he has 36 classmates.

23. If the height of a tower is increased by $\frac{1}{2}$, and that number is reduced by the difference between $\frac{1}{4}$ and $\frac{1}{5}$ of the number, it will equal 30 feet. What is its height?
Ans: $\frac{1}{2} - \left(\frac{1}{4} - \frac{1}{5}\right) = \frac{9}{20}$. If $\frac{9}{20}$ of a number equals 30, then the number is 60 feet.

24. If the length of a fence is increased by $\frac{3}{5}$ and decreased by the difference between $\frac{1}{10}$ and $\frac{1}{20}$, the fence is now 70 feet long. How long was it before? **Ans:** 100 feet.

25. If the length of the fence was increased by $\frac{3}{4}$ and then the whole length was reduced by $\frac{1}{4}$, only 50 feet were left. How long was the length of the fence before?
Ans: If the fence was reduced by one quarter, then $\frac{3}{4}$ is left. If 75 is $\frac{3}{4}$ of a number, then the number is 100. ⌣

Lesson 31 – *One Part a Number of Times Another*

WILLIAM and Henry have 15 battleships. How many battleships does each have, provided William has twice as many as Henry?

Ans: Twice Henry's number equals William's, which, when added to Henry's number, equals three times Henry's number, what they both have, or 15 battleships. If 3 times Henry's number equals 15, then he has 5 and William has 10 battleships.

1. Robert has 3 times as many jets as Sun, and together they have 24. How many does each have?

2. Naz has 4 times as many boats as Ahmad, and together they have 30. How many does each have?

3. Benjamin has 4 times as many points as Oliver, and together they have 20. How many does each have? **A**

4. Mark has 5 times as many points as Oliver, and together they have 60. How many points does each have?

5. Mark has $1\frac{1}{2}$ times as many points as Gene, and together they have 100. How many points does each have?

6. Divide 25 into two parts such that 4 times one part equals the other.

7. Divide 45 into two parts such that 2 times one part equals the other.

8. The sum of two numbers equals 40, and $\frac{1}{3}$ of the larger equals the smaller number. What are the numbers?

9. Emma has 35 flowers: roses and carnations. Four times the number of roses equals the number of carnations. How many does she have of each type?

10. Jill and Kim earned $1200 in one week. How much did each earn if Jill earned twice as much as Kim?

11. A pole, 36 meters in length, was cut into two unequal pieces such that $\frac{1}{3}$ of the longer piece equals the shorter pieces. What is the length of each piece?

12. A pole, 28 meters in length was cut into two unequal pieces such that $\frac{3}{4}$ of the longer piece equals the shorter pieces. What is the length of each piece?

13. In a school that had 35 students, there were $\frac{1}{4}$ as many girls as boys. How many boys and how many girls are in the school?

14. In a class that had 30 students, there were $\frac{2}{3}$ as many girls as boys. How many boys and how many girls are in the school?

15. A man bought a boat and some supplies for $700. The boat cost $\frac{3}{4}$ as much as the supplies. What is the cost of each?

16. A watch and batteries cost $42. What was the cost of each, if $\frac{1}{5}$ of the cost of the watch equals half the cost of the batteries?

17. Jim and Tim lost an envelope containing $24, of which Jim owned $\frac{5}{7}$ as much as Tim. How much did each lose?

18. Marie ate 40 more cherries than Jane, and 5 times what Jane ate equals the number Marie ate. How many cherries did they each eat?

19. Two-thirds of 30 is $\frac{5}{2}$ of the difference between two numbers, and the smaller of them is $\frac{3}{5}$ of the larger. What are the numbers?

20. Divide 86 bugs among three children, so that the second has twice as many as the first and the third has 3 times as many as the first.

21. Divide 66 tickles among Ella, Emma, and June, so that Ella gets twice and Emma three times as many as June.

22. Together Anu, Bose, and Cam earned $700; Anu earned twice as much as Bose, and Bose twice as much as Cam. How much did each earn?

23. The sum of three numbers is 50; the second is 3 times the first, and the third is twice the second. What are the numbers?

24. A turkey, duck, and hen cost $22. The duck cost twice as much as the hen, and the turkey cost 4 times as much as the duck. What is the cost of each?

25. A man bought a kitten, puppy, and a bird for $105 for his daughter. How much did he pay for each, provided the puppy cost 2 times as much as the kitten, and the kitten cost 2 times as much as the bird?

26. A pole is dug in the ground with parts in the mud, air and water. $\frac{2}{3}$ of the length in the air equals the length in the water, and $\frac{3}{4}$ of the length in the water equals the length in the mud. What is the length of each part, supposing the part in the water is 10 meters longer than the part in the mud?

27. Divide some candies among five children, so that the each child gets twice as many as the one before. How many candies do you need?

28. Divide 25 toys among Ella, Emma, and June, so that both June and Emma get twice as many toys as Ella.

29. Divide 24 toys among Ella, Emma, and June, so that Ella gets twice as many as and Emma and June

30. Together X, Y, and Z earned $1000; X earned same as Y, and Y twice as much as Z. How much did each earn?

31. Someone stole $\frac{5}{7}$ of Baldwin's money, and the thief was not caught until he had spent $\frac{4}{5}$ of it; the rest, which was $30 less than Baldwin had left, was given back. How much money did Baldwin have?

    Ans: If the thief spent $\frac{4}{5}$ of what he stole, he had left $\frac{1}{5}$ of what he stole - that is, $\frac{1}{5}$ of $\frac{5}{7}$ of Baldwin's money that was stolen, or $\frac{1}{7}$ of his money. $\frac{2}{7}$ of his money that was not stolen minus $\frac{1}{7}$ of his money, or $\frac{1}{7}$ of his money that was not returned, equals $30. So he had at first $210. ⌣

Lesson 32 – *One Part a Given Number More Than Another*

ALAN and Bob have 25 chocolate bars. How many does each have, if Bob has 5 more than Alan?

Ans: Alan's number plus 5 equals Bob's number. Alan's number is also equal to 25 minus Bob's number. Five plus Bob's number is equal to 25 minus Alan's number. So twice Alan's number is equal to 20, So Bob's number is 15 and Alan's number is 10.

Another way to solve the problem is to subtract 5 from 25, which is 20. Divide 20 by 2 to get 10. Add 5 for Alan, and then we get 15 for Bob and 10 for Alan.

1. Marina has 7 candies more than Boris, and together they have 27. How many do they each have?

2. Stephen got 10 more bug bites than Marta at the camp and together they got 40. How many did each get?

3. The sum of two numbers is 5 and their difference 1. What are the numbers?

4. The sum of two numbers is 65 and their difference 11. What are the numbers?

5. The sum of two numbers is 56 and their difference 40. What are the numbers?

6. Divide number 28 into two parts, such that one part is 6 less than the other.

7. Divide number 40 into two parts, such that one part is 6 less than the other.

8. Divide number 40 into two parts, such that one part is 8 more than the other.

9. Thomas and Reuben each have the same amount of money. Reuben received $9 from his father, and then together they had $45. How much did each have?

10. Ellen and Kate each had the same number of candies. Ellen ate 5 of hers, and now together they have 21 left. How many did each have at first?

11. Two boys found an equal number of green rocks at the beach; one threw away 6 and the other threw away 4, and together they kept 22. How many did they each find?

12. Chris and Ben had equal sums of money. Chris spent $5 and Ben received $7 as a gift, and then together they had $36 left. How much did each have at first?

13. Daniel and Kevin each had the same number of teammates. Daniel lost 6 and 4 of Kevin's teammates changed sides to Daniel, and now together they have 14. How many did each of them have before?

14. Olga and Ivan each had the same number of pebbles; Olga threw away 10, and Ivan gave her 4 of his, and now together they have 24. How many did each have before?

15. Three times Tommy's age increased by 5 years equals Harvey's age, and the sum of their ages is 45 years. How old is each?

16. Divide 48 into two parts such that twice the first part reduced by 6 equals the second part.

17. The sum of two numbers is 55. The larger number equals 3 times the smaller number, reduced by 5. What are the numbers?

18. A pole, 48 meters, was broken into two unequal pieces, such that $\frac{3}{5}$ of the longer piece equals the shorter piece. What is the length of each piece?

19. A pole, 33 meters, was broken into two unequal pieces, such that $\frac{3}{8}$ of the longer piece equals the shorter piece. What is the length of each piece?

20. A locket and chain cost $85. $\frac{3}{10}$ of the cost of the locket, plus $7, equals the cost of the chain. What is the cost of each?

21. Francis has collected 9 more flags than $\frac{1}{2}$ as much as Puja and together they have 42 flags. How many flags does each have?

22. A drill and a saw cost $132. What is the cost of each if the drill cost $\frac{2}{5}$ as much as the saw minus $8?

23. A tower, the height of which was 45 meters, was measured in two unequal parts, and $\frac{3}{5}$ of the longer part plus 5 meters equals the shorter part. What is the length of each part?

24. A group of animals walked 110 miles in three days looking for water. They walked 5 miles farther the second day than the first, and 10 miles farther the third day than the second. How far did they walk each day?

25. There are 42 animals in a field, consisting of horses, sheep, and cows. What is the number of each provided $\frac{1}{2}$ of the number of sheep + 10 equals the number of cows, and $\frac{1}{3}$ of the number of sheep + 10 equals the number of horses.

26. There are 54 instruments in a group consisting of horns, drums, and tuba. The number of tubas are $\frac{1}{2}$ of the drums and the number of drums are $\frac{1}{3}$ the number of horns. How many of each is there?
Ans: 36 Horns, 12 drums and 6 tuba.

27. The sum of two numbers is 46. The larger number equals 3 times the smaller number, reduced by 2. What are the numbers?

28. The sum of two numbers is 46. The larger number equals 3 times the smaller number, increased by 6. What are the numbers?

29. The sum of two numbers is 120. The larger number equals 5 times the smaller number, reduced by 30. What are the numbers?

30. A man bought a kayak, trailer, and oars for $152; for the kayak he paid twice as much as for the oars, plus $8, and for the trailer, 4 times as much as for the oars plus $6. What did he pay for each?⌣

Lesson 33 – *Multiple of Fractions*

ANGEL and Bob together have 34 books, and $\frac{2}{3}$ of Angel's number equals $\frac{3}{4}$ of Bob's number. How many books does each have?

Ans: If $\frac{2}{3}$ of Angel's number equals $\frac{3}{4}$ of Bob's, then $\frac{1}{3}$ of Angel's equals $\frac{1}{2}$ of $\frac{3}{4}$, which is $\frac{3}{8}$ of Bob's. If $\frac{1}{3}$ of Angel's equals $\frac{3}{8}$ of Bob's, then $\frac{3}{3}$ of Angel's equals 3 times $\frac{3}{8}$, which is $\frac{9}{8}$ of Bob' which added to $\frac{8}{8}$ of Bob's, equals $\frac{17}{8}$ of Bob's, for a total of 34 books.

If $\frac{17}{8}$ of some number equals 34, then that number is $\frac{34\times8}{17} = 16$. Bob had 16 and Angel, who had $\frac{9}{8}$ of that, had 18 books.

1. The sum of two numbers is 30 and $\frac{2}{3}$ of the larger number equals the smaller. What are the numbers?

   Ans: If $\frac{2}{3}$ of the larger number equals the smaller, then $\frac{1}{3}$ of larger equals $\frac{1}{2}$ of the smaller, or is equal to $\frac{3}{2}$ of the smaller. Add to that $\frac{2}{2}$ of the smaller, or $\frac{5}{2}$, to get 30. Since $\frac{5}{2}$ of some number equals 30, the smaller number is equal to 12 and larger is 18.

2. The sum of two numbers is 18 and $\frac{1}{3}$ of the larger equals $\frac{2}{3}$ of the smaller number. What are the numbers? **Ans:** 12, 6.

3. The sum of two numbers is 28 and $\frac{1}{3}$ of the smaller equals $\frac{1}{4}$ of the larger. What are the numbers? **Ans:** 12 and 16.

4. The sum of two numbers is 200 and $\frac{1}{5}$ of the smaller equals $\frac{1}{10}$ of the larger. What are the numbers? **Ans:** 100 and 200.

5. The sum of two numbers is 54 and $\frac{2}{7}$ of the larger equals $\frac{3}{4}$ the smaller. What are the numbers? **Ans:** 20 and 16.

6. The sum of two numbers is 24 and $\frac{3}{5}$ of the larger equals the smaller. What are the numbers? **Ans:** 42 and 12.

7. Holmes and Watson together have \$55, and $\frac{2}{3}$ of Holmes's money equals $\frac{4}{5}$ of Watson's. How much does each of them have? **Ans:** Holmes, \$30. Watson, \$25.

8. Divide 46 points between Jose and Kyle so that $\frac{3}{4}$ of Jose's points equals $\frac{2}{5}$ of Kyle's. **Ans:** Kyle, 30; Jose, 16.

9. $\frac{3}{5}$ of the number of apple trees in an orchard equals $\frac{3}{7}$ of the number of peach trees, and in all there are 60 trees. How many of each are there? **Ans:** Apple trees, 25; peach, 35.

10. Twice the sum of two numbers is 30, and 3 times the smaller equals twice the larger. What are the numbers?
Ans: The sum of the numbers is 15 and the smaller is $\frac{2}{3}$ of the larger. So $\frac{5}{3}$ of the larger is 15, and the numbers are 6 and 9.

11. A 630 meter long train was split into two parts such that $\frac{3}{4}$ of the first part equals $\frac{3}{5}$ of the second. What is the length of each part.
Ans: 280 meter and 350 meter.

12. Walter bought a hat and a sweater for $26. $2\frac{1}{2}$ times the cost of the hat equals $\frac{3}{4}$ of the cost of the sweater. What is the cost of each?
Ans: Hat $6; sweater, $20.

13. The difference between two numbers is 6, and $\frac{2}{3}$ of the first equals $\frac{4}{7}$ of the second. What are the numbers? **Ans:** 20 and 14.

14. Rena has 14 books more than Karen. $\frac{2}{5}$ of Rena's equals $\frac{3}{4}$ of Karen's number. How many does each have?
Ans: We find that $\frac{5}{5}$ of Rena's number equals $\frac{15}{8}$ of Karen's number; then $\frac{15}{8}$ of Karen's number, $-\frac{8}{8}$ of Karen's number, or $\frac{7}{8}$ of Karen's number, equals 14. So Rena has 30 and Karen has 16.

15. $\frac{1}{2}$ of the difference between two numbers is 6, and $\frac{1}{8}$ of the first number equals $\frac{1}{4}$ of the second. What are the numbers?
Ans: The difference is 12, and $\frac{1}{2}$ of the first equals the second. So $\frac{2}{2}$ $-\frac{1}{2}$ of the first $= 12$; the first equals 24, and the second, 12.

16. The difference between two numbers is 3, and $\frac{1}{3}$ of the first number equals $\frac{2}{5}$ of the second. What are the numbers?
Ans: If $\frac{1}{3}$ of the first number equals $\frac{2}{5}$ of the second, the first number equals $\frac{6}{5}$ of the second number. The difference between the two numbers is then $\frac{6}{5}$ of the larger and $\frac{5}{5}$ of the smaller, or $\frac{1}{5}$, which equals 2. If one-fifth of some number is 3, then the number is 35, and the larger number is 18.

17. The difference between two numbers is 2, and $\frac{2}{3}$ of the first number equals $\frac{1}{5}$ of the second. What are the numbers? **Ans:** 10 and 12.

18. The difference between two numbers is 45, and $\frac{2}{3}$ of the first number equals $\frac{1}{5}$ of the second. What are the numbers? **Ans:** 15 and 50.
Note—*The following four problems may be difficult for your child to do verbally. Let her write out the steps if she needs to.*

19. The sum of two numbers is 36, and $\frac{3}{4}$ plus 3 of the first number equals $\frac{1}{2}$ of the second number. What are the numbers?

Ans: $\frac{3}{4}$ the first number equals $\frac{1}{2}$ of the second number minus 3. So $\frac{1}{4}$ of the first number is equal to $\frac{1}{6}$ of the second number − one or is equal to $\frac{4}{6}$ of the second number − 4. If the smaller number is ($\frac{4}{6}$ of the second number − 4) then the difference between the number is $\frac{6}{6}$ for the bigger number plus ($\frac{4}{6}$ of the second number − 4) equals $\frac{4}{6}$ minus 4 equals 36. or $\frac{4}{6}$ of the number equals 32, or the larger number is 24 and the smaller number is 12.

20. The difference between two numbers is 8, and $\frac{1}{3}$ of the first number equals $\frac{1}{5}$ of the second number. What are the numbers? **Ans:** 12 and 20.

21. The difference between two numbers is 8, and $\frac{1}{3}$ of the first number equals $\frac{1}{5}$ of the second number. What are the numbers? **Ans:** 12 and 20.

22. The difference between two numbers is 9 , and $\frac{2}{7}$ of the first number plus 4 equals $\frac{1}{3}$ of the second number. What are the numbers? **Ans:** 21 and 30.

23. Big says to Cute, "$\frac{2}{3}$ of my age, + 6 years equals $\frac{3}{4}$ of yours. The sum of our ages is 42 years." What is the age of each?
Ans: If $\frac{3}{4}$ of Cute's age equals $\frac{2}{3}$ of Big's, + 6, $\frac{1}{4}$ of Cute's equals $\frac{8}{9}$ of Big's, + 2, and $\frac{4}{4}$ of Cute's equals $\frac{8}{9}$ of Big's, + 8, which, added to $\frac{9}{9}$ of Big's, equals $1\frac{7}{9}$ of Big's, + 8, which equals 42. So Big's age is 18, and Cute is 24 years old.

24. Five-sixths of the difference between Short's and Big's money is $500, and $\frac{2}{5}$ of Short's equals $\frac{4}{7}$ of Big's money. How much money does each have?
Ans: The difference is $600. Short's equals $\frac{10}{7}$ of Big's; $\frac{10}{7} - \frac{7}{7}$ or $\frac{3}{7}$ of Big's = $600. So Short had $2000; Big, $1400.

25. Little and Big can build $\frac{1}{6}$ of a model in a day. Two times what Ann builds equals what Big builds in a day. How much can each build in one day?
Ans: Three times what Little builds equals what they both can build, or $\frac{1}{6}$ of a model; then one-times what Little builds equals $\frac{1}{3}$ of $\frac{1}{6}$ of a model, or $\frac{1}{18}$ of the model, and two-times what Little builds, or what Big builds, equals $\frac{1}{9}$ of the model.

26. Koo and Kam can build $\frac{1}{4}$ of a nest in a day. Half of what Koo builds equals what Kam builds. How much can each build in one day?

Ans: What two times Kam builds plus one time Koo builds equals what they both build or $\frac{1}{4}$ of the project. What Koo builds equals $\frac{1}{3}$ of $\frac{1}{4}$ of the nest, or $\frac{1}{12}$ of the project. Twice what Kam builds, or what Kam builds, equals $\frac{1}{6}$ of the model.

27. Two birds can do a build a nest in 6 days, and twice what mamma bird does equals what papa bird does. How long will it take each to do it alone?

    Ans: They do $\frac{1}{6}$ of the work in one day; then mamma bird does $\frac{1}{3}$ of $\frac{1}{6}$, or $\frac{1}{18}$ of the work, and papa bird does $\frac{2}{3}$ of $\frac{1}{6}$, or $\frac{1}{9}$ of the work. So it will take mamma bird 18 days, and papa bird 9 days.

28. Three-fourths of 40 is $\frac{3}{5}$ of the number of feathers and sticks that papa bird has. How many does he have of each if 3 times the number of feathers equals 7 times the number of sticks?

    Ans: $\frac{3}{4}$ of 40, or 30, is $\frac{3}{5}$ of the number of both. So he had 50; the number of feathers equals $\frac{7}{3}$ of the number of sticks. So $\frac{10}{3}$ of the number of sticks $= 50$; the number of sticks is 15, and the number of feathers is 35.

29. Two boys fill a tank containing 144 gallons of syrup. $\frac{2}{3}$ of what one pours in equals $\frac{3}{5}$ of what the other pours in. How much does each boy put in?

    Ans: $\frac{3}{5}$ of the quantify poured in by the second equals the quantity poured in by the first. So $\frac{8}{5}$ of the second equals 144 gallons; the second pours in 90 gallons, and the first 54.

30. John and Kyle can write 30 pages of poetry in a week, and $\frac{1}{2}$ of what John can do in a day equals what Kyle can do in one day. How many pages does each write in a week?

    Ans: In a week, Kyle writes $\frac{1}{2}$ of what John writes; $\frac{3}{2}$ of what John writes equals 30 pages. So John writes 20 pages and Kyle 10.

31. Bill can use 6 quarts of paint in 4 days; $\frac{2}{3}$ of what Bill uses equals $\frac{1}{2}$ of what Alan uses, and also $\frac{1}{3}$ of what Carl uses. In what time can Alan and Carl use it alone.

    Ans: Bill uses $\frac{1}{4}$ of it in one day, Alan uses $\frac{1}{3}$, and Carl $\frac{1}{2}$; Alan and Carl will use $\frac{1}{3} + \frac{1}{2}$, or $\frac{5}{6}$, in one day, and to use $\frac{1}{6}$ will take $\frac{1}{5}$ of a day, and to use $\frac{6}{6}$ will take them $\frac{6}{5}$, or $1\frac{1}{5}$ days.

Lesson 34 – *The Proportional Parts*

DIVIDE 30 bones between a lion and a tiger so that their shares will be to each other as 4 is to 6.

Ans: Since the shares are proportionate as 4 is to 6, we divide 30 points into $4 + 6$, or ten equal parts. 4 of these parts, or $\frac{4}{10}$ of 30, will be lion's number, and 6 of these parts, or $\frac{6}{10}$ of 30, will be tiger's number, etc.

1. What part (proportion) is 4 of 10? **Ans:** $\frac{4}{10}$.

2. What part (proportion) is one of 2? **Ans:** $\frac{1}{2}$.

3. What part (proportion) is 4 of 7? **Ans:** $\frac{4}{7}$.

4. What part (proportion) is 3 of 4? **Ans:** $\frac{3}{4}$.

5. If 4 is proportionate to 10, then what has the same proportion to 8? **Ans:** 20.

6. If 3 is proportionate to 7, then what has the same proportion to 4? **Ans:** $\frac{28}{3}$.

7. If 5 is proportionate to 6, then what has the same proportion to 2? **Ans:** $\frac{12}{5}$.

8. If $\frac{2}{7}$ is proportionate to $\frac{3}{7}$, then what has the same proportion to 2? **Ans:** 3.

9. If 2 is proportionate to 5, then what has the same proportion to $\frac{2}{5}$? **Ans:** One .

10. If $\frac{3}{6}$ is proportionate to $\frac{4}{6}$, then what has the same proportion to 3? **Ans:** 4.

11. If $\frac{1}{2}$ is proportionate to $\frac{2}{3}$, then what has the same proportion to 4? **Ans:** 4.

12. Divide 45 coconuts between Barry and Harry so that their shares will be to each other as 3 is to 2.
    Ans: Divide 45 into 5 pieces, which is 9. 9 times 3 or, 27 goes to Barry, and 9 times 2 or, 18 goes to Harry.

13. Divide the number 50 into two parts so that each is to other as 7 is to 3. **Ans:** 35 and 15.

14. In a dog training school consisting of 45 dogs, there are 5 German shepherd for every 4 retrievers. How many retrievers and German shepherd are in the school? **Ans:** 25 German shepherd; 20 retrievers.

15. The sum of two numbers is 40. The larger is to the smaller as 5 is to 3. What are the numbers? **Ans:** 25 and 15.

16. Divide 45 walnuts among three birds so that their shares are in the proportions of 2, 3, and 4.
    Ans: 2 parts + 3 parts + 4 parts = 9 parts; the first has $\frac{2}{9}$ of 45 walnuts, or 10 walnuts, the second $\frac{3}{9}$, or 15 walnuts, the third, $\frac{5}{9}$ or 20 walnuts.

17. Two men bought 10 pounds of fish for $80, the first paying $30, and the second $50. How much of the fish belong to each?
    Ans: The first pays $\frac{3}{8}$ of the cost, and therefore takes $\frac{3}{8} \times 10$ pounds of the fish, or $3\frac{3}{4}$, and the second pays $\frac{5}{8}$, and takes $\frac{5}{8} \times 10$ pounds, or $6\frac{1}{4}$ pounds of the fish.

18. Three women bought 75 books at a garage sale. The money they paid is in proportions of 4, 5 and 6. How many books should each woman get?
    Ans: They pay in proportions of 4, 5, 6; the first pays $\frac{4}{15}$ and takes $\frac{4}{15}$ of 75 books, or 20 books; the second pays $\frac{5}{15}$ and takes 25 books; the third pays $\frac{6}{15}$, and takes 30 books.

19. Divide $44 between Ashok and Kishor so that Kishor will have $3\frac{1}{2}$ for every $2 Ashok has.
    Ans: $3\frac{1}{2}$ and 2 are in the same proportion as 7 and 4; Ashok therefore takes $\frac{7}{11}$ of $44, or $28, and Kishor takes $\frac{4}{11}$, or $16.

20. The sum of two numbers is 50. The first is to the second as $\frac{1}{2}$ is to $\frac{1}{3}$. What are the numbers?
    Ans: One-half equals $\frac{3}{6}$ and $\frac{1}{3}$ equals $\frac{2}{6}$. So the numbers are to each other as $\frac{3}{6}$ to $\frac{2}{6}$, or as 3 to 2; therefore, if we divide 50 into 3 + 2, or 5 equal parts; 3 of these parts, or $\frac{3}{5}$ of 50, will be one number, and $\frac{2}{5}$ of 50 will be the other. So the numbers are 30 and 20.

21. Divide number 49 into two parts which are to each other as $\frac{1}{3}$ is to $\frac{1}{4}$. **Ans:** 28 and 21.

22. The sum of three numbers is 46. What is each of the numbers, if they are to each other as $\frac{1}{2}$, $\frac{2}{3}$, and $\frac{3}{4}$ are to each other?
    Ans: $\frac{1}{2} = \frac{6}{12}$; $\frac{2}{3} = \frac{8}{12}$; $\frac{3}{4} = \frac{9}{12}$. So the numbers are in the proportion

of 6, 8, and 9; the first is $\frac{6}{23}$ of 46, or 12; the second $\frac{8}{23}$, or 16; the third $\frac{9}{23}$, or 18.

23. Divide number 50 into 3 parts which are to each other as $\frac{2}{3}$, $1\frac{1}{2}$, and 2.

Ans: $\frac{2}{3} = \frac{4}{6}$; $1\frac{1}{2} = \frac{9}{6}$; $2 = 1\frac{2}{6}$; numbers 4, 9, and 12 are in the proportion $\frac{4}{25}$ of 50 = 8, the first number; $\frac{9}{25}$ of 50 = 18, the second; $\frac{12}{25} = 24$, the third.

24. Alex, Boyd, and Cathy made \$1000, which they agree to divide in the proportion of $\frac{3}{4}$, $\frac{7}{8}$, and $1\frac{1}{2}$. How much does each receive?

Ans: $\frac{3}{4} = \frac{6}{8}$; $\frac{7}{8}$; $1\frac{1}{2} = 1\frac{2}{8}$ so they divide the money in the proportion 6, 7, 12; Alex receives $\frac{6}{25}$ of \$100, or \$240; Boyd, $\frac{7}{25}$, or \$280, and Cathy, $\frac{12}{25}$ or \$480.

25. Arthur and Bernard agree to pay \$2500 toward building a storage building, which is to be 2 miles from Arthur's business and 8 miles from Bernard's. How much does each contribute, if they pay in proportion to the inverse of their distances?

Ans: The reciprocal of 2 is $\frac{1}{2}$, and the reciprocal of 3 is $\frac{1}{3}$. So they pay in the proportion of $\frac{1}{2}$ to $\frac{1}{3}$, or $\frac{3}{6}$ to $\frac{2}{6}$, or 3 to 2. So Arthur pays \$1500; Bernard, \$1000.

26. If \$420 is divided into two parts which are to each other as $\frac{1}{2}$ is to $\frac{2}{3}$, it will respectively give $\frac{3}{4}$ of Kamal's and $\frac{4}{5}$ of Ben's money. How much do Ahmad and Ben have?

Ans: The parts are as $\frac{3}{6}$ is to $\frac{4}{6}$ or as 3 to 4. So $\frac{3}{7}$ of \$420 = $\frac{3}{4}$ of Kamal's. And $\frac{4}{7}$ of \$420 = $\frac{4}{5}$ of Ben's. Therefore, Kamal's = \$240 and Ben's, \$300.

27. If \$500 is divided into two parts so each is to other as 2 is to 3, it will give $\frac{2}{3}$ of Hans's and $\frac{3}{4}$ Brit's money. How much do Hans and Brit have?

Ans: The parts are as 2 is to 3. So $\frac{2}{5}$ of \$500 = $\frac{2}{3}$ of Hans's. And $\frac{3}{5}$ of \$500 = $\frac{3}{4}$ of Brit's; therefore Hans has \$300, and Brit \$400.

28. Anita's money added to $\frac{1}{2}$ of Bina's money, equals \$2000. How much belongs to each, provided Anita's money is to Bina's as 3 is to 4?

Ans: If Anita's is to Bina's as 3 to 2, we divide \$2000 in two parts, which are as 3 to 4, the first part will be Anita's and the second part $\frac{1}{2}$ of Bina's. So Anita's money is \$1200; Bina's, \$1600. ⌣

Lesson 35 – *Compound Proportions*

IF $\frac{2}{3}$ of a pound of stardust cost $\frac{4}{5}$ of ten dollars, what will $\frac{3}{4}$ of a pound cost?

Ans: This problem is similar to the proportions problems and can be done in several ways. One is to compute the unit cost and the other is to determine the proportion. First we determine how $\frac{2}{3}$ of a pound is related to the material cost $\frac{4}{5}$ of ten dollars. To make a simple comparison, multiply both numerator and denominator of the first fraction with 5 we get $\frac{10}{15}$. Multiply the second fraction with 3 and we get $\frac{12}{15}$. For 12 dollars, we get 10 pounds of stardust. So the cost of the stardust is $\frac{3}{4} \times \frac{12}{10} = \frac{9}{10}$ of a dollar.

1. If 8 chefs use up 8 baskets of rutabagas in 16 weeks, how long will that many baskets last 32 chefs?
   Ans: If 8 chefs take 16 weeks to use the rutabagas, then one chef (who will be slower) will take 8 × 16 weeks. 32 chefs will use it up much faster, so they will take $\frac{8 \times 16}{32} = 4$ weeks.

2. If 6 chefs use up 8 baskets of spinach in 12 weeks, how long will that many baskets last 18 chefs?
   Ans: If 6 chefs take 12 weeks to use up the spinach, then one chef will take 6 × 12 weeks. 18 chefs will use it up much faster, so they will take $\frac{6 \times 12}{18} = 4$ weeks.

3. If 5 workers earn $800 in a certain time, how much will 10 workers earn in $\frac{1}{2}$ the time? **Ans:** $800.

4. If 4 workers earn $800 in a certain time, how much will 8 workers earn in the same time? **Ans:** $1600.

5. If 5 workers earn $800 in a certain time, how much will 8 workers earn in $\frac{1}{2}$ the time? **Ans:** $640.

6. If 6 people out of a party of 10 spent $360 in 3 days for food, then how much will 10 people spend in 5 days?
   Ans: In one day they spent $\frac{360}{6 \times 3} = 20$, so 10 people will spend in one day, $200 and in 5 days, $1000 .

7. How long will 5 tons of hay last 8 horses, if 6 horses eat it in 12 weeks?
   Ans: 9 weeks.

8. How long will 3 barrels of oil last 10 people if 4 people use 4 barrels in 40 weeks? **Ans:** 12 weeks.

9. If 7 men can earn \$2800 in 4 days, how many dollars can 9 men earn in 6 days? **Ans:** \$5400.

10. How long will 6 workers need to build 6 boats if 7 workers can build 3 boats in 12 weeks? **Ans:** 28 weeks.

11. If 10 cows eat 4 acres of grass in 6 days, in how many days will 30 cows eat 8 acres?

    Solution one—One cow can eat 4 acres of grass in 10 times 6 days, or 60 days, and 30 cows can eat 4 acres of grass in $\frac{1}{30}$ of 60 days, or 2 days. If 30 cows eat 4 acres of grass in 2 days, they will eat one acre in $\frac{1}{4}$ of 2 days, or $\frac{1}{2}$ of a day, and they will eat 8 acres in 8 times $\frac{1}{2}$, or 4 days.

    Solution two—If 10 cows eat 4 acres of grass in 6 days, 30 cows, which is 3 times 10 cows, can eat 4 acres of grass in $\frac{1}{3}$ of 6 days, or 2 days. And if they can eat 4 acres of grass in 2 days, they will eat 8 acres, which is 2 times 4 acres, in 2 times 2 days, or 4 days.

12. If 4 programmers need 7 days to write a program, how many programmers are needed to write a program 3 times as large in 6 days? **Ans:** To perform 3 times as large a piece of work will take 12 programmers, 7 days or 84 programmers one day, and to do it in 6 days will take 14 programmers.

13. If 5 men need 8 days to build 20 meters of wall, then how many men can build $\frac{1}{2}$ as much in 2 days? **Ans:** To build the same wall in 2 days, or $\frac{1}{4}$ of 8 days, requires 4 times 5 men, or 20 men; to build $\frac{1}{2}$ as much requires 10 men.

14. How many workers can earn in 10 days of 6 hours each as much as 6 workers can in 20 days of 8 hours each? **Ans:** One man in one hour would earn $\frac{1}{8\times20\times6} = \frac{1}{960}$ of the amount, and in 60 hours would earn $\frac{1}{16}$. So it would require 16 workers.

15. How many deer will eat 5 rose bushes in 5 weeks if 12 deer eat 4 bushes in 4 weeks? **Ans:** 12 deer eat one rose bush in one week. So they would eat 5 rose bushes in 5 weeks.

16. If 3 horses eat $\frac{3}{4}$ of a ton of hay in $\frac{1}{4}$ of a month, how long will $\frac{5}{6}$ of a ton last 5 horses? **Ans:** One horse will eat $\frac{1}{4}$ of a ton in $\frac{1}{4}$ of a month, or one ton in

one month. So he will eat $\frac{5}{6}$ of a ton in $\frac{5}{6}$ of a month, and 5 horses will eat it in $\frac{1}{6}$ of a month.

17. If 4 robots can do a piece of work in 6 days, in how much time will it be completed if they receive the assistance of 5 more robots when the work is half done?

    Ans: It will take 4 robots 3 days to do half the work. One robot will require 12 days to do half the work alone and 9 robots will need only $\frac{12}{9}$ or, $1\frac{1}{3}$ days.

18. How much do 10 melons cost if 4 melons are worth 8 oranges, and 3 oranges cost 9 coins?

    Ans: If 3 oranges are worth 9 coins, one orange is worth $\frac{1}{3}$ of 9, or 3 coins, and 8 oranges, or 4 melons, are worth 8 times 3, or 24 coins. If 4 melons are worth 24 coins, one melon is worth $\frac{1}{4}$ of 24 coins, or 6 coins, and 10 melons are worth 10 times 6 coins, or 60 coins.

19. How many coins will 5 eggplants cost, if 3 eggplants are worth 9 tomatoes, and 4 tomatoes are worth 8 coins?

    Ans: If 4 tomatoes are worth 8 coins, 9 tomatoes are worth 18 coins, and one eggplants is worth 6 coins. So 5 eggplants are worth 30 coins.

20. How much will 10 tomatoes cost, if 5 tomatoes are worth 2 cauliflowers, and 4 cauliflowers are worth 8 coins?

    Ans: If 5 tomatoes are worth 2 cauliflowers, 10 tomatoes are worth 4 cauliflowers, or \$8.

21. How many sheep can a farmer get for 2 cows if 12 sheep are worth 3 cows. **Ans:** 8 sheep.

22. How many oranges can you buy for 20 coins if 4 oranges are worth 8 apples, and 4 apples are worth 8 coins?

    Ans: 8 apples are worth 16 coins and one orange is worth 4 coins. For 20 coins you can buy 5 oranges.

23. How many loaves of bread can you purchase for \$12 if a loaf of bread cost same as 2 pastries, and 3 pastries cost \$6?

    Ans: One pastry is worth \$2, and 2 pastries \$4. So one loaf of bread costs \$4, and you can buy 3 bread loaves for \$12.

24. If 6 sheep are worth 2 cows and 10 cows are worth 5 horses then how many sheep can you buy for 3 horses?

    Ans: 2 cows are worth one horse. So for one horse you can buy 6 sheep, and for 3 horses, 18 sheep.

25. If 5 horses can eat a bag of grain in 12 days, in what time will it be eaten if 7 horses are added when the grain is $\frac{1}{3}$ eaten?

Ans: They eat $\frac{1}{3}$ in 4 days. So 5 horses could eat the rest in 8 days, and one horse could do so in 40 days. $7 + 5$, or 12 horses, will require $\frac{1}{12}$ of 40, or $3\frac{1}{3}$ days, which, added to 4 days, gives $7\frac{1}{3}$ days.

26. If 8 boys can weed a garden in 5 hours, in what time will the job be completed if 3 boys leave when the work is half done? **Ans:** $6\frac{1}{2}$ hours.

27. If 5 sheep are worth 2 cows and 10 cows are worth 5 horses then how many sheep can you buy for 2 horses?

Ans: 2 cows are worth one horse. So for one horse you can buy 5 sheep, and for 3 horses, 15 sheep.

28. If 5 plants need 10 gallons of water in 12 days, and then 3 more plants are planted are added. In how many days will there be only half the water left.

Ans: The 5 plants need $\frac{10}{12}$ of a gallon a day, and each plant needs $\frac{1}{6}$ gallon per day. Now there are 8 plants, so they will all need $\frac{8}{6}$ gallon per day. At this rate 10 gallons will last $10 \div \frac{8}{6} = \frac{30}{4} = 7\frac{1}{2}$ days.

29. If 3 men build 10 meters of wall in 8 days, in what time can 30 meters be built if $\frac{2}{3}$ of the men leave when the work is $\frac{1}{3}$ completed?

Ans: 3 men can build 30 meters, in 3 times 8 days, or 24 days. In 8 days, they have finished $\frac{1}{3}$ of the wall. Now only one man is working and he needs to build the remaining 20 meters. He works at the rate of 10 meters in 24 days. To build 20 meters, it will take him 48 days.

30. If 5 men build 10 meters of wall in 6 days, in what time can 30 meters be built if $\frac{3}{5}$ of the men leave when the work is $\frac{1}{2}$ completed?

Ans: 5 men can build 30 meters, in 3 times 6 days, or 18 days. In 9 days, they have finished $\frac{1}{2}$ of the wall. Now only two men are working and they need to build the remaining 15 meters. They work at the rate of 10 meters in 15 days. To build 15 meters, it will take them $22\frac{1}{2}$ days.

Lesson 36 – *Sharing Problems*

MARK and Bob rented a cottage for $360. Mark stayed there for 4 days, and Bob for 5 days. How much should each pay?

Ans: If 9 days cost $360, then one day will cost $\frac{1}{9}$ of $360, which is $40. Mark's share, will cost 4 times $40, or $160, and Bob's amount, will cost 5 times $40, or $200.

1. Two boys bought 60 ladybugs in a bag for 12 cents; one paid 5 cents and the other 7 cents. How many ladybugs should each get? **Ans:** The first boy should get 25 ladybugs, and the second, 45.

2. Ron and William paid 20 coins for 40 stickers. Of the 20 coins, Ron paid 9 and William paid 11 coins. How many stickers belong to each? **Ans:** 18 to Ron, 22 to William.

3. Three men rented a car for 20 days at the rate of $10 per day. The first used it 5 days, the second 6 days, and the third 9 days. How much should each pay? **Ans:** The first, $50; the second, $60; the third, $90.

4. Mina and Bina rented a truck for $44 to move their things. Mina took her things 12 miles, and Bina 100 miles. How much should each pay, supposing Mina's stuff was 10 times heavier than Bina's stuff? **Ans:** Mina pays $24; Bina, $20.

5. Two businesses rented a storage space for $560 a month; one keeps 10 boxes of machine parts, and the other 36 boxes of books. How much should each pay, provided a box of machine parts weighs twice as much as a box of books?

   Ans: If a box of machine parts weighs twice as much as a box of books, 10 machine part boxes will weigh as much as 20 boxes of books. There are a total $20 + 36 = 56$ boxes of books; so the first pays $200, the second $360.

6. Three men, Alex, Ben, and Carl, bought 144 bananas for $72, of which Alex paid $\frac{1}{6}$, Ben $\frac{2}{6}$, and Carl the rest. How many bananas should each receive?

   Ans: Alex received $\frac{1}{6}$ of 144, or 24; Ben $\frac{2}{6}$ of 144, or 48; Carl $\frac{1}{2}$ of 144, or 72 bananas.

7. Alex and Ben agree to do some construction work for $720. Alex sends 6 full-time employees and Ben sends 15 part-time employees.

How much should each receive supposing 2 full-time employees do as much work as 3 part-time employees?

Ans: If 2 full-time employees do as much as 3 part-time employees, 6 full-time employees, which is 3 times 2 full-time employees, will do as much as 3 times 3 part-time employees, or 9 part-time employees. So 6 full-time employees and 15 part-time employees will do as much as 9 part-time employees + 15 part-time employees, or 24 part-time employees. If 24 part-time employees earn \$72, one part-time employee will earn \$3, and Alex will receive \$270 and Ben, \$450.

8. Anna and Brittany agree to finish a project for \$5400. Anna sends 3 men for 5 days and Brittany sends 4 men for 3 days. How much should Anna and Brittany receive?

    Ans: Three men for 5 days will earn as much as 15 men for one day, and 4 men in 3 days will earn as much as 12 men in one day. So Anna will receive $\frac{15}{27}$ of \$5400, or \$3000, and Brittany $\frac{12}{27}$, or \$2400.

9. Two women rent a pasture for \$100. One keeps 6 horses for 7 days and the other keeps 7 horses for 4 days. How much should each pay?

    Ans: 6 horses in 7 days will eat as much as 42 horses in one day, and 7 horses in 4 days will eat as much as 28 horses in one day. So the first should pay $\frac{42}{70}$, or $\frac{3}{5}$ of \$100, or \$60, and the second $\frac{2}{5}$, or \$40.

10. Alex and Carl agree to work together on a job for \$1400. Alex sends 6 workers for 5 days, and Carl 4 workers for 10 days. How much should each get paid? **Ans:** Alex, \$600; Carl, \$800.

11. Alex and Carl buy an investment together and make \$440 in profit. Alex had put in \$250 for 4 months, and Carl \$150 for 8 months. What is each man's share of the gain?

    Ans: \$250 in 4 months will earn as much as \$1000 in one month, and \$150 in 8 months will earn as much as \$1200 in one month. So Alex gets $\frac{5}{11}$ of \$4400, or \$2000, and Carl $\frac{6}{11}$, or \$2400.

12. Cathy and Don will decorate a house for \$1200. Cathy, with the help of 4 assistants worked for 4 days. Don worked with 3 assistants for 5 days. How much should each get?

    Ans: Cathy, with 4 assistants, for 4 days, will earn as much as 20 workers in one day. And Don, with 3 assistants, for 5 days, will earn as much as 20 workers in one day. So Cathy will receive \$600, Don, \$600.

13. A, B and C are to do some work for $7500. A worked for 4 days. B worked for 5 days, C worked for 6 days. How much of the money should each get?

Ans: A's share is $\frac{4}{15}$ is $2800, B's share is $\frac{5}{15}$ and C's share is $\frac{6}{15}$ of $7500.

14. Alpha, Beta and Gamma are to clear a field for $6200. Alpha brought 3 workers and worked for 4 days. Beta had 4 workers and worked for 5 days, Gamma had 5 workers and worked for 6 days. How much of the money should each get?

Ans: Alpha's workers earn as much as 12 workers in one day; Beta's as much as 20 in one day, and Gamma's as much as 30 workers in one day. So Alpha should receive $1200, Beta $2000, and Gamma $3000.

15. Ed and Fred contract to paint a house for $540. Ed sent 3 workers and they work for 5 days, Fred sent 6 part-timers for 4 days. How much should each get paid if one worker does as much as 2 part-timers?

Ans: 3 workers, or 6 part-timers, for 5 days, will earn as much as 30 part-timers in one day; 6 part-timers for 4 days will earn as much as 24 part-timers in one day. So Ed will receive $300 and Fred $240.

16. In a warehouse which costs $2400 per month, Mark kept 20 cars for 3 weeks, and Noel, 15 trucks. How much should each pay if 3 trucks take up as much space as 4 cars?

Ans: One car takes up as much space as three quarters of a truck. So 20 cars take up as much space as 15 trucks. So they both have to pay one-half of $2400 or $1200 per month.

17. Alex and Don cleared a field using goats and sheep from their farms and earned $760. Alex used 12 goats and Don used 18 sheep. They cleared the field in 4 days. What is value of the daily labor of each goat and sheep, if 3 goats eat as much as 5 sheep?

Ans: Twelve goats, which is 4 times 3 goats, will do as much as 4 times 5, or 20 sheep; then 12 goats and 18 sheep will do as much as 20 sheep + 18 sheep, or 38 sheep; in one day they would earn $\frac{1}{4}$ of $760, or $190. So in one day a goat would earn $\$\frac{50}{6}$, a sheep $5.

18. Ron, Sam, and Tom rent a storage space for $63. Ron keeps 6 boxes, Sam puts in 18 boxes, and Tom 48 boxes. How much should each pay if Ron's box is as heavy as 2 of Sam's boxes and 4 times as much as Tom's boxes? **Ans:** Ron, $18; Sam, $27; Tom, $18.

19. Ed and Fred contract to paint a house for $600. Ed sent 2 workers and they work for 4 days, Fred sent 4 part-timers for 4 days. How much should each get paid if one worker does as much as 2 part-timers? **Ans:** $300 each.

20. In a warehouse which costs $3000 per month, Mark kept 5 cars for 8 weeks, and Noel, 15 trucks for 4 weeks. How much should each get paid if 3 trucks take up as much space as 4 cars?
Ans: One car takes up as much space as three quarters of a truck. So 15 trucks take up as much space as $\frac{15 \times 4}{3}$ = 20 cars. Mark used 5 times 8 or 40 units. Noel used 20 times 4 or 80 units. Mark pays 3000 times $\frac{40}{120}$ or $1000 and Noel pays $2000.

21. One-third of Max's budget plus $\frac{1}{4}$ of Robert's budget, equals $500. What is their budget if Max's budget is to Robert's as 9 is to 8?
Ans: If Max's is to Robert's as 9 is to 8, then $\frac{1}{3}$ of Max's is to $\frac{1}{4}$ of Robert's as 3 is to 2. So if we divide $500 into two parts which are to each other as 3 is to 2, the first part will be $\frac{1}{3}$ of Max's and the second part is $\frac{1}{4}$ of Robert's. So Max's budget is $900; Robert's, $800.

22. Nina and Vic each have a certain number of points. If Nina had 12 more, she would have twice as many as Vic, but if she had 34 more, she would have 4 times as many as Vic. How many does has each have?
Ans: The difference between having 12 more and 34 more is 22. So twice Vic's points equals 22, and Vic's points equals $\frac{1}{2}$ of 22, or 11. Nina's points equal 10.

23. If 3 machines can finish the work in 6 hours, in what time will the job be completed if 1 machine breaks when the work is one-third done?
Ans: Each machine will take 18 hours to do the work. In 2 hours, the 3 machines have done one-third the work. Now, there are only 2 machines working. They work at the rate of $\frac{1}{9}$ work per hour. The amount of work left is $\frac{2}{3}$. It will take 6 hours to finish.⌣

Lesson 37 – *Bigger and Equal Number*

A MAN gave $4 each to some kids. Had he given them $7 each, it would have taken $36 more. How many kids were there?

Ans: If he had given $3 more than before, then it would have taken $36 more. So there were as many kids as 3 is contained in 36, which is 12.

1. A teacher gave her students 2 tickets each, and had 26 tickets left. If she had given them each 4 tickets, there would have been none left. What is the number of students and tickets?

   Ans: Since she had none left after giving 4 tickets each, then that means that 26 tickets is equal to 2 tickets per student, which gives 13 students in the class. Now we find the number of tickets by multiplying 2 by 13, and then adding 26, or by multiplying 4 by 18.

2. A teacher gave her children 5 notebooks each and had 90 notebooks left. Had she given them 8 each, it would have taken all her notebooks. What is the number of children and the amount of notebooks the teacher has?

   Ans: Giving the children 3 extra used up all 90 leftover notebooks. That means there were 30 children. 8 times 30 is 240, the number of notebooks she had before.

3. Diana gave some kids 6 books each, and had 25 books left. Had she given them 8 books each, she would have had 3 books left. How many kids were there?

   Ans: To give them 2 books more apiece would have required 25 − 3, or 22 books more. So there were 11 kids.

4. Nadia bought some tomatoes, at the rate of 5 cents each. If she had paid 3 cents each, they would have cost 14 cents less. How many tomatoes did she buy?

   Ans: If 2 cents less had been paid for the tomatoes, they would have cost 14 cents less. So she bought 7 tomatoes.

5. A woman wishing to buy some wire, found that if she bought it at 10 cents a meter, she would be short 9 cents, but if she bought it at 7 cents a meter, she would have 9 cents left. How much money did she have?

   Ans: The difference in price is 18 cents; the difference in price for one yard is 3 cents, so she must have bought 6 meters; 6 meters, at 7 cents a meters, cost 42 cents, which, added to the 9 cents left, equals 51 cents.

6. A coach divided 28 balls between an equal number of boys and girls, giving 3 to each girl and 4 to each boy. What is the number of boys and girls?

   Ans: He gave to one girl and one boy 3 plus 4, or 7 balls. So there were as many of each as 7 is contained in 28, which is 4.

7. An artist bought an equal number of acrylic and oil paints for $81, paying $4 each for the acrylics, and $5 each for the oils. How many of each did he buy?

   Ans: For one acrylic and one oil he paid $9. So for $81 he bought 9 of each.

8. A boy spent $36 for an equal number of comic books and CDs, paying $4 for comic book, and $2 for each CD. How many of each did he purchase?

   Ans: For a book and a CD he spent $6. So for $36 he bought 6 of each.

9. Susan and Robert each caught a certain number of fish. If Susan had 10 more, she would have twice as many as Robert, but if she had 30 more, she would have 4 times as many as Robert. How many does has each have?

   Ans: The difference between having 10 more and 30 more is 20, and the difference between twice Robert's number and 4 times Robert's number is twice Robert's number. So twice Robert's number equals 20, or Robert has 10, and Susan's has 10.

10. A driver bought gas at 3\frac{1}{2}$ a gallon, and found he was $6 short of having enough money to pay for it. If the gas price was $2 a gallon, he would have had $9 left. How much money did he have?

    Ans: The difference in the whole cost is $15, the sum of $6 and $9; the difference in the cost per gallon is 1\frac{1}{2}$ which means he bought 10 gallons, and at $2 a gallon it would cost $20. So he had $20 + $9 = $29.

11. Jack wishes to buy a network cable. If he pays $3 a meter, he is short by $6 to pay for it, but if he pays $2.50 a meter, he will have $5 left. How many meters of cable does he need?

    Ans: The difference in the whole cost is $11; the difference per meters is $.50. So he bought 22 meters and had $60.

12. A woman gave $60 to some children; to each boy she gave $2, and $4 to each girl. How many were there of each, provided there were 3 times as many boys as girls?

Ans: If one boy receives $2, 3 boys will receive $6, and one girl and 3 boys will receive $4 + $6, or $10, and they all received $60. So there were as many times one girl and 3 boys as 10 is contained in 60, or 6. So there were 6 girls, and 6 times 3, or 18, boys.

13. Mike, Don, and Kevin picked snails from the garden for $60; Mike receives $$1\frac{1}{2}$$, Don $2, and Kevin $$2\frac{1}{2}$$ a day. How many days did they work, and how much did each receive?

Ans: They received for one day's work $6, and so were at work 10 days; Mike received $15, Don $20, and Kevin $25.

14. Simon and Hal agree to do a piece of work, Simon receiving $200 a day and Hal $300 a day; Simon works twice as many days as Hal, and they receive $7000. How many days did each work?

Ans: Simon working 2 days and Hal working one day, receive $700. Hal worked 10 days, and Simon 20.

15. Two girls had an equal sum of money. One bought some candies at 4 cents each and had 12 cents left. The other bought twice as many candies for 3 cents each and had 2 cents left. How much money did they each have?

Ans: It takes 2 extra cents to buy 2, 3 cent candies than one 4 cent candy. The second girl spent 10 more cents so the first girl must have bought 5 candies and spent 20 cents. The second girl got 10 candies and spent 30 cents. Each started with 32 cents.

16. A teacher divided 56 candies between an equal number of boys and girls, giving 4 to each girl and 3 to each boy. What is the number of boys and girls.

Ans: She gave to one girl and one boy 3 plus 4, or 7 candies. So there were as many of each as 7 is contained in 56, which is 8.

17. Jack and Jill agree to get water from the river, each receiving $10 a bucket. Jill works twice as hard and together they receive $300. How many buckets did each fetch? **Ans:** Jill 20, Jack 10 buckets. ⌣

Lesson 38 – *Rate Problems*

ALAN and Ben both need 10 days to do the same work alone. Guess how long it would take them if they work together? **Ans:** 5 days.

1. Rumple can do the work in 2 days. Bumble can also do it in 2 days. Guess how long would it take them together? **Ans:** One day.

2. Rumple takes 10 days and Bumble needs 20 days to do the work alone. Guess how long it would take them if they work together? **Ans:** $8\frac{2}{3}$ days. *The guess should be less than 10, the smaller of the two numbers.*

3. Speedy needs 6 days to do the work, Poky needs 9 days. Guess how long it would take them if they work together? **Ans:** $3\frac{3}{5}$ days.

4. Jokey needs 8 days to do the work. How much work does she do in 2 days? **Ans:** $\frac{1}{4}$.

5. Stickey needs 10 days to do the work. How much work does she do in 2 days? **Ans:** $\frac{1}{5}$.

6. Sleepy can do a piece of work in 4 days. What part of it can he do in one day? **Ans:** $\frac{1}{4}$.

7. Bookey can read an article in $\frac{1}{3}$ of a day. How much can he read in one day? **Ans:** One article.

8. Beady can write 10 pages in 4 days. How many pages can he write in a week?
   Ans: If he writes 10 pages in 4 days, then in one day he writes $\frac{10}{4}$ pages. In seven days he can write 7 times $\frac{10}{4}$ or, $17\frac{1}{2}$ pages.

9. Three workers can build a house in 102 days. How long would it take five workers to build the same house? **Ans:** $61\frac{1}{5}$ days.

10. A builder can build $\frac{3}{8}$ of a deck in a week. How long will it take him to build the whole deck? **Ans:** $2\frac{2}{3}$ weeks.

11. Red fairy can finish her visit to the flowers in $2\frac{1}{3}$ days. What part of it can she finish in one day? **Ans:** $\frac{3}{7}$.

12. If Jason and Jessica can mow $\frac{4}{9}$ of a field of grass in one day, how long will it take them to mow the whole field? **Ans:** $2\frac{1}{4}$ days.

13. Ang can do a piece of work in 3 days, and Chan can do the same work in 6 days. What part can each do in one day? **Ans:** Ang, $\frac{1}{3}$; Chan, $\frac{1}{6}$

14. If Chan can do a piece of work in 3 days, and Kevin in 6 days, how much can they together do in one day? **Ans:** $\frac{1}{2}$.

15. If Chan and Kevin can do $\frac{3}{6}$ of a piece of work in one day, how long it will take to do all of it? **Ans:** 2 days.

16. Digger can finish the project in 8 days, and Miner in 6 days. How many days would it take them both?
    Ans: In one day they can both do $\frac{1}{8} + \frac{1}{6} = \frac{7}{24}$ part of the work, and in $\frac{24}{7}$ or $3\frac{3}{7}$ days they can do all the work.

17. Andy can paint a house in 5 days, and Chan in 6 days. How many days will they take working together? **Ans:** $2\frac{8}{11}$ days.

18. Andy can make a model in 4 days, and Chan in 7 days. How many days will they take working together? **Ans:** $2\frac{6}{11}$ days.

19. Ed can draw a plan in 6 days, and Fred in 8 days. How long will it take them both to do it? **Ans:** $3\frac{3}{7}$ days.

20. Cathy can build a robot in 3 days, Carla in 4 days, and Kevin in 6 days. How many days will it take them to build it if they work together? **Ans:** $1\frac{1}{3}$ days.

21. A tank has two pipes. The tank can be filled by the first pipe in 12 hours, and in $\frac{2}{3}$ of the time by the second one. How long it will take to fill it with both pipes?
    Ans: $\frac{2}{3}$ of 12 equals 8; the first fills $\frac{1}{12}$ of it in one hour, the second $\frac{1}{8}$ of it in one hour. So both will fill $\frac{1}{12} + \frac{1}{8}$, or $\frac{5}{24}$, in one hour. Both will fill it in $\frac{24}{5}$ or $4\frac{4}{5}$ hours.

22. Sanjay can make a model city in 6 days, Sanjay and Baldev can make it in 4 days. In what time can Baldev make it alone?
    Ans: Sanjay can make $\frac{1}{6}$ of it, and Sanjay and Baldev together can make $\frac{1}{4}$ of it. If Baldev alone can make $\frac{1}{12}$ of it in one day. Baldev can complete it in 12 days.

23. Kamal, Baldev, and Kevin can move a house full of stuff in 3 days. If Kamal can do it in 6 days, and Baldev in 8 days, in what time can Kevin do it alone?
    Ans: In one day they can move $\frac{1}{3}$; Kamal can move $\frac{1}{6}$ in one day, Baldev $\frac{1}{8}$, and Kamal and Baldev $\frac{1}{6} + \frac{1}{8}$, or $\frac{7}{24}$ so Kevin in one day can move $\frac{1}{3} - \frac{7}{24}$, or $\frac{1}{24}$. So Kevin can move it all in 24 days.

24. A pound of tea lasted a woman and her son 3 months. It would have lasted the woman alone 4 months. How long would it last the son

alone?

Ans: In one month together they will drink $\frac{1}{3}$, and the woman will drink $\frac{1}{4}$. So the son alone will drink $\frac{1}{3} - \frac{1}{4}$, or $\frac{1}{12}$ in one month. So it will last the son 12 months.

25. Aster, Blue Bell and Carnation all do work at the same speed. If they work together they can finish the job in 4 days. How long does it take them if they each work alone?

    Ans: They can do $\frac{1}{4}$ of the work in one day and each can do $\frac{1}{3}$ of that in a day or, $\frac{1}{12}$. If it takes one day to do $\frac{1}{12}$, then it will take 12 days for one working alone.

26. If 6 bees can gather pollen from 12 gardens in a day, how much can 8 bees gather in the same time?

    Ans: One bee will be able to gather from 2 gardens in one day. 8 bees will be able to gather from 16 gardens in the same time.

27. If 10 men can lay 30 sections of pipe in a one day, how many sections of pipe can 12 men lay in the same time? **Ans:** One man can lay 3 sections in one day, then 12 men can lay 36 sections of pipe in one day.

28. Ash, Bose, and Darla can dig and plant a garden in 6 days, Ash and Bose in 8 days, and Bose alone in 12 days. How long would it take each working alone?

    Ans: In one day they can dig $\frac{1}{6}$ of the garden, and Ash and Bose can dig $\frac{1}{8}$ of the garden in the same time. So Darla can dig by herself $\frac{1}{6} - \frac{1}{8}$, or $\frac{1}{24}$, in one day; Bose can do $\frac{1}{12}$ in a day, and Ash and Darla can dig $\frac{1}{8}$ of the garden in one day. So Ash can do $\frac{1}{8} - \frac{1}{12}$, or $\frac{1}{24}$ in a day. So it will take Ash 24 days, Bose 12 days, Darla 24 days.

29. If 3 horses, or 4 donkeys, can do a piece of work in 12 days, in what time can 3 horses and 4 donkeys do it?

    Ans: If 3 horses or 4 donkeys can do the work in 12 days, 3 horses and 4 donkeys will do the work in $\frac{1}{2}$ of 12 days, or 6 days.

30. If Alex can do a piece of work in $\frac{1}{3}$ of a day, and Tina in $\frac{1}{4}$ of a day, how long will it take both to do it?

    Ans: Working together Alex and Tina can do $\frac{1}{3} + \frac{1}{4} = \frac{7}{12}$ of the work in one day. If in one day they do $\frac{7}{12}$, then to do the whole work will take them $\frac{12}{7}$ or $1\frac{5}{7}$ days.

31. Kyle can stack a cord of wood in $\frac{3}{4}$ of a day and Dina in $\frac{4}{5}$ of a day. In what time can they stack a cord working together?

Ans: Kyle can stack $\frac{4}{3}$ of a cord, and Dina can stack $\frac{5}{4}$ of a cord, so Kyle and Dina can stack $\frac{4}{3} + \frac{5}{4}$, or $\frac{31}{12}$, of a cord in one day. Working together, they can stack a cord in $\frac{12}{31}$ of a day.

32. Don can build a fence in 9 days, and Don and Jay, in 6 days. How long will it take Jay to make what is left after Don has built $\frac{2}{3}$ of it?
Ans: We find that Jay can build the fence in 18 days. So he can build $\frac{1}{3}$ of it, which is what remains after Don has built $\frac{2}{3}$ of it, in $\frac{1}{3}$ of 18 days, or 6 days.

33. Two big tractors, or 3 small tractors, can plant an acre in $\frac{1}{6}$ of a day. How long will it take 3 big tractors and 2 small tractors to plant it?
Ans: If 2 big tractors can plant an acre in $\frac{1}{6}$ of a day, they can plant 6 acres in one day. one big tractor can plant $\frac{1}{2}$ of 6 acres, or 3 acres, and 3 big tractors can plant 9 acres in a day. If 3 small tractors can plant 6 acres, one small tractor can plant 2 acres, and 2 small tractors can plant 4 acres. So 3 big tractors and 2 small tractors can plant 13 acres in a day, and they can plant one acre in $\frac{1}{13}$ of a day.

34. Shawn, Shanon, and Kyle can clean up the garage in 6 days, and Shawn and Shanon in 9 days. After the three had worked for 2 days, Kyle left. How long does it take Shawn and Shanon to finish the work?
Ans: Shawn, Shanon, and Kyle did $\frac{1}{3}$ of it in the first 2 days. So there remained $\frac{2}{3}$ of the work when Kyle left. Shawn and Shanon can do the whole work together in 9 days. So they can do $\frac{2}{3}$ of it in $\frac{2}{3}$ of 9 days, or 6 days.

35. Marie can make a dress in 6 days, Sally in $\frac{1}{2}$ of the time, and Nan in $\frac{2}{3}$ of the time. In what time can Marie and Sally finish it, after the three had worked $\frac{2}{3}$ of a day?
Ans: Sally can make it in 3 days, and Nan in 4 days. So the three will make $\frac{1}{6} + \frac{1}{4} + \frac{1}{3} = \frac{9}{12}$ of it in a day, and after working $\frac{2}{3}$ of a day, $\frac{1}{2}$ of it was still left. Marie and Sally can make $\frac{1}{6} + \frac{1}{3} = \frac{1}{2}$ of it in one day. So it will take one day for Marie and Sally to finish it.

36. Ang, Bill, and Kyle can build a detailed scale model of their school in $\frac{1}{4}$ of a month. Ang and Kyle in $\frac{1}{2}$ of a month, and Kyle in $\frac{2}{3}$ of a month. After they had all worked for one month, Ang left. In what time could Bill and Kyle finish it?
Ans: Ang, Bill, and Kyle, in one month, can build $\frac{1}{3}$ of the model, and Ang and Kyle can build $\frac{1}{6}$ of it, Kyle $\frac{1}{8}$. So Kyle and Bill can

build $\frac{1}{8} + \frac{1}{6}$, or $\frac{7}{24}$ of the model in one month, and to build $\frac{1}{24}$ of it will take them $\frac{1}{7}$ of a month; to build $\frac{16}{24}$, or what is left, will take them 16 times $\frac{1}{7}$, or $\frac{16}{7}$, or $\frac{23}{7}$ months.

37. A boy receives \$3 a day for properly brushing his teeth, and loses \$1 for each day he does not brush his teeth. At the end of 80 days, he receives \$50. How many days he did not brush his teeth?

Ans: Had he brushed all 30 days, he would have received 30 times \$3, or \$90. That means he lost \$90 minus \$50, which is \$40, by not brushing. Every day he was lazy he lost \$3, plus \$1, his penalty a total of, \$4. If in one day he loses \$4, to lose \$40 it will take as many days as 4 is contained in 40, which is 10. So he did not brush his teeth for 10 days.

38. A student agreed to work for \$20 a day, on condition that every day he did not come in he should forfeit \$5. How many days did he work, if at the end of 25 days he received \$300?

Ans: Had he worked all 25 days, he would have received \$500; he therefore lost \$200. Every day he did not work he lost \$25, therefore he was idle as many days as \$25 is contained in \$200, or 8 days. So he worked for $25 - 8 = 17$ days.

39. A boy agreed to carry 32 cups of coffee to the party guests. His mom told him that she would pay him 5 cents for every cup, on condition that for each one he spilled he would be fined 10 cents. He received \$1 when the party was over. Did he spill any coffee? How many times?

Ans: Had he carried them all safely, he would have received \$1.60, so he lost 60 cents; for each spilled cup he lost 5 cents + 10 cents, or 15 cents. So he spilled 4 cups out of 32.

40. Robert agreed to carry 50 cupcakes to school for 10 cent each, on condition that he should lose 25 cents for each one he ate on the way. He received 400 cents for taking the cupcakes to school. How many did he eat on the way?

Ans: Had he carried them all, he would have received 500 cents, so he lost 100 cents; for each one eaten he lost 25 cents, so he ate 4 cupcakes.

41. The contractor was hired to build a house on the condition that for every day he worked he would receive \$300, and for every day he did not work he would be fined \$100 for not working. At the end of 30 days he received \$7000. How many days did he work?

Ans: Had he worked the whole time, he would have received $9000. Instead he received $7000, so he lost $2000. Every day he did not work he lost $400, so he was idle 5 days, and worked 25 days.

42. The head of a catfish is 10 inches long and the tail is as long as the head, plus $\frac{1}{2}$ of the body and the body is as long as the head and tail both. What is the length of the fish.
Ans: The tail is equal to $= \frac{1}{2}$ of the body $+$ 10 inches. Add to that the head to get the length of the body, which is body $= \frac{1}{2}$ of the body $+$ 20 inches. So $\frac{1}{2}$ the body is equal to 20 inches. The fish is 50 inches long.

43. The head of a shark is 8 inches long, the tail is as long as the head, plus $\frac{1}{2}$ the length of the body. The body is as long as the head and tail. What is the length of the shark?
Ans: $\frac{1}{2}$ of the body $+$ 8 inches $=$ the tail; adding the length of the head, $\frac{1}{2}$ of the body $+16$ inches $=$ the length of the body, so $\frac{1}{2}$ of the length of the body is 16 inches, the length of the body is 32 inches, and the shark is 64 inches long.

44. The head of a perch is 4 inches long, the tail is as long as the head plus $\frac{1}{2}$ the length of the body. The body is as long as the head and tail. What is the length of the perch?
Ans: $\frac{1}{2}$ of the body, $+$ 4 inches $=$ the tail. So $\frac{1}{2}$ of the body, $+$ 8 inches $=$ the length of the body; $\frac{1}{2}$ of the length of the body is 8 inches, the length of the body is 16 inches, and the perch is 32 inches long.

45. The tail of a pike weighs 3 ounces, the head weighs as much as the tail, plus $\frac{1}{4}$ of the weight of the body, and the body weighs twice as much as the head and tail. What is the weight of the fish?
Ans: $\frac{1}{4}$ of the body, $+$ 3 ounces $=$ the head; $\frac{1}{4}$ of the body, $+$ 6 ounces $= \frac{1}{2}$ of the body, so $\frac{1}{4}$ of the weight of the body $=$ 6 ounces The body weighs 24 ounces and the pike weighs 36 ounces.

46. The head of a trout weighs 2 pounds. The tail weighs 2 pounds more than the head plus $\frac{1}{3}$ of the body, and the body weighs as much as the head and tail together. What is the weight of the fish?
Ans: Weight of the tail $=$ weight of the body minus 2 pounds. $\frac{1}{3}$ of the body $+$ 4 pounds also equals the weight of the tail. The So $\frac{2}{3}$ of the weight of the body $=$ 6 pounds. So the tail weighs 7 pounds, the body 9 pounds, and the fish, 18 pounds.

47. Wormy receives $250 a day for his work, and pays $50 a day for his expenses; at the end of 40 days he has saved $5000. How many days did he work, and how many days he did not work?

Ans: He can save $200 each day, and in 40 days he can save $8000, so he loses $8000 − $5000 = $3000. So each day he does not work he loses $250, so to lose $3000, it would take 12 days. She he worked for 28 days and rested for 12 days.

48. Squirmy receives $80 a day (5-day week) for his work, and pays $350 a week for expenses. At the end of some time he has saved $1250. What is the number of days he worked?

Ans: He can save $50 in a week, so it took him 25 weeks to save $1250.

49. Soupy agreed to work for a certain time for $6000, on condition that for each day he was out he should forfeit $200; at the end of the time he received $3000. How many days did he work, supposing he received $200 a day for his work?

Ans: If he received $200 a day, and agreed to work for $6000, he agreed to work as many days as $200 is contained in $6000, or 30. For every day he was out, he lost $200, his wages plus the penalty. He was off as many days as $400 is contained in 3000 or, $7\frac{1}{2}$ days.

Lesson 39 – *Combination Problems*

FORTY cups of lemonade contain 2 pounds of sugar. How much fresh water must be added to these 40 pounds so that 6 pounds of the new mixture contains $\frac{1}{5}$ pounds of sugar?

Ans: If 6 pounds of the lemonade contains $\frac{1}{5}$ pounds of sugar, then to contain one pounds of sugar, there must be 5 times 6 or 30 pounds of the lemonade. To contain 2 pounds of sugar, there must be 2 times 30 pounds, or 60 pounds of the lemonade. But we have 40 pounds that contain 2 pounds of sugar. We add 20 pounds of water to make it 60 pounds. The amount of sugar did not change.

1. If 50 pounds of sea-water contains 2 pounds of salt, how much fresh water must be added to these 50 pounds so that 10 pounds of the new mixture contains $\frac{1}{3}$ of a pound of salt?
   Ans: To contain one pound of salt there must be 30 pounds of the mixture, and to contain 2 pounds of salt there must be 60 pounds of the mixture. So add 10 pounds of water.

2. In a mixture of silver and copper weighing 60 ounces, there are 4 ounces of copper. How much silver must be added so that there would be $\frac{1}{3}$ ounces of copper in 6 ounces of the mixture?
   Ans: There will be one ounce of copper in the mixture. So it will require 72 ounces of the mixture to contain 4 ounces of copper; $72 - 60 = 12$ ounces, the quantity of silver that must be added.

3. A car dealer has 100 vehicles, consisting of trucks and cars, and there are 40 cars. How many trucks must she sell so that there are 5 trucks to every 4 cars?
   Ans: 40 cars is 10 times 4 cars; therefore there will be 10 times 5 trucks, or 50 trucks; 50 trucks + 40 cars = 90 vehicles. So she must sell 10 trucks.

4. In a school of 80 students there are 32 girls. How many boys must have left now that there are 5 boys to 4 girls?
   Ans: 32 girls is 8 times 4 girls, so there will be 8 times 5 boys, or 40 boys; 40 boys + 32 girls = 72 students. So 8 boys left.

5. If 62 pounds of sea-water contains 2 pounds of salt, how much salt must be added so that 42 pounds of sea-water will contain 2 pounds of salt?
   Ans: 60 pounds of fresh water is mixed with 2 pounds of salt. 40

pounds of fresh water is mixed with 2 pounds of salt. If 40 pounds contains 2 pounds of salt, to keep the same ratio between salt and water, 60 pounds must have 3 pounds of salt. So we need to add one pound of salt to the first mixture.

6. If 50 pounds of sea-water contains 2 pounds of salt, how much salt must I add to these 50 pounds so that 40 pounds of the new mixture contains 4 pounds of salt?

   Ans: If 36 pounds are mixed with 4 pounds, 48 pounds must be mixed with $5\frac{1}{3}$ pounds. So the added amount is: $5\frac{1}{3}$ pounds $-$ 2 pounds, or $3\frac{1}{3}$ pounds.

7. In a mixture of gold and silver, weighing 50 ounces, there are 3 ounces of silver. How much gold must be added so that there will be $\frac{1}{4}$ ounces of silver to 5 ounces of gold?

   Ans: If there is $\frac{1}{4}$ ounces of silver to 5 ounces of gold, to one ounce of silver there will be 20 ounces of gold, and to 3 ounces of silver there will be 60 ounces of gold; in the mixture there are $50 - 3$, or 47 ounces of gold. So $60 - 47$, or 13 ounces of gold must be added.

8. In a school with 60 students, 20 are girls. How many boys must leave the school so that there will be 10 girls to every 25 students?

   Ans: If there were 10 girls to 25 students, there will be 20 girls to 50 students, or 20 out of 70. The number of student right now is 80 with 20 girls. So 10 boys must leave to create the 20 to 50 ratio.

9. Arslan has $200 in gold and silver, and for every $60 of gold he has $40 of silver. How much gold must be added so that there is $90 of gold for $30 of silver?

   Ans: Since the amount of gold is to silver as 6 is to 4, and there are $200 in all, we find that there are $120 of gold and $60 of silver. After the additions, since 3 times the silver equals the gold, 3 times $80, or $240, is the gold, and $240 - $120, or $120, equals the amount added.

10. A coin collector has 40 coins, consisting of copper and silver, and for every 7 coins of copper there are 3 of silver. How many silver coins she buy so that for every 4 copper coins there are 2 silver coins?

    Ans: $\frac{7}{10}$ of $40 - 28$, the copper coins; $\frac{3}{10}$ of $40 = 12$, the silver coins; $\frac{1}{2}$ of $28 = 14$, the silver after addition. So $14 - 12 = 2$, the number to be added.

11. An art collector has 100 pieces of art, consisting of sculptures and paintings. He has 2 sculptures for every 3 paintings. How many sculptures must he sell so that he has 2 sculptures to every 6 paintings?

Ans: $\frac{2}{5}$ of 100 = 40, the number of sculptures; $\frac{3}{5}$ of 100 = 60, the number of paintings; $\frac{1}{3}$ of 60 = 20, the number of sculptures after selling. So 40 − 20, or 20, is the number he must sell.

12. There are 50 students in a certain school, consisting of girls and boys. The ratio of boys to girls is 8 boys to 2 girls. How many boys must leave the school so that there will be 6 boys to 2 girls?

Ans: $\frac{8}{10}$ of 50 = 40, the boys; $\frac{2}{10}$ of 50 = 10, the girls; 3 times 10 = 30, the number of boys left. So 40 − 30 = 10, the number of boys that must leave school.

13. A man spends 60 cents for an equal number of apples and pears, paying 3 cents each for apples and 2 cents each for pears. How many pears must he give away so that those remaining may be to apples as 2 is to 3?

Ans: There were as many of each at first as 3 + 2, or 5, is contained in 60, or 12; $\frac{2}{3}$ of 12 = 8, the number of pears after selling; 12 − 8 = 4, the number of pears he must give away.

14. A tree 90 meters in length fell during a storm and broke into two parts such that $\frac{1}{4}$ of the shorter part equaled $\frac{1}{5}$ of the longer. How much must be cut from the longer part of the tree so that $\frac{1}{4}$ of it may equal $\frac{1}{5}$ of the shorter part?

Ans: The two parts are 40 and 50, then after cutting a piece from the longer, $\frac{1}{5}$ of 40, or 8 feet = $\frac{1}{4}$ of the rest, so the rest is 32 feet. So there must be 50 − 32, or 18 feet, cut from the longer.

15. A boy bought 24 red and green tickets, and $\frac{2}{3}$ of the number of red tickets equals $\frac{2}{5}$ of the number of green tickets. How many more red tickets must be purchased, so that $\frac{3}{5}$ of the number of red tickets may equal $\frac{2}{3}$ of the number of green tickets?

Ans: $\frac{5}{8}$ of 24 = 15, the number of green tickets; $\frac{3}{8}$ of 24 = 9, the number of red tickets; $\frac{5}{3}$ of 15 = 25, the number after the purchase. So 25 − 9, or 16, is the number of red tickets to be purchased.

16. A man rode his bike downhill at the speed of 10 miles per hour, then rode his bike back up the hill at the speed of 5 miles per hour. He was gone for 6 hours. How far did he go?

Ans: If he goes 10 miles an hour, he will go one mile in $\frac{1}{10}$ of an hour. And if he returns at 5 miles an hour, he will return one mile in $\frac{1}{5}$ of an hour. So to go and return one mile up the hill and down, it takes him $\frac{1}{5} + \frac{1}{10}$ or, $\frac{3}{10}$ of an hour. Therefore, in 6 hours he can go and return as many miles as $\frac{3}{10}$ is contained in 6, or 20 miles. So he rode his bike 20 miles from where he started.

17. How far can a person ride a bike at the rate of 9 miles per hour, provided he is gone only 10 hours, and he rides back at the rate of 6 miles an hour?
    Ans: To go and return a mile takes $\frac{1}{9} + \frac{1}{6}$, or $\frac{5}{18}$ of an hour. So in 10 hours he can go and return $10 \div \frac{5}{18}$ or 36 miles.

18. How many miles will I sail in a boat, going at the rate of 15 miles an hour, provided I am gone only 9 hours, and return at the rate of 12 miles an hour?
    Ans: To go and return one mile takes $\frac{1}{15} + \frac{1}{12}$, or $\frac{3}{20}$ of an hour. So in 9 hours I can go $9 \div \frac{3}{20}$, or 60 miles.

19. A steamboat, which sails in still water at 12 miles an hour, goes down a river whose current is 4 miles an hour, and is gone 6 hours. How far did it go?
    Ans: The rate going is $12 + 4$, or 16 miles an hour; the rate returning is $12 - 4$, or 8 miles; $\frac{1}{16} + \frac{1}{8} = \frac{3}{16}$ of an hour. So in 6 hours it went 32 miles.

20. A boat sails down the river at 10 miles an hour with a down river current of 2 miles an hour. How far can it go provided it is gone only 5 hours?
    Ans: The rate going is 12 miles per hour; the rate returning is 8 miles; $\frac{1}{12} + \frac{1}{8} = \frac{5}{24}$ of an hour. So in 5 hours it went 24 miles.

21. Eight people rent a bus to ride to Lancaster, but by taking 4 more people the expense for each is reduced by $\frac{3}{4}$ of a dollar. What do they pay for the bus?
    Ans: If the expense of one is reduced by $\$\frac{3}{4}$, the expense of 8 is reduced 8 times $\$\frac{3}{4}$, or $6, which the 4 new people pay. 4 people pay $6 then 12 people will pay 3 times $6, or $18.

22. Ten tourists hire a coach for a certain sum of money, but by taking in 5 more persons, the expense of each is reduced by 5 of a dollar. What did the coach cost them?
    Ans: If the expense of one tourist is diminished 5 dollars, the expense

of 10 tourists is diminished $50. So 5 tourists pay $50, one tourist pays 10, and 15 would pay $150.

23. Twenty people hire a boat for sailing, but before they start, 12 in the party decide not to go. Because of this, the expense for those who go is increased by $3 per person. What did they pay for the boat?

    Ans: The expense of 8 persons is increased 8 × 3, or $24. So 12 persons pay $24, and 12 + 8, or 20 persons, would pay $40 for the boat.

24. Suppose that a contractor uses an acre of land for 4 houses, and leaves one acre of land for roads for every 2 houses. How many houses can he build on 15 acres?

    Ans: If for every 4 houses, he uses one acre for the lots, then for one house he uses $\frac{1}{4}$ of an acre. And if for every 2 houses he allows one acre for roads, then for one house he uses an extra $\frac{1}{2}$ an acre. So one house requires $\frac{1}{2} + \frac{1}{4}$, or $\frac{3}{4}$ of an acre, and on 15 acres he could build as many houses as $\frac{3}{4}$ is contained in 15, or 20 houses.

25. Suppose that for every 3 houses, a builder uses one acre of land, and allows one acre of land for roads for every 2 houses. How many houses can he build on 20 acres?

    Ans: For one house he uses $\frac{1}{3}$ of an acre for building and leaves $\frac{1}{2}$ an acre for roads of , so every house requires $\frac{1}{3} + \frac{1}{2}$, or $\frac{5}{6}$, of an acre, and on 20 acres he can build as many houses as $\frac{5}{6}$ is contained in 20, or 24.

26. Suppose that for every 4 houses a builder builds he should use one acre of land and also allow one acre for roads for every 3 houses. How many houses could he build on 140 acres?

    Ans: For every house he allows $\frac{1}{4} + \frac{1}{3}$, or $\frac{7}{12}$ of an acre; on 140 acres he can keep as many houses as $\frac{7}{12}$ is contained in 140, or 240.

27. If a builder uses one acre of land for every 4 houses and allows one acre of roads for every 5 houses, how many acres will it require to build 60 houses?

    Ans: She allows $\frac{1}{4} + \frac{1}{5}$, or $\frac{9}{20}$ of an acre for each house. So 60 houses will require 60 times $\frac{9}{20}$, or 27 acres.

28. A contractor builds 72 houses on her land. For every 4 houses she uses one acre and keeps one acre for roads for every 6 houses. How many acres is her land?

Ans: She allows for each house $\frac{1}{4} + \frac{1}{6}$, or $\frac{5}{12}$ of an acre. So 72 houses will require 30 acres.

29. If a builder builds 40 houses on 18 acres of land, and allows one acre for every 4 houses, how many acres for roads are to be used per house?
Ans: He uses 10 acres for 40 houses, and has $18 - 10$, or 8 acres left for the roads for 40 houses. So for 40 houses would have for roads $\frac{1}{10}$ of 8 acres, or $\frac{4}{5}$ of an acre per house.

30. A builder builds 48 houses on 14 acres of land. He reserves one acre of land for every 6 houses. How many acres will he use for every 16 houses?
Ans: 48 houses will require 8 acres of roads, and 6 acres will be left for lots. So for 16 houses, or $\frac{1}{3}$ of 48, he will use $\frac{1}{3}$ of 6 acres, or 2 acres.

31. A party of 15 people meet for dinner at a hotel, but before paying the bill, 5 of the party leave. Now each person's bill is increased by $10. What was the bill?
Ans: If each person's bill is increased by $10, then 10 persons left will pay 10×10, or $100 extra. This extra money should have been paid by the 5 persons who left without paying, or $\frac{100}{5} = \$20$ per person. The total bill was $300.

32. Diana gave Lily 24 clips, which is $\frac{3}{5}$ of what Lily already had, and $\frac{3}{5}$ of what Diana had left. How many clips did each have at first?
Ans: If 24 is $\frac{3}{5}$ of Lily's clips, then Lily had 40. If 24 is $\frac{3}{5}$ of what Diana had left, then Diana had 40 left so she had 64 at first.

33. What is the height of a pole with a 10-meter-long shadow if at the same time a pole 10 meters tall casts a shadow $2\frac{1}{2}$ meters long?
Ans: If a shadow, $2\frac{1}{2}$ feet long requires a pole 10 feet long, then to cast a shadow 10 feet long, or 4 times $2\frac{1}{2}$ feet, will need a pole of length 4×10 feet, or 40 feet.

34. A man lost $\frac{4}{5}$ of his money, and then gained $\frac{3}{4}$ as much as he lost, leaving him with $200. How much money did he have at first?
Ans: He had left $\frac{1}{5}$, and gained $\frac{3}{4}$ of $\frac{4}{5}$, or $\frac{3}{5}$. He then had $\frac{4}{5}$, which equals $200. So at first he had. $250.

35. A man lost $\frac{3}{5}$ of his money, and then gained $\frac{1}{3}$ as much as he lost, leaving him $60. How much money did he have at first? **Ans:** $80.

36. A merchant exchanged 7 machines for 6 tractors. How much were the machines worth if 5 tractors cost $3500?

Ans: If 5 tractors cost $3500, then one tractor is worth $700 and 6 tractors are worth $4200, which is the same as what 6 machines cost.

37. A store had a sale and sold $\frac{1}{2}$ of their chairs and 10 desks. After the sale, they found that they still had 15 chairs and $\frac{1}{3}$ of the desks. How many of each did the store own?

Ans: If the store sold $\frac{1}{2}$ of their chairs, $\frac{1}{2}$ of the chairs are left, which equals 15. So it owned 2 times 15, or 30 chairs. If $\frac{1}{3}$ of the desks remained, they sold $\frac{2}{3}$ of them, which equals 10. So they had at first 15 desks.

38. Stephen lost 12 of his paint brushes, then found $\frac{1}{2}$ as much as he lost, and then had $\frac{3}{4}$ as much as he had at first. How much did he have at first?

Ans: He found 6 brushes, so he had $12 - 6$, or 6 brushes fewer than he had at first; but he had only $\frac{3}{4}$ as much as at first, so 6 brushes equals $\frac{1}{4}$ of what he had at first; therefore he had 24 brushes at first.

39. Maria gave some money to a charity, and found that she had $10 left, which is $\frac{1}{5}$ of what she had at first. How much did she give away?

Ans: $10 is $\frac{1}{5}$ of what she had, so she had $50. She had at first $50, and then had left $10. So she gave away $50 - 10$, or $40.

40. To $\frac{1}{2}$ the cost of Bubble's scooter you add $80, the sum will equal $\frac{2}{3}$ of the cost. What is the cost of his scooter.

Ans: $80 equals the difference between $\frac{2}{3}$ and $\frac{1}{2}$, or $\frac{1}{6}$ of the cost. So the cost is $480.

41. Zack paid $80 for some barrels of monkeys. $\frac{3}{8}$ of $80 is 3 times the number of barrels he purchased. What was the price of a barrel?

Ans: $\frac{3}{8}$ of 80, or 30, is 3 times the number of barrels. So there were 10 barrels, at $8 a barrel.

42. Phil received 10 cookies, then ate $\frac{2}{5}$ of what he received, and then had $\frac{3}{2}$ as many as he had at first. How much did he have at first?

Ans: $\frac{3}{8}$ of 10, or 6, equals $\frac{1}{2}$ of what he had at first. So he had 12 cookies.

43. Shawn has 8 coins and Sevi has 7, and 6 times what they both have is equal to the number that Ali has, increased by 10. How many coins does Ali have?

Ans: $8 + 7 = 15$; 6 times 15, or 90, equals Ali's number $+ 10$. So Ali has 80 coins.

44. Andrew can do as much work in 2 days as Bill can in one day or Kyle in 6 days. In how many days can Bill do as much as Kyle can in 18 days?

    Ans: If Andrew can do as much work in 2 days as Bill can in 4 days, or Kyle in 6 days, then Bill can do as much in 4 days as Kyle can in 6 days, and Bill can do as much in 3 times 4 days, or 12 days, as Kyle can in 18 days, which is 3 times 6 days.

45. Sophia bought a number of meters of silk at the rate of 3 meters for $10, and as much more at the rate of 4 meters for $10, and sold it all at the rate of 8 meters for $30 and making a profit of $50 on all. How many meters did she buy?

    Ans: If 3 meters cost $10, then 1 meter cost $\frac{10}{3}$. If 4 meters cost $10, then one meter cost $\frac{10}{4}$. So 2 meters cost $\frac{10}{3} + \frac{10}{4} = \frac{70}{12}$. She sold 8 meters for $30, so she sold 2 meters of both kinds for $\frac{90}{12}$, and therefore gained $\frac{20}{12}$, or $\frac{10}{6}$, on 2 meters. So to gain $50 she must sell 60 meters.

46. A boy bought some apples at the rate of 4 for one dollar, and as many more at the rate of 5 for one dollar. He sold them all at the rate of 10 for $2, losing $5. How many of each kind did he buy?

    Ans: One apple cost $\frac{1}{4}$ dollar, the other cost $\frac{1}{5}$ of a dollar. So 2 apples cost $\frac{1}{4} + \frac{1}{5}$, or $\frac{9}{20}$ of a dollar. He sold one for $\frac{1}{5}$ dollar, or 2 for $\frac{2}{5}$ dollar. So on one of each kind he lost $\frac{9}{20} - \frac{2}{5}$, or $\frac{1}{20}$, and to lose $5 it would require 100 of each kind.

47. A store owner bought some toys at $2 apiece, and twice as many balls at $4 apiece, and then sold them all at $3 each, losing $10. How many of each kind did he buy?

    Ans: As often as he paid $2 for one toy he paid $8 for 2 balls, so one toy and 2 balls cost $10, and 3 were sold for $9. So he lost on one toy and 2 balls $1, and to lose $10 he must sell 10 times one toys and 2 balls, or 10 toys and 20 balls.

48. A woman bought some ribbon at $5 a meter, and as much more at the rate of $7 a meter, and sold it all at $8 a meter. How much did she buy if she made a profit of $20?

    Ans: She gained $2 on one meter. So, to gain $20, there were $\frac{20}{2}$, or 10 meters.

49. Albert bought some pineapples at $2 each and as many more at $4 each, and sold them at the rate of 2 for $8, gaining $12. What is the number he bought?

Ans: He paid $6 for 2 pineapples, and sold 2 for $8, and thus gained $2 on 2 pineapples. So to gain $12, which is 6 times $2, he sold 6 times 2 pineapples, or 12 pineapples.

50. Ian bought some tea at 4 francs a pound, and as much more at 8 francs, and sold it all for 7 francs a pound, gaining 40 francs. How many pounds of each kind did he have?

Ans: The average price per pound is 6 francs. So the gain on each pound is one franc, therefore he must have bought 40 pounds of tea, or 20 of each. ⌣

Lesson 40 – *Mixed Problems*

A MAN has 2 cooking pots, but only one cover for both. The first pot weighs 12 ounces. If the first pot is covered, it will weigh twice as much as the second, but if the second pot is covered it will weigh 3 times as much as the first. What is the weight of the second pot and the cover?

Ans: By the last condition of the problem, 3 times 12, or 36 ounces equals the weight of the second pot and the cover. Added to 12 ounces, the weight of the first pot plus the weight of the second pot and its cover equals 48 ounces.

By the second condition of the problem, twice the weight of the second pot equals the weight of the first pot and cover, which added to the weight of the second pot, equals 3 times the weight of the second pot, which equals the weight of all, or 48 ounces. The second pot weighs one-third of 48 or 16 ounces.

1. A man has two cups, but only one cover for both. The first cup weighs 10 ounces. If the first cup is covered, it will weigh 3 times as much as the second, but if the second cup is covered, it will weigh 5 times as much as the first. What is the weight of the second cup and the cover.
   Ans: Weight of second cup and cover = 50 ounces; 60 ounces = the weight of all; 4 times the weight of the second = 60 ounces. So 15 ounces = the weight of the second cup, and 35 ounces is the weight of the cover.

2. A woman bought two pendants, a gold one and a silver one, and a chain. The chain and gold pendant cost 4 times as much as the silver pendant. The chain and the silver pendant cost twice as much as the gold pendant. What is the value of each, if the silver pendant is worth $30?
   Ans: Cost of gold pendant and chain = $120; $150 = cost of all; 3 times the cost of the gold pendant = $150; gold pendant costs $50, and the chain $70.

3. A trainer bought a horse, colt, and saddle. If the horse is saddled, it will be worth 5 times as much as the colt, but if the colt is saddled, it will be worth $\frac{1}{2}$ as much as the horse. What is the value of the horse and the saddle, supposing the colt is worth $50?
   Ans: By the first condition, $5 \times 50 = \$250$ equals the cost of the horse and saddle; $250 + $50 = $300, the cost of all; by the second

condition, $\frac{3}{2}$ of the cost of the horse = \$300. So the horse cost \$200, the saddle \$50.

4. The head of a fish is 10 inches long; 7 times the length of the head equals the length of its body and tail, and 3 times the length of the tail equals the length of the head and body. What is the length of the tail and body respectively.
Ans: Length of the body and tail = 10 × 7 = 70 inches 70 inches + 10 inches = 80 inches, the length of the fish; 4 times the length of tail = 80 inches; the tail = 20 inches, the body 50 inches.

5. Andrew went to his brother and borrowed as much money as he had, then spent \$4. He then went to his other brother and did the same, and then had \$4 left. How much money did he have at first?
Solution one—After borrowing as much as he had at first, he had twice his money, and then spending \$4, he had twice his money minus \$4; after borrowing as much as he had the second time, he had 4 times his money at first, minus \$8, and after spending \$4, he had 4 times his money minus \$12, which equals \$4. So, at first, he had \$4.
Solution two—Since he had \$4 left, before spending \$4 at the second store, he had \$4 + \$4, or \$8; but $\frac{1}{2}$ of this he borrowed, so he had $\frac{1}{2}$ of \$8, or \$4, when he left the first store; but he had spent \$4 there, so, before spending these \$4, he had 4 + 4, or \$8; but one-half of this he had just borrowed, so, at first, he had $\frac{1}{2}$ of \$8, or \$4.

6. A girl went to her mom, borrowed as much money as she had, and spent \$8; she then went to her dad, borrowed as much as she had, and spent \$12, and then had no money left. How much money did she have at first?
Ans: When she left mom she had twice her money minus \$8. When she left dad she had 4 times her money minus \$28; since nothing remained, $\frac{1}{4}$ of \$28, or \$7 = her money at first.

7. Ronnie went to a bank, borrowed as much money as he had, and spent \$800. He then went to a second and a third bank borrowed same as what he had and each time spent \$800, and then had no money left. How much did he have at first?

8. A boy bought a hammer for \$30, which was $\frac{1}{3}$ of what he paid for wood and nails. $\frac{1}{5}$ of what he paid for the wood and nails equals what the nails cost. How much did the wood and nails cost?

Ans: The wood and nails cost $90; the cost of the nails = $120; the nails cost $18.

9. Reynolds went to a hotel, cashed a check for as much money as he had, and spent $20. He then went to a second and third hotel, did the same, and had $60 left. How much money did he have at first if what was left was equal to 8 times his money minus $140?
   Ans: When he left the third hotel he had 8 times his money minus $140, which equals $60. So 8 times his money = $200, his money = $25.

10. Andre went to a bank, borrowed $1000, and then spent $800; doing the same at a second and third bank, he found he had doubled his money. How much money did he have at first?
    Ans: At each bank he borrowed $200 more than he spent. So from 3 banks he would borrow 3 times $200, or $600 more than he spent, and since this doubled his money, he had at first $600.

11. James went to a store, borrowed $10 from Jane, and then spent $12. He did the same with money from his brother and sister, and then had no money left. How much money did he have at first?
    Ans: After he got money from his brother and sister, he had his money minus $6. And since no money remained, he had $6 at first.

12. A man spent $5 for socks, which was $\frac{1}{5}$ of what he paid for a tie and shoes, and twice what he paid for the tie equals what he paid for shoes and socks. How many of each kind did he buy, provided the socks cost $\frac{1}{2}$ a dollar, the tie $1, and the shoes $3 each? **Ans:** 10 socks, 10 ties and 5 shoes.

13. Victor can do as much in 6 days as Bob can in 2 days, and Bob can do as much in 5 days as Carlo can in 15 days. In how many days can Victor do as much as Carlo can in 4 days?
    Ans: Victor can do as much in 3 days as Bob in one day, and Bob can do as much in one day as Carlo in 3 days. So Victor can do as much in 4 days as Carlo can in 4 days.

14. Amie can do 3 times as much in a day as Bunny, and Bunny can do twice as much as Carol. In how many days can Amie do as much as Carol can in 4 days?
    Ans: If Amie can do 3 times as much in a day as Bunny, and Bunny can do twice as much in a day as Carol, then Amie can do 3 times twice as much as Carol, or 6 times as much as Carol. So Amie can

do as much in one day as Carol does in 6 days, and Amie can do as much in $\frac{1}{6}$ of a day as Carol can in one day, and a can do as much in $\frac{4}{6}$, or $\frac{2}{3}$ of a day, as Carol can in one days.

15. A store has 102 pairs of pants in its inventory, consisting of jeans, slacks and sweats. It has $\frac{3}{4}$ as many jeans as slacks, and $\frac{4}{5}$ as many slacks as sweats. How many of each does the store have?

   Ans: If there are $\frac{3}{4}$ as many jeans as slacks, $\frac{3}{4}$ of the number of sweats equals the number of jeans. And if there are $\frac{4}{5}$ as many slacks as sweats, $\frac{4}{5}$ of the number of sweats equals the number of slacks, so $\frac{51}{20}$ of the number of sweats equals 102. So there were 40 jeans, 30 slacks, and 32 sweats.

16. Diana and Annie collected avocados that fell on the ground. One-half of Diana's avocados equals the number Annie collected, and $\frac{1}{2}$ of Annie's equals Emma's. Altogether they have 28 avocados. How many has each?

   Ans: Diana has 4 times as many as Emma, and Annie twice as many. So 7 times Emma's equals 28, Emma has 4, Annie 8, and Diana 16.

17. Alan earned $\frac{2}{3}$ times as much as Bobbie, and Bobbie earned $\frac{3}{4}$ times as much as Cathy, and they altogether they earned $108. How much did each of them earn?

   Ans: Alan earned $\frac{2}{3}$ of $\frac{3}{4}$, or $\frac{2}{4}$ as much as Cathy; then $\frac{2}{4}$ of what Cathy earned, or what Alan earned $+ \frac{3}{4}$ of what Cathy earned, or what Bobbie earned, $+ \frac{4}{4}$ of what Cathy earned, equals $\frac{9}{4}$ of what Cathy earned, which is $108. So Alan earned $24; Bobbie, $36; Cathy, $48.

18. Reuben bought 9 roses worth 4 dollars apiece. Jackson bought 8 peonies worth 3 dollars apiece all of which he gave to Reuben for a part of his roses. How many roses does Reuben have left?

   Ans: The peonies were worth 24 dollars, for which you could get 6 roses at 4 dollars each. So there remained $9 - 6 = 3$ roses.

19. A teacher had 50 students in one classroom, and $\frac{4}{5}$ of that number in an another classroom. Then $\frac{1}{2}$ of the students in each classroom went into the other. How many are in each classroom?

   Ans: He had 40 students in the second class, One-half of 20 from second class went into the first. 25 from the first class went into the second. So each class had 45 students.

20. A man sold his car and bike for \$2000. $\frac{4}{5}$ of this is 8 times what his bike cost and the car cost 10 times as much as the bike. What is the cost of each?

Ans: $\frac{4}{5}$ of \$2000 is \$1600, which was 8 times the cost of the bike. So the bike cost \$200, and the car cost \$1800.

21. Andrea had 30 bunnies, and Lucy gave her 10 more; then Andrea gave her best friend 7, her other best friend a certain number, and now she has 13 left. How many did she give her second best friend?

Ans: $30 + 10 = 40$, the number she had; $40 - 7 = 33$; $33 - 13 = 20$, the number she gave her second best friend.

22. Adrian and Bob each had 30 candies. Adrian gave Bob 10 of his, and Bob gave Adrian 6 of his, and then ate a certain number, so that Adrian had 12 more than Bob. How many did Bob eat?

Ans: After Adrian gave Bob 10 and Bob gave Adrian 6, Adrian had 4 less and Bob 4 more than at first. So Adrian had 26 and Bob 34; then after Bob ate a certain number, $26 - 12$, or 14, remains. So Bob ate $34 - 14$, or 20 candies.

23. Adrian and Fysal each had 40 dollars; Adrian gave Fysal 10 of his, and Fysal gave Adrian twice as many of his, and then, spending a certain number, had twice as many as Adrian gave him. How many did he spend?

Ans: After Adrian gave Fysal 10 dollars and Fysal gave Adrian 20, Adrian had 10 more and Fysal had 10 less than at first. So Adrian had 50 and Fysal had 30; then after Fysal spent a certain number he had twice 10, or 20. So he spent $30 - 20$, or 10 dollars.

24. Two times a certain number, $+ 10$, equals 3 times the sum obtained by increasing the number by 2. What is the number?

Ans: Two times a number, $+ 10$, equals 3 times the number $+ 2$, which is 3 times the number, $+ 6$; then 3 times the number, $- 2$ times the number, or once the number, equals $10 - 6$, or 4.

25. A car and a truck need a quantity of gas in 3 weeks. How long will it last each, provided the car uses only $\frac{2}{3}$ much as the truck?

Ans: We find that $\frac{5}{3}$ of what the truck needs equals what they both can use in a week, or $\frac{1}{3}$. So the truck will use $\frac{3}{15}$ of it in a week, and the car $\frac{2}{15}$. So the truck will use it in 5 weeks, the car in $7\frac{1}{2}$ weeks.

26. Two computers count votes for 15 hours, and $\frac{2}{3}$ of what one counts equals $\frac{2}{5}$ of what the other counts. How long will it take each to count all of the votes?

Ans: In one hour they can count $\frac{1}{15}$ of it; since $\frac{2}{3}$ of what the first counts is $= \frac{2}{5}$ of what the second counts, then $\frac{8}{5}$ of what the second counts $=$ what they both count in one hour, or $\frac{1}{15}$. So the second counts $\frac{5}{120}$, or $\frac{1}{24}$ in an hour, the first $\frac{3}{120}$, or $\frac{1}{40}$ in an hour. So the first can count it in 40, and the second in 24 hours.

27. Three men, A, B, and C, together can build a roof on a house in 12 days, and their rates of working are $\frac{1}{2}$, $\frac{1}{3}$, and $\frac{1}{4}$. How long would it take each alone to build the roof?

    Ans: Together they can build $\frac{1}{2} + \frac{1}{3} + \frac{1}{4} = \frac{1}{12}$ of a roof in one day, which, divided into three parts, which is as $\frac{1}{2}$, $\frac{1}{3}$, and $\frac{1}{4}$, or as 6, 4, 3, gives the respective parts each can do in a day. So it will take A 26, B 39, and C 52 days.

28. The distance from Mount Joy to Harrisburg is 25 miles, and $\frac{4}{5}$ of this distance is $\frac{5}{8}$ of $\frac{4}{9}$ of the distance from Harrisburg to Minton. What is the distance to Minton?

    Ans: $\frac{4}{5}$ of 25 miles $= 20$ miles; $\frac{5}{8}$ of $\frac{4}{9} = \frac{5}{18}$; since 20 miles is $\frac{5}{18}$ of the distance to Minton, the whole distance is 72 miles.

29. John and Michael can do 60 experiments in 6 weeks, and $\frac{1}{2}$ of what John can do in a day equals what Michael can do in a day. How long will it take each to do all the experiments?

    Ans: They will do $\frac{1}{6}$ of the experiments in a week. And $\frac{3}{2}$ of what John does equals what they both can do in one week, or $\frac{1}{6}$. So John does it in 9 weeks, Michael in 18 weeks.

30. The distance from Philadelphia to Lancaster is 68 miles, and $\frac{1}{4}$ of this, increased by 2 miles, equals $\frac{4}{7}$ of the distance from Lancaster to Harrisburg minus one mile. What is the distance to Harrisburg?

    Ans: $\frac{1}{4}$ of 68 miles $+ 2$ miles $= 19$ miles plus one mile, equals $\frac{4}{7}$ of the distance to Harrisburg. So the distance is 35 miles.

31. Frank can paint 3 rooms in 4 days; $\frac{2}{3}$ of what Frank paints equals $\frac{1}{2}$ of what Glenn paints, and also $\frac{1}{3}$ of what Kyle paints. After the three had been painting $\frac{6}{13}$ of a day, Frank and Kyle painted the rest. How long did it take them?

    Ans: Kyle can paint $\frac{1}{4}$ of it in a day, Frank $\frac{1}{3}$ of it, and Kyle $\frac{1}{2}$; Frank, Glenn, and Kyle can paint $\frac{1}{2} + \frac{1}{3} + \frac{1}{4} = \frac{13}{12}$ of it in a day. So, after painting $\frac{6}{13}$ of a day there will remain $\frac{1}{2}$ of it for Frank and Kyle to paint; Frank and Kyle can paint $\frac{1}{3} + \frac{1}{2} = \frac{5}{6}$ of it in a day, and to paint $\frac{1}{2}$ of it will take them $\frac{3}{5}$ of a day.

32. Ivan lost $15, and then earned $\frac{1}{3}$ as much as he had left, and then had $\frac{1}{2}$ as much as he had at first. How much did he have at first?
    Ans: After losing $15 he had his money minus $15, and after winning $\frac{1}{3}$ as much as he had left, he had $\frac{4}{3}$ of his money, minus $\frac{4}{3}$ of $15, which, equals $\frac{1}{2}$ of his money. So $\frac{4}{3}$ of his money, minus $\frac{1}{2}$ of his money, or $\frac{5}{6}$ of his money equals $\frac{4}{3}$ of $15, or $20, and his money was $24.

33. Fysal lost $22, and then earned $\frac{1}{4}$ as much as he had, and then had $\frac{1}{3}$ as much as he had at first. How much did he have at first?
    Ans: After losing $22, $\frac{5}{4}$ of what he had left = $\frac{1}{3}$ of what he had at first. So what remained was $\frac{4}{15}$ of what he had at first; $\frac{15}{15} - \frac{14}{15}$ of what he had at first = $22. So he had $30 at first.

34. Andy, had a certain sum of money, found another $20, and then lost $\frac{1}{3}$ of what he then had, and then had twice as much as he had at first. How much did he have at first?
    Ans: After finding $20, $\frac{2}{3}$ of what he then had = twice what he had at first. So what he then had equals 3 times what he had at first. And the difference, or twice what he at first had, equals $20. So he had $10 at first.

35. A man, had some money, borrowed $30, and then losing $\frac{1}{4}$ of what he then had, found that he has 8 times as much as at first. How much did he have at first?
    Ans: After borrowing $30, $\frac{3}{4}$ of what he then had = 3 times what he had at first. So what he then had is 4 times what he first had. And the difference, or 3 times what he at first had, equals $30. So he had at first $10.

36. A girl spent $44 and then got a job and earned $\frac{2}{3}$ as much as she had left. Now she has $\frac{3}{4}$ as much as what she started with. How much did she have at first?
    Ans: After she spent $44, $\frac{5}{3}$ of what remained = $\frac{3}{4}$ of what she had at first. So what remained = $\frac{9}{20}$ of what she had at first, and $\frac{20}{20} - \frac{9}{20}$, or $\frac{11}{20}$, = $44, $80.

37. A man went to a store and spent $21, and then borrowing $\frac{1}{5}$ of what he had left, had $\frac{1}{2}$ as much as he had at first. How much money did he have at first?
    Ans: After spending $21, $\frac{6}{5}$ of what was left = $\frac{1}{2}$ of what he had at

first. What was left $= \frac{5}{12}$ of what he had at first; $\frac{12}{12} - \frac{5}{12}$ or $\frac{7}{12}$ of what he had at first $= \$21$. So he had $\$36$ at first.

38. Jillian can paint 6 rooms in 8 days; $\frac{2}{3}$ of what Annie paints equals $\frac{1}{2}$ of what Glenn paints, and also $\frac{1}{3}$ of what Kyle paints. After the three had been painting $\frac{6}{13}$ of a day, Dylan and Carl painted the rest. How long did it take them?

Ans: Carl can paint $\frac{1}{4}$ of it in a day, Dylan $\frac{1}{3}$ of it, and Carl $\frac{1}{2}$; Dylan, Glenn, and Carl can paint $\frac{1}{2} + \frac{1}{3} + \frac{1}{4} = \frac{13}{12}$ of it in a day. So, after painting $\frac{6}{13}$ of a day there will remain $\frac{1}{2}$ of it for Dylan and Carl to paint; Dylan and Carl can paint $\frac{1}{3} + \frac{1}{2} = \frac{5}{6}$ of it in a day, and to paint $\frac{1}{2}$ of it will take them $\frac{3}{5}$ of a day.

39. A, B, and C have a picnic. A brings 2 dishes, B 3 dishes, and C who contributes $\$25$ to be divided between A and B instead of bringing food. How much do A and B get?

Solution one—If 3 persons eat 5 dishes, each eats $\frac{5}{3}$ of the food. So A provided C with $2 - \frac{5}{3}$, or $\frac{1}{3}$ of a dish, and B provided C with $3 - \frac{5}{3}$, or $\frac{4}{3}$ of a dish. If for $\frac{5}{3}$ of a dish C pays $\$20$, for $\frac{1}{3}$ of a dish, what A provides, he will pay $\frac{1}{5}$ of $\$20$, or $\$4$, and for $\frac{4}{3}$ of a dish, what B provides, $\$16$.

Solution two—This problem can be solved by dividing the money that C pays between A and B, in proportion to the number of dishes each provides, instead of dividing in the proportion of the number of dishes each provides C. Thus they would divide the $\$20$ between A and B, in the proportion of 2 to 3, the number of dishes which A and B provide respectively.

40. John brought 2 loaves of bread for a pot-luck dinner, and Ross brought 4 loaves, while Zack contributed $\$5$ to be divided between John and Ross. How much of it should each receive?

Ans: Each person ate 2 loaves, so John furnished and ate his own bread; therefore Ross should receive all the money.

41. The seller mixed some coffee worth $\$6$ a pound with an equal quantity worth $\$10$ a pound. He then sold the mixture for $\$12$ a pound, and made a profit of $\$640$. What was the quantity of each kind?

Ans: The average price per pound is $\$8$. So the gain on each pound is $\$12 - \$8$, or $\$2$. So there must have been as many pounds of the mixture as 2 is contained in 640, which is 320 pounds of each. Out of 320 pounds, the expensive type was $320 \times \frac{10}{16} = 200$ pounds.

42. Andrea brought 3 eggs for a big omelet and Harris, 5 eggs while Jill contributed $8 to be divided between Andrea and Harris. How much shall each receive, provided Andrea and Harris eat the same number and Jill eats 2 more eggs than each of them?

Ans: Andrea and Harris each eat 2 eggs, and Jill eats 4 eggs. So Andrea gives Jill 3 − 2, or 1 egg, and Harris gives Jill 5 − 2, or 3 eggs. If Jill pays $8 for 4 eggs, for one egg she will pay $2, and for 2 eggs, the number that Andrea gave, she will pay $4, For 3 eggs, the number that Harris gave, she will pay $6.

43. A, B, and C eat 14 cookies, of which A brought 5, B brought 9, and C added $24. How much of the money ought A and B each to receive, if B eats twice as many as A, and C eats twice as many as B?

Ans: A gave C 3 cookies, B 5, and C paid $24 for 8 cookies. So for 3, the number he got, he would pay $9; for 5, the number B provided, he would pay $15.

44. Two merchants, A and B, had a certain number of suits to sell. They bought 30 suits more, and then sold $\frac{1}{4}$ of the suits, and then had 3 times as many as at first. How many suits each had, if $\frac{1}{2}$ of A's number equals $\frac{1}{3}$ of B's?

Ans: $\frac{3}{4}$ of the number of suits they had, after buying 30 suits, = 3 times what they had at first; the number they had after buying = 4 times what they had at first. So the difference, or 3 times what they had at first, = 30 suits. They had 10 suits at first, of which A owns 4 suits, B 6 suits.

45. Mr. Bowman mixed some nuts worth $5 a pound with an equal quantity worth $9 a pound. He then sold the mixture for $10 a pound, and made a profit of $6. What was the quantity of each kind?

Ans: The average price per pound is $7. So the gain on each pound is $10 − $7, or $3. So there must have been as many pounds of the mixture as 3 is contained in 300, which is 200; therefore, 100 pounds of each.

46. A hare is 30 meters ahead of a coyote, and runs 3 meters while the coyote runs 6. How many meters must the coyote run to catch the hare?

Ans: For every meter the hare runs, the coyote runs 2. So to gain one meter he runs 2, and to gain 30 meters he must run 30 times 2 or, 60 meters.

47. Stephen is 40 steps ahead of James, and takes 5 steps to James's 7. How many steps must James take to catch Stephen, supposing their steps are equal?

Ans: James takes 7 steps to gain 2, and to gain 40 he must take as many times 7 steps as 2 is contained in 40, or 20. So he must take 20×7, or 140 steps.

48. A hare takes 2 leaps while a coyote takes 1, but one of the coyote's leaps equals 4 of the hare's. How much does the coyote gain on the hare in taking one leap?

Ans: Since one of the coyote's leaps equals 4 of the hare's and he takes one leap while the hare takes 2, he gains $4 - 2$, or 2 leaps.

49. A hare is 30 leaps ahead of a coyote. He takes 4 leaps while the coyote takes 2, but 2 of the coyote's leaps equal 8 of the rabbit's. How many leaps must the coyote take to catch the hare?

Ans: Since 2 of the coyote's leaps equal 8 of the hare's, for the hare to run as fast as the coyote it must take 8 leaps while the coyote takes 2 leaps, by the problem, the hare takes only 4 while the coyote takes 2. The coyote gains $8 - 4$, or 4 of the hare's leaps in taking 2 leaps. To gain one leap he must take $\frac{1}{4}$ of 2, or $\frac{1}{2}$ of a leap. To gain 30 leaps, the distance the hare is ahead, he must take 30 times $\frac{1}{2}$ of a leap, or 15 leaps.

50. A fox is 40 leaps ahead of a coyote, and takes 3 leaps while the coyote takes 2, but 2 of the coyote's leaps equal 4 of the fox's. In how many leaps will the coyote catch the fox?

Ans: The coyote gains one leap on the fox in taking 2 leaps. To gain 40 leaps he must take 40 times 2 leaps, or 80 leaps.

51. A thief running away is 20 steps ahead an officer who is trying to catch him. The thief takes 6 steps while the officer takes 5, but 5 of the officer's steps equal 8 of the thief's. How far will the thief run before he is overtaken?

Ans: The thief loses 2 steps in taking 6 steps. So to lose 20 steps, which is. 10 times 2 steps, he must take 10 times 6 steps, or 60 steps.⌣

Lesson 41 – *Time Problems*

WHAT is the time of day right now if the time past midnight equals $\frac{1}{3}$ the time from midnight to noon?

Ans: $\frac{1}{3}$ of the time from midnight to noon, which is 12 hours, is 4 hours. So it is 4 o'clock in the morning.

1. What is the time of day right now provided $\frac{1}{2}$ of the time past midnight to now equals the time to noon?

   Ans: Assume it is T o'clock now. $\frac{1}{2}$ of the time past midnight plus the other half, plus the time to from T o'clock to noon equals 12 hours. This means that each of these segments is equal in time. So $\frac{1}{2}$ of the time past midnight is one-third of 12 hours or 4 hours. The time now is 8 hours past midnight of 8 o'clock.

2. What is the time of day right now, supposing $\frac{2}{3}$ of the time past midnight to now equals the time to noon?

   Ans: The line M-N represents the time from midnight to noon, and M-T present time from midnight to now. $\frac{2}{3}$ of M-T is equal to T-N, which, added to $\frac{3}{3}$ of M-T = $\frac{5}{3}$ of M-T, which equals M-N, or 12 hours, and $\frac{3}{3}$ of M-T = $\frac{36}{5}$ = $7\frac{1}{5}$ hours. So it is 7:12 A.M.

3. What time of the day is it, if $\frac{1}{3}$ of the time past midnight equals the time past noon?

   Ans: In this problem, M-N represents the time from midnight to noon, M-T the time past midnight, and N-T the time past noon. Then $\frac{1}{3}$ of M-T = N-T, which, subtracted from $\frac{3}{3}$ of M-T = $\frac{2}{3}$ of M-T, which equals M-N, or 12 hours. So $\frac{1}{3}$ of M-T = 6 hours, which equals N-T. It is 6 o'clock P.M.

4. What time is it if $\frac{1}{5}$ of the time past midnight equals the time past noon? **Ans:** 3 o'clock P.M.

5. What time of the day is it if $\frac{1}{7}$ of the time past midnight equals the time to midnight again?

   Ans: If $\frac{1}{7}$ of the time past midnight equals the time to midnight again, $\frac{8}{7}$ of the time past midnight equals 24 hours. So $\frac{1}{7}$ of the time past midnight, which equals the time to midnight again, equals $\frac{1}{8}$ of 24 hours or 3 hours. So it must be 9 P.M.

6. What time of the day is it if $\frac{3}{5}$ of the time past midnight equals the time to midnight again?

166

Ans: $\frac{5}{5} + \frac{3}{5}$, or $\frac{8}{5}$ of the time past midnight = 24 hours. The time is 3 P.M.

7. What time of the day is it if $\frac{1}{3}$ of the time to noon equals the time past midnight?
Ans: $\frac{3}{3} + \frac{1}{3}$, or $\frac{4}{3}$ of the time to noon, equals 12 hours. So it is 3 A.M.

8. A person, when asked the time of day, said $\frac{1}{5}$ of the time past noon equals the time to midnight. What was the hour?
Ans: $\frac{5}{5} + \frac{1}{5}$, or $\frac{6}{5}$ of the time past noon = 12 hours. So $\frac{1}{5}$ of the time past noon, or 2 hours. = the time till midnight. So it is 10 P.M.

9. Andre studied for his test $\frac{3}{7}$ of the time past noon which equals the time past midnight. At what hour did he stop his study?
Ans: $\frac{7}{7} - \frac{3}{7}$, or $\frac{4}{7}$ of the time past noon = 12 hours. So $\frac{3}{7}$ of the time past noon, which is the time past midnight = 9 hours. So it was 9 A.M. when he stopped studying.

10. What time after 12 o'clock, are the hour and the minute-hands of a watch exactly together
Note—*The tip of the minute hand moves at the rate of 12 5-minute (There are 12 five-minute sections in 60 minutes.) spaces per hour. The hour hand moves at the rate of 1, 5-minute spaces per hour. (There are 12 five-minute spaces in 12 hours.*
Ans: Think of the tip of the minute hand as moving at a speed of 60 spaces per hour. The tip of the hour hand moves at the speed of 5 spaces per hour. At 1 P.M. they are 5 spaces apart, with hour hand at 1 and minute hand at 12.
The hour hand is ahead and the minute hand is gaining on the hour hand at the rate of 60 - 5 = 55 spaces per hour. The distance between the two is 5 spaces, and it will take the minute hand $\frac{5}{55} = \frac{1}{11}$ hour to catch up to the hour hand. $\frac{1}{11}$ hour is same as $\frac{60}{11}$ or $5\frac{5}{11}$ minutes after 1:00 P.M.

11. What time after 2 o'clock are the hour and minute-hands of a clock together?
Ans: At 2 P.M. they are 10 spaces apart, with hour hand at 2 and minute hand at 12. The hour hand is ahead and the minute hand is gaining on the hour hand at the rate of 60 - 5 = 55 spaces per hour. The distance between the two is 10 spaces, and it will take the minute

hand $\frac{10}{55} = \frac{2}{11}$ hour to catch up to the hour hand. $\frac{2}{11}$ hour is same as or $10\frac{10}{11}$ minutes after 2:00 P.M.

12. What time after 5 o'clock are the hour and minute-hands of a clock together?

   Ans: At 5 p.m. they are 25 spaces apart, with hour hand at 5 and minute hand at 12. The hour hand is ahead and the minute hand is gaining on the hour hand at the rate of 55 spaces per hour. The distance between the two is 25 spaces, and it will take the minute hand $\frac{25}{55} = \frac{5}{11}$ hour to catch up to the hour hand. $\frac{5}{11}$ hour is same as or $27\frac{3}{11}$ minutes after 5:00 P.M.

13. How many times in 12 hours are the minute and hour hand together?
   Ans: First time they are together is just after 1:05, then at about 2:10, then at about 2:15, so on for a total of 11 times.

14. A man, when asked for the hour of the day, replied that it was between 4 and 5 o'clock, and that the hour and minute-hands were together. What was the time?
   Ans: $21\frac{9}{11}$ minutes after 4 P.M.

15. A person, when asked the time of day, said $\frac{3}{5}$ of the time to midnight equals the time past midnight. What was the time?
   Ans: $\frac{5}{5} + \frac{3}{5}$, or $\frac{8}{5}$ of the time to midnight = 24 hours. So $\frac{3}{5}$ of the time to midnight which = the time past midnight = 9 hours., 9 A.M.

16. A math teacher, when asked the time of day, replied that $\frac{1}{6}$ of the time to midnight equaled $\frac{1}{2}$ of the time past noon. What was the time?
   Ans: 3 times the time past noon equals the time to midnight. So 4 times the time past noon equals 12 hours, 3 P.M.

17. What is the hour of day when twice the time to midnight equals $\frac{2}{3}$ of the time to noon?
   Ans: $\frac{2}{3}$ of the time to noon equals twice the time to midnight. So time to noon equals 3 times the time to midnight. So each segment is 3 hours long. So it is 9 hours. to noon, or 3 A.M.

18. One-half of the time past 9 o'clock A.M. equals $\frac{1}{3}$ of the time to midnight. What is the time?
   Ans: We find the time past 9 o'clock equals $\frac{2}{3}$ of the time to midnight; then $\frac{3}{3} + \frac{2}{3}$, or $\frac{5}{3}$ of the time to midnight, equals the time from 9 o'clock till midnight, which is 15 hours. So it is 9 hours to midnight, or 3 P.M.

19. When asked the hour of day, a man replied that $\frac{1}{4}$ of the time past 3 o'clock equaled $\frac{1}{2}$ of the time to midnight. What was the hour?
Ans: 3 times the time to midnight equals 12 hours − 3 hours, or 9 hours. So 2 times the time to midnight, which equals the time past 3 o'clock = 6 hours. So it must be 9 P.M.

20. A man, when asked the hour of the day, replied that $\frac{1}{8}$ of the time past 2 o'clock equals $\frac{1}{2}$ of the time to midnight. What was the hour?
Ans: 5 times the time to midnight = 10 hours. So it must be 10 P.M.

21. At what time between 7 and 8 o'clock are the hour and minute-hands of a watch exactly together.
Ans: At 7 p.m. they are 35 spaces apart, with hour hand at 7 and minute hand at 12. The hour hand is ahead and the minute hand is gaining on the hour hand at the rate of 60 - 5 = 55 spaces per hour. The distance between the two is 35 spaces, and it will take the minute hand $\frac{35}{55} = \frac{7}{11}$ hour to catch up to the hour hand. $\frac{7}{11}$ hour is same as $\frac{60 \times 7}{11}$ minutes, or $38\frac{2}{11}$ minutes after 7:00 p.m.

22. In how many minutes after 4 o'clock will the hour and the minute hands be 5 minute-space apart?
Ans: At 4 o'clock the hour and minute hands are 4 spaces apart, but the minute hand only needs to gain 3 spaces to be 5 minute-space from the hour hand. To gain 3 spaces it will need $\frac{180}{11}$ minutes, or $16\frac{4}{11}$ minutes. It may also go 5 minute spaces beyond, which gives $27\frac{3}{11}$ minutes.

23. In how many minutes after 4 o'clock will the hour and minute hands be 5 minutes apart?
Ans: At 4 o'clock the hour and minute hands are 20 spaces apart. The minute hand gains on the hour hand at the rate of 55 spaces per hour. To gain 20 spaces, it needs $\frac{20}{55}$ hours, or $21\frac{9}{11}$ minutes. So $21\frac{9}{11}$ minutes − 5 minutes, or $16\frac{9}{11}$ minutes after 4 o'clock they will be 5 minutes of time apart; also in $21\frac{9}{11}$ + 5 min., or $26\frac{9}{11}$ min.

24. A math teacher, when asked the hour of day replied that $\frac{2}{3}$ of the time past noon equaled $\frac{4}{5}$ of the time to midnight, minus $\frac{4}{5}$ of an hour. What was the time?
Ans: We find that the time past noon equals $\frac{3}{5}$ of the time to midnight, minus $\frac{6}{5}$ of an hour. $1\frac{1}{5}$ of the time to midnight, minus $\frac{6}{5}$ of an hour, equals 12 hours and $1\frac{1}{5}$ of the time to midnight will equal $6\frac{6}{5}$

hours, so $\frac{5}{5}$ of the time to midnight equals 6 hours; therefore it is 6 o'clock P.M.

25. A person, when asked the hour of the day, replied that 2 hours ago the time past noon was $\frac{1}{3}$ of the time to midnight 2 hours so. What is the time?

Ans: We find $\frac{4}{3}$ of the time to midnight 2 hours so + 2 hours + 2 hours, equals 12 hours. So, $\frac{4}{3}$ of the time to midnight, 2 hours so, equals 8 hours, and $\frac{1}{3}$ of the time to midnight 2 hours so, which was the time past noon 2 hours ago, equals $\frac{1}{4}$ of 8 hours, or 2 hours. So the time now is 2 hours + 2 hours, or 4 hours past noon, or 4 o'clock P.M.

26. A person, when asked the time of day, replied that $\frac{2}{3}$ of the time past midnight, 2 hours ago, equaled $\frac{3}{5}$ of the time to midnight, 3 hours and 20 minutes so. What is the time?

Ans: $\frac{8}{5}$ of the time to midnight, 3 hours and 20 minutes so $= 18\frac{2}{3}$ hours. So the time past midnight, 2 hours ago, is 7 hours; the time now, 9 A.M.

27. My friend's watch loses 2 minutes in 3 hours, and mine gains 20 minutes a day; they were set with correct time yesterday noon, and are now half an hour apart. What time is it?

Ans: My friend's watch loses $\frac{2}{3}$ of a minute in an hour while mine gains $\frac{5}{6}$ of a minute in an hour. So in one hour after they were set they will be $\frac{2}{3} + \frac{5}{6}$, or $\frac{3}{2}$ of minute apart, and to be 30 minute apart will require $30 \div \frac{3}{2}$, or 20 hours. So the time is 20 hours from yesterday noon, or 8 A.M. today.

Lesson 42 – *Age Problems*

JAREN is 35 years old and Diana is 5. In how many years will Jaren be 6 times as old as Diana?

Ans: The difference in their ages is 30 years. This of course stays the same as they get older. Right now Jaren is 7 times as old as Diana, or the difference in the age is equal to six times the age of Diana. That will be when she is $30 \div 5 = 6$ years old. In one year from now Diana will be 6 years old, and Jaren will be 6 times as old as she or, 36 years old.

1. James is 29 years old and Ellen is 9. In how many years will James be 3 times as old as Ellen?
   Ans: The difference in their ages is 20 years. If James is 3 times as old as Ellen, then the difference which is 2 times Ellen's age is equal to 20 years. So Ellen will be 10 and in one year James will be 30 years old.

2. Alex is 30 years and Paula is 6 years old; in how many years will Alex be 4 times as old as Paula?
   Ans: The difference between their ages is 24 years, which, at the required time, will be 3 times Paula's age. So Paula's age will then be 8 years, and the time will be 2 years.

3. If Lin is 4 times as old a Li, and the sum of their ages is 50, then how old are they?
   Ans: Li's age plus Lin's age which is 4 times Li's age equals 5 times Li's age is equal to 50, so Li is 10 years old and Lin is 40 years old.

4. If Jack is 6 times as old a Lin, and the sum of their ages is 35, then how old are they?
   Ans: Jack's age plus Lin's age which is 6 times Lin's age equals 7 times Jack's age is equal to 35, so Jack is 5 years old and Lin is 30 years old.

5. Eva is 6 years old, and her mother is 7 times as old. In how many years will her mother be 5 times as old?
   Ans: The difference in age is 36 years which, at the required time, will be 4 times Eva's age. So she will then be 9 years old, and the time will be 3 years.

6. Morton is 10 years old and Moses is 30. How long has it been since Moses was 5 times as old as Morton?

Ans: The difference of ages is 20 years, which at the required time, was 4 times Morton's age. So Morton's age was 5 years, and the time was 5 years ago.

7. Jacob is twice as old as his son who is 20 years old. How long has it been since Jacob was 5 times as old as his son?
   Ans: The difference in ages is 20 years; which, at the required time, Jacob was 4 times the age of his son. So the son was 5 years old, and it was 15 years ago.

8. Inez is $\frac{1}{4}$ as old as her aunt, who is 40 years of age. How many years since Inez was $\frac{1}{7}$ as old as her aunt?
   Ans: The difference in ages is 30 years, which, at the required time, was 6 times Inez's age. So Inez was 5 years old, and the time was 5 years ago.

9. Jason is 5 times as old as John, and the difference in their ages is 20 years. In how many years will Jason be 3 times as old as John?
   Ans: 5 times John's age, which equals Jason's age, minus John's age, equals 4 times John's age, or 20 years. So John's age is 5 years, and in 5 years Jason's age will be three times John's age.

10. Jaren is 4 times as old as William, and the sum of their ages is 25 years. In how many years will Jaren be 5 times as old as William?
    Ans: 4 times William's age, which equals Jaren's age, added to William's age = 5 times William's age, which is 25 years. Jaren's age is 20 years, William's 5 years. So in 5 years Jaren will be three times as old as William.

11. Two-thirds of A's age equals $\frac{4}{5}$ of B's age, and the difference between their ages is 10 years. How long has it been since A was 3 times as old as B?
    Ans: If $\frac{2}{3}$ of A's age = $\frac{4}{5}$ of B's age, $\frac{6}{5}$ of B's age = A's age; therefore A's age is 60 years, and B's age 50 years. 45 years ago A was three times as old as B.

12. One-half of Marilyn's age equals $\frac{1}{3}$ of Nella's age, and the difference of their ages is 10 years. In how many years will $\frac{1}{3}$ of Marilyn's age equals $\frac{1}{4}$ of Nella's age?
    Ans: $\frac{1}{2}$ of Marilyn's = $\frac{1}{3}$ of Nella's. So Marilyn's age = $\frac{2}{3}$ of Nella's, and $\frac{3}{3} - \frac{2}{3}$, or $\frac{1}{3}$ of Nella's age equals 10 years. So Nella's is 30

years old, and Marilyn's is 20 years old. At the required time, $\frac{1}{3}$ of Marilyn's $= \frac{1}{4}$ of Nella's, or Marilyn's $= \frac{3}{4}$ of Nella's. So $\frac{4}{4} - \frac{3}{4}$, or $\frac{1}{4}$ of Nella's $= 10$ years., and Nella's $= 40$ years. So the time is $40 - 30$, or 10 years.

13. Two-tenths of B's age equals $\frac{4}{5}$ of C's age, and the sum of their ages is 30 years. In how many years will B be 3 times as old as C.
Ans: If $\frac{2}{10}$ of B's age equals $\frac{4}{5}$ of C's age, the B's age equals 4 times C's age. The sum of B's and C's age equals 5 times C's age which is equal to 30 years. So B is 24 years old and, C's age 6 years; at the required time C's age is 9 years. So the time is $9 - 6$, or 3 years.

14. Two-thirds of Daniel's age equals $\frac{3}{4}$ of Mark's age, and the sum of their ages is 68 years. How long has it been since $\frac{2}{3}$ of Daniel's age equaled $\frac{4}{5}$ of Mark's age
Ans: $\frac{2}{3}$ of Daniel's age equals $\frac{3}{4}$ of Mark's age, then Daniel is $\frac{9}{8}$ times as old as Mark. The sum of their ages then is one times Mark's age plus $\frac{9}{8}$ times Mark's age which is equal to 68. We get $\frac{17}{8}$ times Mark's age equal to 68 years or Mark's age equal to 32 years and Daniel's age is 36 years. At the required time, Mark's age was 20.

15. A's age equals 4 times B's, but in 5 years A's age will be only 3 times B's. How old is each?
Ans: Four times B's age equals A's age, so, the difference of their ages is 3 times B's age, and B's age equals $\frac{1}{3}$ of the difference of their ages. In 5 years, 3 times B's age equals A's age, so, twice B's age equals the difference of their ages, and once B's age then equals $\frac{1}{2}$ of the difference. Therefore, 5 years is the difference between and $\frac{1}{3}$ of the difference of their ages, or $\frac{1}{6}$ of the difference of their ages. And $\frac{6}{6}$, or the difference of their ages, is 6 times 5, or 30 years. If 3 times B's age equals 30 years, B's age is $\frac{1}{3}$ of 30 years, or 10 years, and A's age is 4 times 10, or 40 years.

16. John is 5 times as old as Oliver, but in 8 years he will be only 3 times as old. How old are they?
Ans: The difference in their ages is 4 times Oliver's, and once Oliver's $= \frac{1}{4}$ of the difference. In 8 years, the difference will equal twice Oliver's, and once Oliver's will equal $\frac{1}{2}$ of the difference; therefore 8 years is the difference between $\frac{1}{2}$ of the difference and $\frac{1}{4}$ of the difference of their ages, or $\frac{1}{4}$ of the difference. So the difference of

their ages is 4 times 8, or 32 years, Oliver's age is 8 years, and John's 40.

17. Anne is $\frac{1}{4}$ as old as her aunt, but in 20 years she will be $\frac{1}{2}$ as old. How old are they?
   Ans: The difference in ages = 3 times Anne's, and Anne's age = $\frac{1}{3}$ the difference. In 20 years, the difference will equal Anne's age. So the difference in their ages minus $\frac{1}{3}$ of the difference, or $\frac{2}{3}$ of the difference, equals 20 years; therefore the difference of their ages is 30 years Anne's age is 10 years, and her aunt's 40.

18. Jeffery is $\frac{1}{5}$ as old as his uncle, but in 25 years he will be $\frac{3}{5}$ as old. How old are they?
   Ans: The difference of their ages = 4 times Jeffery's age, and once Jeffery's age = $\frac{1}{4}$ of the difference. In 25 years, the difference will equal $\frac{2}{3}$ of Jeffery's age, and once Jeffery's age will equal $\frac{3}{2}$ of the difference. So $\frac{3}{2}$ of the difference minus $\frac{1}{4}$ of the difference, or $\frac{5}{4}$ of the difference, equals 25 years; therefore the difference is 20 years. Jeffery's age is 5 years, and his uncle's 25.

19. Ten years ago, when I first met Mr. Morgan, I was $\frac{1}{4}$ as old as he, but now I am $\frac{1}{2}$ as old as he is. How old are we?
   Ans: The difference of our ages equaled 3 times my age, and my age equaled $\frac{1}{3}$ of the difference. In 10 years my age = the difference. So the difference minus $\frac{1}{3}$ of the difference, or $\frac{2}{3}$ of the difference, is 10 years; therefore the difference is 15 years. My age is 15 years, and Morgan's 30.

20. Sixteen years ago, when Andy married, he was $1\frac{1}{2}$ times as old as his wife. Now she is $\frac{3}{4}$ as old as him. What is the age of each?
   Ans: She is 30, he is 40.

21. Twenty-five years ago Will, was $\frac{1}{7}$ as old as his uncle, but 5 years ago he was $\frac{1}{3}$ as old. How old are they both now?
   Ans: The difference in their ages 25 years ago equaled 6 times Will's, and Will's age equaled $\frac{1}{6}$ of the difference. In 20 years, or 5 years ago, twice Will's age = the difference, and his age = $\frac{1}{2}$ of the difference. So $\frac{1}{2}$ of the difference minus one of the difference, or $\frac{1}{3}$ of the difference, equals 20 years; therefore the difference is 60 years Will's age is 30 + 5, or 35 years, and his uncle's age is 95 years.

22. Four years ago B's house was four times as old as his barn. Two years from now, it will be only twice as old. How long ago was each built?
Ans: The difference in age 4 years ago equaled 3 times the age of the barn, and the age of the barn equaled $\frac{1}{3}$ of the difference. Once the difference will equal the age of the barn. So once the difference minus $\frac{1}{3}$ of the difference, or $\frac{2}{3}$ of the difference, equals 6 years; therefore the difference is 9 years. The barn has been built 7 years ago, and the house 16.

23. Three years ago, Emma's sister was $\frac{1}{5}$ of her age. In 7 years Emma's sister will be $\frac{3}{5}$ of her age. How old are each?
Ans: Three years ago, Emma was 5 times as old as her sister, so $\frac{1}{4}$ of the difference will equal sister's age, and the sister's age will be $\frac{3}{2}$ of the difference. $\frac{3}{2}$ the difference minus $\frac{1}{4}$ of the difference, or $\frac{5}{4}$ of the difference, equals 10 years. Therefore the difference is 8 years, the sister's age is $2 + 3$, or 5 years, and Emma's age is 13 years.

24. The difference in ages of two men is 28 years. In 12 years, the younger one will be half the age of the older one. How old are they both?
Ans: One is 44 years old and the younger is 16 years old.

25. The difference in ages of two men is 30 years. In 12 years ago, the younger one was $\frac{1}{11}$ the age of the older one. How old are they both?
Ans: 12 years ago, the difference between their ages was 10 times the age of the age of younger one. So the younger one then was 3 years old. He is now 15 and the older one is $15 + 30 = 45$ years old.

26. The difference in ages of two men is 23 years. In 21 years, the younger one will be half the age of the older one. How old are they both?
Ans: In 21 years, the difference between their ages will equal half of the age of older one. So the older one will be 2 times 23 or 46 years old. So right now he is 25 years old and the younger one is 2 years old.

27. Two years ago Mr. Smith was 5 times as old as his son John will be 2 years so, and 3 years so his age will equal 15 times John's age 3 years ago. What is the age of each?

28. A boy, when asked his age, replied that if 11 years ago his age had been increased by $\frac{1}{4}$, it would then have been $\frac{1}{3}$ of what it now is. What is his age?

Ans: $\frac{5}{4}$ of the boy's age 11 years ago $= \frac{1}{3}$ of his age now; $\frac{4}{15}$ of his age now $=$ his age then. So $\frac{11}{15}$ of his age now $= 11$ years. His age then was 4 years, and now is 15 years.

29. A woman, when asked her age, said that if her age were increased by its $\frac{1}{5}$, the sum would equal 3 times her age 12 years ago. What was her age?
    Ans: $\frac{6}{5}$ of her age now $= 3$ times her age 12 years ago, and $\frac{2}{5}$ of her age now $=$ her age 12 years ago, and $\frac{3}{5}$ of her age now $= 12$ years. So she was 20 years old.

30. A person, when asked his age, said that if his age in 4 years is reduced by its $\frac{2}{3}$, the rest will equal $\frac{1}{2}$ of his. age 4 years ago. What was his age?
    Ans: His age 4 years ago $= \frac{2}{3}$ of his age 4 years so. So $\frac{1}{3}$ of his age 4 years so $= 8$ years. His age 4 years $= 24$ years; $24 - 4 = 20$ years, his age now.

31. A boy, when asked his age, replied that if my age in 3 years is reduced by its $\frac{2}{5}$, the rest will be $\frac{3}{4}$ of my age now. What was his age?
    Ans: Three-fifth of his age 3 years so $= \frac{3}{4}$ of his age now. So $\frac{5}{4}$ of his age now $=$ his age 3 years so. So $\frac{1}{4}$ of his age now $= 3$ years, his age now, 12 years.

32. Said Ellen to Frank, "My age is 5 years more than yours, but 4 years ago my age was $\frac{1}{2}$ of what yours will be in 4 years." What was the age of each?
    Ans: Ellen's age, minus 4 years, is $\frac{1}{2}$ of Frank's, plus 2 years; but Ellen's age $=$ Frank's $+ 5$ years, and Ellen's age, minus 4 years $=$ Frank's age plus one year. So Frank's age $+$ one year $= \frac{1}{2}$ of Frank's, $+ 2$ years. So $\frac{1}{2}$ of Frank's age is one year, Frank is 2 years old, and Ellen is 7 years old. ⌣

You are now a whiz at fractions. Ready for percents?

About the authors
Michael Levin M.D.
Charan Langton M.S.

Michael is a practicing physician specializing in childhood developmental and psychiatric problems. Together Michael and his wife, Charan Langton, an electrical engineer, have coauthored several books on childhood education. Their goal has been to find the most effective educational techniques and bring them to market. Their first book - The Reading Lesson - is one the most popular books for teaching children to read.

With verbal math book series they bring a most child-friendly and effective method for helping children become proficient in math.

Information on the reading and math books is available at

www.readinglesson.com
www.mathlesson.com